Portrait of the Poor

AN ASSETS-BASED APPROACH

Orazio Attanasio
and Miguel Székely
Editors

Distributed by the Johns Hopkins University Press
for the Inter-American Development Bank

Washington, D.C.
2001

Latin American Research Network
Inter-American Development Bank

The Inter-American Development Bank created the Latin American Research Network in 1991 in order to strengthen policy formulation and contribute to the development policy agenda in Latin America.

Through a competitive bidding process, the network provides grant funding to leading Latin American research centers to conduct studies on economic and social issues selected by the Bank in consultation with the region's development community.

Most of the studies are comparative, which allows the Bank to build its knowledge base and draw on lessons from experiences in macroeconomic and financial policy, modernization of the State, regulation, poverty and income distribution, social services, and employment.

Individual country studies are available as working papers and are also available in PDF format on the Internet at *http://www.iadb.org/oce/RED_working_papers.cfm*

© 2001   **Inter-American Development Bank**
            1300 New York Avenue, N.W.
            Washington, D.C. 20577

Cover: J.R. Ripper/Social Photos © www.socialphotos.com

To order this book, contact:
IDB Bookstore
Tel: 1-877-PUBS IDB/(202) 623-1753
Fax: (202) 623-1709
E-mail: idb-books@iadb.org
www.iadb.org/pub

The views and opinions expressed in this publication are those of the authors and do not necessarily reflect the official position of the Inter-American Development Bank.

Cataloging-in-Publication data provided by the
Inter-American Development Bank
Felipe Herrera Library

    Portrait of the poor : an assets-based approach / Orazio Attanasio and Miguel Székely, editors.

p. cm.
Includes bibliographical references.
ISBN:1886938970

1. Poor—Latin America.   2. Poverty—Latin America.   3. Human capital—Latin America.
I. Attanasio, Orazio.   II. Székely, Miguel.   III. Inter-American Development Bank.

339.46 P24—dc21   LCCN: 01-132817

TABLE OF CONTENTS

ACKNOWLEDGMENTS

The authors are indebted to Ricardo Hausmann and Juan Luis Londoño for helping to launch the initial stages of this project. We also thank Rodolfo de la Torre, who helped put together earlier versions of the papers upon which the book is based. Finally, we would like to thank Norelis Betancourt, Raquel Gómez, Rita Funaro and John Dunn Smith, without whom it would have been impossible to put this volume together.

PREFACE

Reducing poverty is the greatest challenge facing Latin American policymakers today. In the 1990s, macroeconomic reform helped put much of the region on a growth trend, yet the ranks of the poor continued to swell. Today, most countries have levels of poverty that far exceed expectations given their levels of development. Not surprisingly, poverty reduction is a program priority at the Inter-American Development Bank and the World Bank, and tops the national agendas of many countries in the region.

Countries have not been indifferent to the plight of the poor. But traditional poverty reduction programs or safety nets have done little to alleviate the problem, largely because they address the consequences rather than the causes of poverty. Policymakers must learn to look beyond the most obvious manifestation of the problem—low incomes—and ask what prevents all people from having the same opportunities. This book asks that very question and comes up with an innovative, assets-based approach to this pressing regional concern.

Portrait of the Poor paints a whole new picture of poverty in Latin America. Low incomes are just the silhouette of the problem. Learning more about why poor people earn less makes for a more complete portrait. This book finds the key in unequal access to education, credit and the other income-generating assets of human, physical and social capital. Evidence from case studies on Bolivia, Brazil, Chile, Colombia, Costa Rica and Peru supports this finding. The result is a vicious circle in which people with few productive assets receive lower wages because they lack assets, which in turn prevents them from accumulating the assets they need to improve their incomes in the future.

The policy implications of this approach are vast. To begin with, the limitations of even the most efficient and well-targeted traditional social programs become clear. Policies based on a broader approach that impacts the distribution of assets, their use or even the prices paid for them in the marketplace would seem more effective.

Portrait of the Poor redefines poverty as a problem that comes from flaws in an overall economy. It is not a problem of individuals, but of the context in which these individuals operate. If the context does not change, then it is unlikely that traditional public policies or economic growth alone can make measurable advances in the fight against poverty. This book exposes this stark reality and points the way to a new policy direction.

Guillermo Calvo
Chief Economist
Inter-American Development Bank

CHAPTER ONE

Going beyond Income:
Redefining Poverty in Latin America

Orazio Attanasio and Miguel Székely[1]

Poverty reduction remains one of the main challenges for Latin America at the dawn of the 21st century. Most countries in the region are classified as middle income by international standards, and yet they register poverty rates well above what would be expected given their GDP per capita. The reason for this "excess poverty" lies in the high level of inequality in the distribution of resources. Income inequality has not declined during the 1990s in any of the countries in Latin America for which comparable data for more than two points in time are available.[2] Combined with the meager growth of most of these countries, this accounts for why poverty has remained at such high levels in the region.

Traditionally, governments have addressed this problem by implementing poverty alleviation programs that involve social safety nets designed to provide temporary relief for the poor. However, these programs do not attack the causes of poverty. Moreover, the traditional approach has almost always neglected general equilibrium effects that can change, sometimes in pernicious ways, interactions among individual households and social networks. Some Latin American countries have pioneered poverty programs with additional investment components for human capital through education and health.[3] However, more often than not, such programs provide only short-term relief because they have not been adequately institutionalized to last over the long term.

[1] Orazio Attanasio is a Professor of Economics at University College in London and an associate of the Institute of Fiscal Studies and the National Bureau of Economic Research. Miguel Székely is an economist with the IDB Research Department.
[2] See Székely and Hilgert (1999).
[3] A recent example is the *Progresa* program in Mexico, which combines cash transfers with support for keeping children in school and investing in health and nutrition.

Implementation of these policies has been influenced by the economics literature on poverty, which has emphasized that the main policy problem is to effectively target resources to the poor.[4] Although this kind of policy response is adequate and necessary in periods of economic crisis and negative shocks, it entails a rather reductionist approach to the problem because it often restricts policies to providing only temporary support. Poverty in Latin America and beyond, however, is most often a structural problem caused by the way the whole economic system operates. Therefore, it can only be tackled effectively with policies that modify the economic environment in ways that allow all people in society to take advantage of available opportunities.[5] The first step toward developing such policies is to focus on the mechanisms that generate inequality and poverty, and construct an analytical framework that identifies the structural mechanisms at play.

The main argument that underlies this book is that poverty in Latin America—or at least the "excess poverty" given the region's income levels—is a problem caused mainly by high levels of inequality. This chapter will document that income inequality in the region is, to a large extent, a reflection of very skewed distribution of income-earning assets, the most important being human capital.[6] To understand what causes income inequality, it is first necessary to determine why the distribution of income-generating assets is so unequal. But if one takes an asset-based approach to poverty, the central question becomes: Why are some people able to accumulate the most productive assets, while others are prevented from doing so? Is it that there are market imperfections, or does the pattern reflect rational decisions that take into account expected returns on a given asset and alternative opportunities? If the evidence were to point to the existence of market imperfections, then poverty reduction policies could be reoriented to trying to eliminate those problems.

---

[4] See the review in Székely (1998).
[5] This argument is developed in detail in IDB (1998).
[6] This is not to say that inequality in returns (to human capital and other assets) does not play an important role. Indeed, the *increase* in inequality observed in the last 15 years is largely a reflection of changes in the return to human capital and its variance. Here, however, we focus on the issue of inequality in the *stocks* and its causes.

An Asset-Based Approach to Poverty: A Simple Framework for Analysis

Poverty is normally measured using income as the welfare indicator, mainly for two reasons. The first is that income provides some indication of a person's capability to achieve a certain standard of living. The second is that information is more readily available on income than it is for other variables. In fact, among the possible options, income is not necessarily the best alternative, but it has been widely used to measure poverty, mainly because of its availability.[7]

Public policies aimed at reducing poverty have concentrated on increasing incomes through a variety of instruments, or even "subsidizing" incomes directly through cash transfers. Some poverty alleviation programs have included other mechanisms, such as directly providing the poor with a range of services, under the assumption that, if the problem is lack of income, the solution is to provide income or transfers in kind.

Although this standard approach might be adequate in certain circumstances, such as periods of economic stagnation, natural disasters or unexpected negative income shocks, it does not solve the basic problem because it is focused on the "consequences" of poverty rather than on its causes. The standard approach is better framed in terms of providing insurance against some types of shocks, and as such it is subject to a variety of problems, ranging from moral hazard to the crowding out of private insurance schemes. Moreover, these types of schemes provide benefits for rather short periods of time, and when they are discontinued they leave the poor in the same (or a very similar) position as when they started. On the other hand, there are situations when providing insurance against certain types of shocks interacts in a virtuous way with the incentives to accumulate human capital. It has been argued, for instance, that temporary income shocks can induce poor households to withdraw children from school, therefore permanently hampering the accumulation of human capital. The rest of this section sketches a simple framework for analyzing the poverty problem from a wider perspective.

---

[7] The vast majority of the 111 works on poverty measurement in Latin America reviewed by Londoño and Székely (1997) used income as the welfare indicator.

Going beyond Income

In general terms, income is a function of the combination of four crucial elements: (i) the stock of income-earning assets owned by each individual; (ii) the rate at which these assets are used for producing income; (iii) the market value of income-earning assets; and (iv) transfers and bequests independent of the income-earning assets owned. Thus, family per capita income—which is the welfare indicator traditionally used in Latin America to classify the population into poor and non-poor—can be expressed in general terms as:

$$y_i = \frac{(\sum_{i=1}^{j} \sum_{a=1}^{l} A_{a,i} R_{a,i} P_a) + \sum_{i=1}^{k} T_i}{n} \qquad (1)$$

where y is the household per capita income of individual i, A is a variable representing the stock of asset type a, owned by individual I, R is a variable representing the rate at which asset type a is used by individual i, and P is the market value per unit of asset type a. The variable j represents the number of income-earners in the household to which individual i belongs, l is the number of different types of assets, and k is the number of individuals in the household obtaining income from transfers or bequests, while n is the size of the household to which i belongs.

Equation (1) should then be complemented with equations describing the accumulation of each asset. The process of accumulation, obviously, would be asset-specific. For instance, in the case of human capital, it would depend on the rate of utilization of that asset (if a child goes to work, he or she will not be able to go to school). Furthermore, it might depend on the availability of other assets. For instance, the parent's human capital or access to "social capital" in the form of credit or other help from the community might facilitate the process of accumulation of the child's human capital. Finally, accumulation might depend on the shocks households receive and how these may be alleviated by contingent transfers T. For instance, certain types of temporary shocks could induce very poor households to withdraw their children from school to provide additional income. Transfers targeted at counteracting these types of shocks could be particularly useful. However, publicly provided insurance could induce moral hazard and could also crowd out private transfers and affect the interaction among households.[8]

Traditional poverty alleviation programs have been aimed at T_i, in a way that is typically independent from the individual's capacity to obtain income (and on the possible effects of such transfer; on A, R or P). On the other hand, policies aimed at affecting A, R or P will have much deeper and permanent effects on poverty because they address the long-term income-earning capacity of individuals. Each of these elements will now be defined in more detail.

To simplify the framework and make the analysis tractable from an empirical point of view, A is classified into three types of assets: human capital, physical capital, and social capital. Under human capital is included the set of skills that are needed to produce a good or service. The most widely used proxy for quantifying these skills is years of formal education. Other types of skills acquired through training are more difficult to measure, and information on labor market experience is also seldom available. Therefore the definition of human capital is limited to years of schooling.

"Physical" capital refers to the monetary value of any form of financial asset, money holdings, property, and capital stock used for production. This type of capital can play different roles, in that it can be used to buffer temporary shocks or produce income, and it can be accumulated for long-term objectives such as financing consumption after retirement.

Regarding social capital, a conventional definition by Robert Putnam (1993) is adopted that refers to the set of norms and social networks that facilitate collective action among individuals. Unlike other forms of capital, social capital inheres in the structure of relations between persons and among persons, so it is the most difficult to quantify.[9] Moreover, this type of capital is different from the others, as its accumulation does not depend directly on individual decisions.

---

[8] See Attanasio and Ríos-Rull (2001).
[9] See Coleman (1990). Among the three assets defined here, social capital is by far the most controversial in terms of definition. Following the case study for Bolivia included in this book, the definition is derived from Putnam (1993): "Social capital refers to features of social organization, such as trust, norms and networks that can improve the efficiency of society by facilitating coordinated actions."

Ownership or access to any of these assets implies that an individual has the potential capacity to generate income at some point in time, but the income that is actually generated depends on the use of the asset. For instance, in the case of human capital, the years of schooling of an individual will only be translated into income if there is labor market participation [that is, $R>0$ in equation (1)]. Physical capital becomes an income when the dividend or return generated by the stock is made liquid, while social capital has a positive effect on y_i when social relations are used to actually generate income.

On the other hand, the market price of each income-earning asset [P in equation (1)] operates somewhat independently from individuals themselves because it is determined by supply, demand and institutional factors, in which the relative weight of each individual is negligible. Prices are therefore set by the economic system, and they become relevant to the individual in the process of deciding whether to seek income and accumulate a certain type of capital.[10] However, in the design of policies that might have large effects on the accumulation of certain types of capital, the general equilibrium on its return should also be taken into account.

According to the definition used here, T_i refers to the market value of public and private transfers and bequests.

Scope for Policy Action

As already mentioned, most poverty alleviation policies are aimed at the T_i component of equation (1). But interventions through T_i may have an effect on incomes that is not totally independent of A and R, for several reasons. First, government transfers that target the poor may take A into account for defining its population of beneficiaries. Second, certain types of policies may result in increases in A when they are directly aimed at enhancing human capital or providing credit for production. Additionally, they may provide incentives for affecting R by requiring that individuals use the income-earning assets they own for receiving a benefit. But T can also have negative

---

[10] Birdsall, Pinckney and Sabot (1999) develop a model in line with this argument, where they sort out the interaction between returns to labor, the incentives to the use of human capital, and income distribution.

effects, either directly, by altering the incentive structure faced by individual households, or indirectly through general equilibrium effects. If the transfer program is large enough, general equilibrium effects can also affect the prices and returns of various programs.[11]

Unfortunately, these last considerations are often ignored in the design of actual transfer programs. And even when the potentially beneficial effects of these policies on A and R constitute the stated aim of the program, if the program itself is temporary in nature it would not be suitable for it to have an impact on long-run decisions. As a consequence, these programs rarely result in a substantial improvement in people's long-term income-earning capacity. That is, the programs are not able to eliminate the restrictions that prevent the poor from accumulating A.

A good example is the case of poverty alleviation policies with a human capital component that transfers income through scholarships. The logic under which most of these programs operate is that children in poor families are not able to accumulate human capital because the family does not have the money to send children to school. Costs range from transportation and materials to the income foregone by the family because the child does not participate in the labor market. So, if the family is provided with an income subsidy in monetary terms or in kind, it will be able to finance these costs and keep the child in school.

The above approach would be a sufficient solution if the transfer of resources was permanent, if the family could rely on it with certainty through the child's full process of human capital accumulation, and if low income was the only restriction that households face. But in practice, such programs are neither permanent nor fully reliable in the long run, and most importantly, they usually do not address the main constraints that prevent an (efficient) accumulation of human capital. These may include the absence of efficient credit or insurance markets that allow people to diversify idiosyncratic risk, and force the household to adopt relatively unproductive invest-

---

[11] For instance, Heckman, Lochner and Taber (1998) consider a dynamic general equilibrium model in which optimal human capital accumulation decisions are affected by factor prices and, in turn, aggregate supply effects affect factor prices. Cameron and Heckman (1998) estimate a model of schooling decisions for males in the United States.

ment strategies.[12] It is therefore crucial when designing a transfer scheme with a particular goal—for instance, to improve school enrollment of a certain age group—to understand the main structural reasons why such a goal is not achieved by households in the first place.

Credit programs constitute another example of programs that may have only temporary effects for the poor. One can readily imagine how providing credit through a poverty alleviation program would lead to an increase in consumption rather than productive investment, which was the original target. This would occur, for instance, if, in addition to credit problems, the poor were subject to an income constraint (because their incomes are lower than what is required to satisfy the family's basic needs) and to severe and uninsurable uncertainty. People living close to subsistence level have a very high marginal utility of current consumption, while the return on potentially productive investments can be very uncertain. The program could be effective if it addressed the main reason for the lack of insurance markets and credit, the presence of asymmetric information and induced moral hazard.[13]

These examples should make clear the usefulness of framing the problem of intervention for poverty reduction in terms of equation (1). Within this framework, one may think of several ways in which policy action could increase the incomes of the poor. First, policies may be aimed at increasing T_i through some type of income transfer. As stressed above, these solutions are unlikely to be beneficial in the long run. Moreover, one should consider carefully the effects (beneficial or otherwise) that they might have on the other variables in the equation. Second, policies could be aimed at generating a price structure that produces higher rewards for the assets typically owned by the poor. This is obviously a very unrealistic target, especially if one operates in an open economy. Third, policies may provide incentives

---

[12] This argument has been made several times in development economics in relation to the diversification of rural investment. It has been argued that in many underdeveloped countries, rural households plant relatively inefficient crops because of the lack of insurance mechanisms. A similar argument may hold for investment in human capital, even though it is a long-run investment.

Another common restriction that interacts with liquidity constraints and risk is the indivisibility of investment. Galor and Zeira (1993) argue that some investments (including human capital) require a minimum amount of resources to make them worthwhile. If such resources are unavailable and individuals face credit constraints, they might rationally choose not to make the investment at all and use the available resources for less productive ventures.

[13] This is the idea behind the popular Grameen banks.

for modifying the rate at which the existing assets are used for generating income. Again, the design of these types of policies requires a complete understanding of the incentives and mechanisms at play in the process of asset accumulation and utilization. Fourth, policies may be focused on increasing the capital stock. Fifth, if the restrictions that the poor face in accumulating income-earning assets were identified, policies could be aimed at eliminating or easing the constraints.

The main issue to stress here is that any of the first four alternatives will only be able to improve the standard of living of the poor to a limited extent if the restrictions on accumulation remain unaltered. If the restrictions remain unchanged, any action through the first four options will in some sense imply "swimming against the tide," because the economic context will continue to impose restrictions on enhancing the long-term income-earning capacity of the poor. On the other hand, if policies were to focus on eliminating those restrictions, they would have a more permanent effect, and in fact, any of the other four options considered above would perhaps be redundant. This strategy, however, imposes the greatest challenge because it implies changes to the whole economic system. But precisely because of its broad effects, it is the only real option for tackling the causes of poverty and providing some solutions to the problem.

The ultimate objective of each of the six country studies included in this book is to provide empirical evidence on the link between assets and poverty and, whenever possible, to identify the restrictions faced by the poor in accumulating income-earning assets. Rather than exhausting this topic, the present aim is to take some steps toward showing its potential as an alternative policy approach to poverty reduction and analysis.[14] But even before illustrating this argument empirically, it is necessary to clarify the magnitude of poverty in Latin America.

Magnitude of the Problem: Poverty in Latin America in the 1990s

Poverty reduction remains one of the greatest challenges facing Latin America today. Based on the 18 countries included in this analysis, which include

---

[14] For the link between asset distribution and other development indicators such as the rate of economic growth, see Birdsall and Londoño (1997).

around 93 percent of the total population of the region, the average poverty rate is 40 percent.[15] In terms of absolute numbers of poor, around 180 million Latin Americans in 1996 lived below the $2 per day poverty line.[16]

The estimates presented here are believed to be the first covering all 18 countries and going beyond 1995. The estimates are produced by following the methodology of Londoño and Székely (1997), henceforth LS, which is adequate for international comparisons.[17] The method consists of scaling up household per capita incomes in the surveys to match 1985 private consumption per capita from the National Accounts, adjusted for purchasing power parity (PPP) and using a poverty line of two 1985 PPP-adjusted dollars-per-day per person to classify the population into poor and non-poor.[18] It must be stressed that calculating poverty in this way normally yields estimates below calculations made with local poverty lines.[19] The value of the poverty indexes obtained is more useful for ranking countries in international comparisons rather than for obtaining the best poverty estimate for each individual country. It should also be mentioned that since this chapter is based on micro data in all 18 countries, the estimates have a high degree

---

[15] The data are representative at the national level for all countries except Argentina and Uruguay, where the household surveys covered only urban areas but still include around 85 percent and 91 percent of the population, respectively. As for the timing of the surveys, one (for Nicaragua) refers to 1993, four to 1995 (Ecuador, El Salvador, Paraguay, and Uruguay), seven to 1996 (Argentina, Bolivia, Brazil, Chile, Dominican Republic, Jamaica, and Mexico), five to 1997 (Costa Rica, Colombia, Panama, Peru, and Venezuela) and one to 1998 (Honduras). The working paper version of this chapter provides more information on each of the surveys used. It can be accessed at *http://www.iadb.org/RES/publications_list.cfm?CODE=R-376*. Some of these surveys were obtained through MECOVI, a program sponsored by the World Bank, the IDB, and ECLAC to collect and organize the existing household surveys in Latin America and to promote the implementation of new ones. The rest of the surveys were obtained directly from country statistical offices.

[16] Note that the absolute number of poor obtained by following the method used by Londoño and Székely (1997) is a point estimate specific to this methodology. Székely et al. (1999), for instance, show that with the application of other methods for computing poverty, the number of poor in the region can range between 50 and 280 million. The Londoño and Székely method is followed for the present results because it appears to be the best option for international comparisons. In any case, the conclusion that poverty in Latin America is extremely high by international standards holds with any of the methodological options considered in Székely et al. (2000).

[17] Londoño and Székely (1997) documented changes in poverty and inequality in Latin America and the Caribbean for 1970-95. They considered information for 13 countries, covering around 83 percent of the population in the region. Apart from having wider coverage of the region's

of comparability. However, due to differences in survey characteristics, samples, questionnaires and so on, *full* comparability across countries is not guaranteed.

Figure 1.1 shows that poverty rates range from more than 70 percent in Nicaragua, El Salvador and Bolivia to less than 20 percent in Argentina, Chile and Venezuela. Argentina and Uruguay have some of the lowest proportions of poor, but it should be remembered that these two countries do not include observations for rural areas, so there is an underestimation of poverty as compared with other national samples. Paraguay and Honduras are also among the poorest countries, with more than 60 percent of the total population below the PPP-adjusted poverty line of $2 per day. After Honduras, there is a group of three countries (Brazil, Panama and Ecuador), all with poverty rates between 40 percent and 50 percent. Some of the countries included in this group, especially Brazil and Panama, have GDP per capita above the Latin American average, which in international comparisons classifies them as middle-income countries. Therefore, it is rather surprising that they have such high poverty rates. A similar argument applies to Colombia, Mexico, and Jamaica, which have poverty rates between 22 percent and 30 percent. These rates are high considering that these upper-middle-income countries have some of the highest GDP per capita in the region. The reason for the mismatch between poverty and average income is

population, there are other differences between this study and LS. The first is that seven additional countries are included; the second is that information on the Bahamas and Guatemala (included in LS), is not included in this chapter. Third, more recent household survey data are used for the countries that are included in both studies.

[18] The PPP adjustment is made for two reasons. The first is to express the incomes of all countries in the same units in order to apply the same poverty line. Secondly, and more importantly, there are differences between surveys as to the degree of under-reporting of incomes. Private consumption in the National Accounts is a good proxy of the resources available to households for purchasing goods and services, so by scaling incomes up to this aggregate it is possible to obtain a more comparable series across countries than would be possible with the raw data. This methodology implicitly assumes that under-reporting is proportional to current income and that the factor of proportionality is the same across the distribution of income. If rich households under-report a larger portion of their income, the method will underestimate poverty.

[19] Since PPP private consumption per capita for 1996 and 1997 was only available in a preliminary form for Latin America, the poverty estimates for the countries with household surveys for these years or 1998 should be taken as preliminary. They are subject to change if the aggregates in the National Accounts are modified with more recent data.

Figure 1.1. Poverty in Latin America, mid-1990s

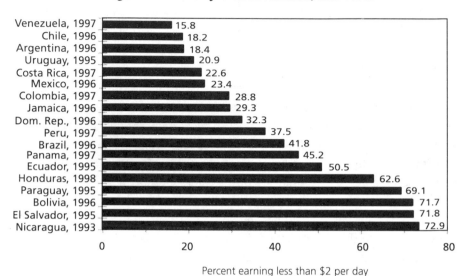

Percent earning less than $2 per day

that all these countries have very high inequality levels. Following these countries, a group comprised of Uruguay, Venezuela, Chile, and Argentina has rates between 15.8 percent and 20 percent, which are still rather high for their GDP per capita.

Poverty, Inequality and Income-Earning Assets

One simple way to explicitly link poverty, inequality and assets is to perform the decomposition of poverty indexes suggested by Székely (1998, Chapter 4). This splits poverty into three components when the population is divided into subgroups according to certain criteria: an "income" component, a "between-group" inequality element, and a "within-group" inequality term. Following this methodology, after classifying the population into subgroups according to a characteristic of the population for which household surveys provide information, poverty indexes from the family of additively decomposable indexes (such as the head count ratio used in Figure 1.1) can be expressed as:

$$S = S_B + S_W + S_\mu \qquad (2)$$

where S is a decomposable poverty index, S_B is the between-group component, S_W is the within-group term and S_μ is the income component. S_μ/S measures the proportion of poverty due to lack of resources to satisfy each individual's basic needs; it is the poverty that would remain even if income were distributed equally among the population. If average income is greater than the poverty line, the value of this component equals zero. S_W/S is the proportion of poverty associated with the inequality within each subgroup and is regarded as the proportion of poverty "not explained" by the characteristic chosen to classify the population. It is the poverty that would remain if mean income were above the poverty line and there were no differences among the average incomes of the subgroups. Finally, S_B simulates the poverty that would remain if there were no differences within groups and average income was above the poverty line. The statistic S_B/S is the proportion of poverty associated with between-group inequalities and can be regarded as the proportion of poverty "explained" by the characteristic chosen to classify the population into subgroups. If there are no differences between groups, this statistic equals zero. $S_B/S+ S_W/S$ is therefore the proportion of poverty due to inequality.

All the countries in Figure 1.1 have average private consumption per capita (which has been used as a welfare indicator to measure poverty) above the poverty line of $2 a day. Therefore, $S_\mu/S=0$, which implies that poverty in Latin America is not a matter of lack of resources. If income were perfectly equally distributed among the population there would actually be no poverty.[20] Poverty is therefore accounted for by inequality in the distribution of resources.

Table 1.1 presents the value of the S_B/S statistic obtained by dividing the population according to a range of population characteristics. As mentioned above, this statistic shows how much poverty is associated with the inequality between groups. The poverty not accounted for by this statistic, is therefore attributable to within-group differences. For most of the 18 countries surveyed, there is information on every person's sector of activity, oc-

---

[20] Note that the decomposition relies on a static simulation that does not account for the possibility that if income were perfectly distributed, average income would perhaps be lower or higher.

Table 1.1. Poverty Due to Between-Group Inequalities

(Percent of total poverty)

Country	Inequality between					
	Sectors of activity	Occupations	Age groups	Male-Female headed hh's	Education level	Rural/ Urban
Argentina	10.4	19.9	4.0	0.0	34.4	
Bolivia	4.8	21.3	0.2	0.1	35.8	13.0
Brazil	10.5	24.8	2.2	0.4	32.4	9.7
Chile	17.9	45.7	1.7	0.2	47.8	13.5
Colombia	12.9	22.9	0.9	0.0	33.3	15.7
Costa Rica	13.5	26.1	3.0	0.4	35.3	13.5
Dom. Rep.	5.0	14.3	1.4	0.8	16.8	8.4
Ecuador	5.9	10.4	1.2	0.1	17.6	7.8
El Salvador	12.0	16.5	0.1	0.3	26.2	4.1
Honduras	14.7	26.8	3.0	0.0	34.5	17.0
Jamaica			7.1	2.9	15.8	7.2
Mexico	25.7	40.3	3.2	1.1	46.9	30.2
Nicaragua		1.2	0.6	0.1	15.6	3.0
Panama	5.2	14.7	0.7	0.2	21.4	7.9
Paraguay	13.9	18.4	4.0	0.3	26.3	13.0
Peru	13.3	20.6	0.2	0.9	32.4	19.6
Uruguay	6.7	19.6	2.1	0.5	18.8	
Venezuela	9.1	21.4	0.6	0.3	23.5	
Average	**11.3**	**21.5**	**2.0**	**0.5**	**28.6**	**12.2**

Source: Authors' calculations based on household survey data. The methodology used for estimating poverty and the poverty line is the same as in Figure 1.1.

cupation, age, sex, education level, and rural/urban location. Each of these characteristics is used to classify the population into subgroups by taking the characteristics of the household head as a reference and performing the decomposition in equation (2), using the same methodology as in Figure 1.1 to estimate poverty.

With respect to the age of the household head, life-cycle theories suggest that the income profile of individuals is hump-shaped. Thus, households headed by relatively old individuals would normally be poorer because earnings decline with age due to productivity reductions, and also because pensions and transfers for retirement tend to be of limited value. Similarly, households headed by relatively young individuals also are expected to earn low incomes because of low labor market experience and relatively large family size. Therefore, in relatively young or aging economies, poverty would normally be expected to be associated with age differences, while in countries in the middle stages of the demographic transition these disparities would be less important. Table 1.1 shows that on average, 2 percent of the total poverty in the region can in fact be attributed to age differences, a figure that is quite low. In line with the theoretical argument, the countries that are most advanced (Argentina and Uruguay) and at the initial stages of the demographic transition (Honduras and Paraguay) have relatively higher S_B/S statistics for this characteristic. Age differences are apparently not an important source of poverty in Latin America because most of the countries in the region are entering the middle stages of the transition, when most of the population is of working age.

It is usually believed that poverty is also strongly associated with gender differences. This is because there is a growing proportion of households headed by single females. Women generally receive lower remuneration for performing the same tasks as men due to discrimination, and also because households tend to invest less in women, thus hindering their income-earning capacity. However, the results in Table 1.1 indicate that only a very small portion of total poverty in the region is associated with gender differences (on average, .5 percent). Rather than providing conclusive evidence against the argument that female heads of household are disadvantaged, the result shows that the number of female-headed households is still small in the region. These households are typically underrepresented in household surveys because the head is self-reported, and because they are in fact highly vulnerable and tend to merge into other households, forming extended units. Only the female-headed households headed by relatively educated women at the upper spectrum of the distribution actually survive as such, and they appear in the data as independent units.

One of the most common explanations for poverty in developing countries is the presence of an urban bias through an unfavorable allocation of public goods and the presence of adverse terms of trade. According to the evidence in Table 1.1, rural/urban differences account on average for around 12.2 percent of the poverty in the region, but they are associated with around 30 percent and 20 percent in Mexico and Peru, respectively. Thus, particularly in these countries, the geographic location among urban and rural areas is an important determinant of poverty.

Another common argument is that poverty is determined by the sector of activity in which the poor work, and thus by the structure of the economy. The poor tend to have access to sectors with lower productivity, and as argued above, they may also choose less profitable but also less risky activities in certain sectors. On average, 11.3 percent of the total poverty in the region is actually accounted for by differences among sectors. As compared with rural/urban differences, the disparities between sectors are less important.

Occupational disparities are also usually regarded as being important determinants of poverty because people's income-earning possibilities are strongly related to the ownership of human and physical capital assets, which determine the chances of overcoming the barriers to entry into certain occupations. Occupational indicators provide some information on the access to human, physical and social capital that is required to be able to perform certain activities. Among the characteristics for which information is available, occupation is actually the second most important in terms of poverty. Table 1.1 shows that 21.5 percent of the poverty in the region is associated with differences across occupational groups. However, there are cases such as Mexico and Chile, where these inequalities account for more than 40 percent of total poverty. Due to the connection between asset ownership and occupation, the result is suggestive of the link between the distribution of assets and poverty.

With regard to educational differences, the poor are rarely able to finance the private costs of schooling, even when there is public free access to these services. In countries where formal education and skills are concentrated, unskilled labor is relatively more abundant and poorly paid, while skilled labor is scarce and highly rewarded. The price structure reflects the interaction between an unequal distribution of these assets and the demand for skills. Table 1.1 confirms that quite a significant proportion of poverty in Latin America is associated precisely with income differences across education groups. On average, 28.6 percent of total poverty would be eliminated if there were no disparities between education groups. In Mexico, Honduras, Costa Rica, Chile, Bolivia and Argentina, more than one-third of the overall poverty rate is accounted for by educational differences. Thus, having more or less skills is a stronger determinant of poverty than being located in rural areas, being employed in relatively unproductive sectors of activity, belonging to female-headed households, or living in households with relatively young or old heads. The results illustrate that there is a powerful link between poverty and the distribution of human capital.

Poverty and Assets

The results discussed above indicate that the "excess poverty" in many Latin American countries (given their average per capita income) can be explained by high levels of inequality. This is in turn likely to be linked to high levels of inequality in income-generating assets, and in particular human capital. This section takes a closer look at the number of years of formal schooling, which is one of the main components of human capital and is probably the most important income-earning asset. Specifically, within the context of equation (1) the distribution of the stock is examined, as well as its use by different sectors of the population and the prices paid for it in the market. Second, and more importantly, the argument about the connection between poverty and the restrictions on accumulating assets is illustrated by examining the process of human capital accumulation and by providing some evidence on what constraints the poor face in acquiring it. Among the three income-earning assets considered in this book, human capital is chosen because it is the asset for which high-quality information is available.

Distribution, Use and Remuneration of Human Capital

It is not surprising that the poor typically have low schooling levels. The household survey data documents this for the 18 Latin American countries in the sample. Figure 1.2 presents the results by ordering countries according to their GDP per capita level.[21] The figure includes the average years of schooling of all adults between 25 and 65 years of age in three different quintiles. Clearly, adults at the lower end of the income distribution have acquired much less human capital than individuals in the same age-range in the upper quintiles.

---

[21] This and the following figures order countries from low to high PPP-adjusted GDP per capita.

Figure 1.2. Years of Schooling of Adults, 25-65, by Quintile

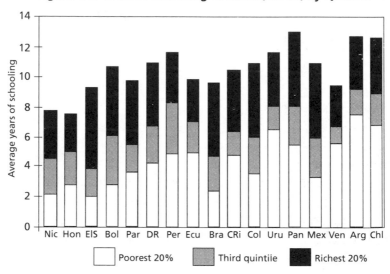

On average, adults in the first quintile have 4.4 years of schooling. Those in the middle quintile have 6.6 years, while those located in the richest quintile have 10.5 years. The average difference between the poorest and richest 20 percent is 6.1 years, but there is a wide variety across countries. While in Venezuela the difference is around four years, in Brazil, Colombia, El Salvador, Panama, Mexico and Bolivia, the gap is of more than seven years. Since education is one of the main determinants of income, it is clear that income-earning capacity in terms of human capital is very poorly distributed in the region. Even the differences between the poorest 20 percent and the third quintile are quite high (they range from 1.6 years in Uruguay to 3.4 years in Peru). So, in terms of equation (1), the figure provides evidence on the highly skewed distribution of one of the elements in A.

Human capital is very unequally distributed among males, but there is no evidence that there are differences in the rate at which this asset is used to produce income. In fact, labor force participation rates for all countries and education groups are very close to 90 percent. However, the story for females is totally different. Figure 1.3 presents female labor force participation rates for the 25-65 age range. The data clearly show that there are very large differences across education groups. On average, the participation rate

**Figure 1.3. Female Formal Participation Rates
by Schooling Level**
(In percent)

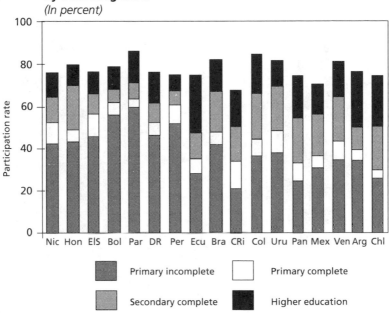

for females with incomplete primary schooling is 39 percent, while the rates for those with secondary and higher education are 61.8 percent and 77.4 percent, respectively. The differences in participation rates between the highest and lowest education levels seem to increase with GDP per capita and are greatest in Chile, Panama, Costa Rica, Ecuador, Venezuela and Colombia, where there is a gap of more than 45 percentage points.

Thus, in the case of females, a low level of human capital is clearly associated with a low rate of use. In terms of equation (1), this illustrates that A and R can be closely linked. It is important to stress that this evidence does not imply that women belonging to poorer sectors of the population work less. The information only means that a much smaller proportion of women with little education, and who typically belong to the lower spectrum of income distribution, is remunerated for their labor in the market. In fact, women with few years of education may devote more hours to work, but few of those hours relate to work for which retribution in monetary terms is received.

**Figure 1.4. Female Formal Participation Rates
by Schooling Level**
(In percent)

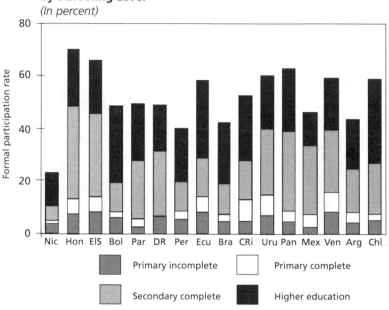

The comparison becomes even more dramatic when comparing female labor force participation in the formal sector. Figure 1.4 reveals that the differences across education groups are even greater in this case. The average formal participation rate among females with incomplete primary education is 5.6 percent, while the average among the highly educated is 52 percent. So, the differences in use arise not only because females with lower income-earning capacity use their human capital at a lower rate, but also because those who participate in the labor market do so in jobs that typically have less stability, fewer benefits, and are of lower quality.

Obviously, the link between the distribution of schooling and labor force participation is the return to the use of human capital. Females with low education levels choose not to participate in the labor market because the incentives to participate might not be enough in comparison with home production. However, for females with higher education levels, the rewards that the market offers are attractive enough to induce a higher proportion of them to use this asset.

Table 1.2 provides some evidence on the returns to education in Latin

Table 1.2. Returns to Education in Latin America during the 1990s

Country	Year	Coefficients from OLS regression				
		Primary incomplete	Primary complete	Secondary incomplete	Secondary complete	Higher education
Argentina*	1996	0.12	0.21	0.34	0.60	1.03
Bolivia*	1990	-0.14	-0.06	0.11	0.21	0.49
	1991	-0.14	-0.06	0.11	0.21	0.49
	1993	0.09	0.17	0.36	0.66	1.11
	1995	0.06	0.16	0.25	0.56	1.13
Brazil	1992	0.12	0.26	0.47	0.84	1.54
	1993	0.10	0.24	0.47	0.82	1.50
	1995	0.45	0.82	1.17	1.72	2.50
	1996	0.41	0.76	1.13	1.65	2.39
Chile	1990	0.19	0.36	0.66	0.97	1.72
	1992	0.20	0.33	0.61	1.02	1.83
	1994	0.27	0.44	0.67	1.11	1.87
	1996	0.19	0.38	0.67	1.08	1.92
Colombia	1997	0.19	0.55	0.82	1.28	2.10
Costa Rica	1989	0.22	0.42	0.70	1.04	1.51
	1991	0.11	0.27	0.53	0.84	1.47
	1993	0.30	0.43	0.65	0.88	1.55
	1995	0.21	0.37	0.57	0.84	1.44
Dom. Rep.	1996	0.30	0.49	0.63	0.75	1.39
Ecuador	1995	0.23	0.49	0.90	1.26	1.64
El Salvador	1995	0.26	0.49	0.73	1.17	1.77
Honduras	1992	0.15	0.38	0.71	1.11	1.82
	1996	0.24	0.54	0.70	1.23	1.90
	1998	0.17	0.40	0.59	1.79	1.92
Mexico	1989	0.33	0.68	1.05	1.47	1.90
	1992	0.43	0.82	1.27	1.72	2.37
	1994	0.24	0.52	0.88	1.39	2.05
	1996	0.09	0.40	0.93	1.65	2.43
Nicaragua	1993	0.40	0.55	0.71	0.99	1.47
Panama	1991	-0.07	0.04	0.22	0.47	0.96
	1995	0.06	0.14	0.33	0.56	1.09
	1997	-0.03	-0.06	0.00	0.23	0.96
Paraguay	1995	0.32	0.71	1.07	1.63	2.26
Peru	1991	0.00	-0.02	0.08	0.12	0.31
	1994	0.03	0.08	0.27	0.34	0.73
	1997	0.22	0.29	0.50	0.56	1.09
Uruguay*	1989	0.03	0.12	0.27	0.32	0.52
	1992	0.27	0.51	0.81	0.99	1.47
	1995	0.18	0.36	0.73	0.93	1.46
Venezuela	1995	0.35	0.55	0.73	0.98	1.44
	1997	0.27	0.43	0.58	0.88	1.59
Average LAC	**1997**	**0.18**	**0.37**	**0.61**	**0.95**	**1.52**

Source: Authors' calculations based on household survey data.
*Surveys with urban coverage.

America [this is the *P* component of equation (1)]. The table shows the coefficients of a standard OLS Mincer regression where the dependent variable is the log hourly wage of each individual, while the independent variables are experience (proxied by age six minus years of schooling), experience squared, and a vector of dummies representing five different education levels.[22] The returns to education are determined by a variety of factors and are less subject to individual preferences and decisions.

Not surprisingly, Table 1.2 shows that the returns to education increase considerably by level. This suggests that the poor not only have low incomes because of their few years of education, but also because their schooling is rewarded less in the market. The rich receive a larger income not only for having greater stocks of human capital but also because they own the types of education that are valued most.

Table 1.2 shows that having incomplete primary schooling implies, on average, an income 18 percent higher than that for people with no schooling. Complete primary education yields a return of 37 percent, while incomplete and complete secondary education have returns of 61 percent and 95 percent, respectively. The greatest returns are observed for higher education, with 152 percent on average. The largest differences in returns between the lowest and highest schooling levels are observed in Brazil, Chile, Colombia and Mexico.

This evidence illustrates the circularity between asset ownership, use, and return. The poor have the smallest stocks of human capital. They receive the lowest rewards not only for having a small stock but also because the returns are non-linear and increase with the size of the stock. Finally, due to the low returns, the poor (and specifically women) end up using the asset at a lower rate.

Interestingly, this circularity is reinforced when individuals join together into families. Table 1.3 plots the correlation between the years of education of the household head (who typically is male) and his (her) spouse. As can be seen, the correlation is positive and high. It ranges from .39 in the case of Venezuela to .96 in Argentina. Thus, individuals with low human

---

[22] The regression is estimated for all adults in the 25-65 age range and does not correct for sample selection biases due to participation. However, the conclusions about the changes in the returns to education and the differences between low and high schooling levels do not change substantially when corrections to the bias are attempted.

Table 1.3. Correlation Coefficients

Country	Correlation of years of schooling	Correlation of income
Argentina	0.96	0.60
Bolivia	0.68	0.35
Brazil	0.59	0.52
Chile	0.60	0.51
Colombia	0.57	0.03
Costa Rica	0.50	0.34
Dom. Rep.	0.52	0.42
Ecuador	0.60	0.26
El Salvador	0.62	0.42
Honduras	0.55	0 16
Mexico	0.62	0.36
Nicaragua	0.59	0.59
Panama	0.47	0.51
Paraguay	0.59	0.53
Peru	0.62	0.45
Uruguay	0.46	0.34
Venezuela	0.39	0.50
Average LAC	**0.58**	**0.50**

Source: Authors' calculations.

capital tend to form households with others with similar levels, and vice versa. The second column in the table presents the correlation between the income earned by the head of the household and his (her) spouse. This correlation not only accounts for assortative mating in terms of education, but also incorporates the effect of participation. In all cases, the correlation is positive and quite high, indicating that individuals with low income-earning potential tend to form households with individuals who have similarly low income-earning capacity. This translates into low family incomes, and perhaps more importantly, into restricted capacity to finance the accumulation of human capital for younger generations. For the well educated, on the other hand, the correlation reinforces a *virtuous* circle between asset ownership and family formation.

Table 1.2 estimates the returns to education for several years for the countries for which more than one comparable household survey for the 1990s is available. With few exceptions, the returns to all education levels have been increasing. Moreover, returns have increased more for the highest levels. It should be noted, however, that these shifts are in line with a worldwide trend and are not exclusive of the region. Where Latin America stands out is in the large differences in returns between low and high schooling levels.

Obviously the simple description of the data reported here does not constitute the whole story. Research should be developed in several directions that are beyond the scope of this chapter. First, the returns to education should be corrected for selection biases in several dimensions. Second, and related to this, there might be important differences between observed wages and the price of different skills (an argument recently stressed in Heckman, Lochner and Taber, 1998). Finally, in considering the incentives to invest in human capital, one should also consider the general equilibrium effects that large changes in the supply of some skills might have on their prices. While all these issues are extremely important, the evidence presented here is sufficient to show that inequality in the stock of human capital and its use is, at least given the current returns to education, crucial in explaining inequality in Latin America.

Why Do the Poor Accumulate Less Human Capital than the Rich?

Following the argument presented above, the key question regarding poverty in terms of equation (1) is what are the restrictions that the poor face in accumulating human capital. To turn to this question it is first useful to take a closer look at the process of human capital accumulation.

Figure 1.5 plots the difference in average years of schooling between children in the highest and lowest quintiles for four different age groups (12, 15, 18 and 21 years of age). In Uruguay, for instance, there is no difference for children age 12 between the top and bottom 20 percent of the income distribution. The average gap at this age is one year, with the largest difference of 1.6 years in Brazil. But the differences start widening in higher age groups. Among 15-year olds, the average difference between the poorest and richest 20 percent is 1.4 years, but the gap increases to 2.7 and 3.8 years for children aged 18 and 21, respectively. So, education differences between

Figure 1.5. Difference in Average Years of Education between Richest and Poorest Quintile

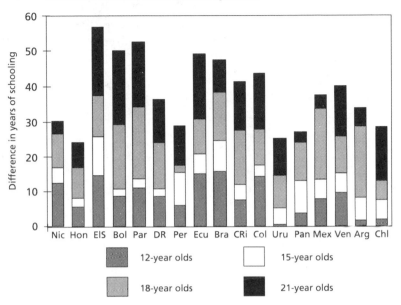

the tails of the distribution start becoming apparent at around age 15 (note also that in general, the differences are smaller for countries with higher GDP per capita).

There is extensive literature on the determinants of schooling,[23] and there seems to be a consensus that family background plays a key role in the process of human capital accumulation. Table 1.4 documents the association between some indicators of family background and schooling attainment. The coefficients are presented from a regression performed on 15-year olds, where the dependent variable is the average years of schooling, and the independent variables are the years of schooling of the mother and father, respectively, and household income per capita (excluding the income of the person in question in case he/she is an income earner). The table also in-

---

[23] See Behrman (1999) for a recent review.

Table 1.4. Regression Coefficients: Dependent Variable Years of Schooling

| Country | Year | Coefficient independent variables | | | |
		Mother's schooling**	Father's schooling**	Household per capita income***	R-Squared**
Argentina*	1996	8.43	3.70	5.15	9.36
Bolivia*	1990	5.37	7.74	3.98	12.26
	1991	5.37	7.74	3.98	12.26
	1993	7.47	5.20	-0.62	11.35
	1995	3.99	3.76	-1.45	4.85
Brazil	1992	19.98	12.05	0.00	26.97
	1993	19.96	11.95	0.13	25.88
	1995	18.86	11.24	6.61	25.86
	1996	18.10	11.10	8.74	26.07
Chile	1990	8.23	4.08	0.01	10.37
	1992	9.83	1.89	-0.02	7.40
	1994	7.25	2.36	0.00	7.34
	1996	7.48	2.25	0.00	9.03
Colombia	1997	22.31	5.15	0.00	24.31
Costa Rica	1989	16.27	4.17	0.04	12.00
	1991	16.90	7.08	-0.12	20.93
	1993	20.62	4.45	0.07	26.37
	1995	12.04	4.43	0.05	15.29
Dom. Rep.	1996	18.84	3.34	1.10	16.97
Ecuador	1995	19.81	6.49	0.00	21.12
El Salvador	1995	20.69	9.27	3.43	17.73
Honduras	1992	18.48	6.01	10.80	22.79
	1996	18.33	10.25	6.75	23.99
	1998	18.97	8.14	-0.31	15.10
Mexico	1989	20.76	12.07	0.00	21.04
	1992	14.94	12.27	0.00	12.73
	1994	19.94	20.56	0.57	15.41
	1996	21.65	17.58	0.03	14.57
Nicaragua	1993	20.06	13.30	5.19	18.85
Panama	1991	14.24	4.36	2.81	17.05
	1995	14.48	0.88	9.12	19.82
	1997	12.42	4.88	4.01	15.21
Paraguay	1995	22.61	3.39	0.00	16.15
Peru	1991	11.23	2.01	31.04	14.92
	1994	9.02	4.33	17.18	15.74
	1997	6.23	8.89	20.20	21.35
Uruguay*	1989	7.22	2.44	26.15	8.04
	1992	8.49	2.56	0.00	6.25
	1995	6.21	4.95	0.00	6.80
Venezuela	1995	17.10	4.54	0.11	18.28
	1997	10.90	7.61	0.08	12.52

Source: Authors' calculations based on household survey data.
*Surveys with urban coverage.
**Coefficient multiplied by 100.
***Coefficient multiplied by 10,000.

cludes a column with the R^2 from the regression. This statistic averages 16 percent, but reaches 26 percent for Brazil, indicating that the association between a child's educational attainment and family background can be very important. As is common in this type of regression, the coefficient for the mother's schooling is in most instances higher than the father's. The table includes results for more than one year whenever possible, but there seems to be no clear pattern of change during the 1990s.

There are several (not mutually exclusive) possible interpretations for the result that parental background has an effect on the schooling of children. One possibility is that more educated parents put more input into their children's education, which facilitates their achievement of academic goals. Alternatively, it is possible that less educated parents face binding liquidity constraints that prevent them from borrowing the amounts necessary to see their children through a certain number of years of schooling and therefore enjoying the high returns to education.

While it is difficult to distinguish between these alternative hypotheses without a structural model of education choices and additional evidence that would control for selection biases, there is evidence in some household surveys favoring the latter explanation.[24] Specifically, surveys for Bolivia, Costa Rica, Chile, El Salvador, Paraguay and Venezuela include a question asking children and young adults not enrolled in school why they are not attending. The answers to these questions could constitute a first step towards discriminating among the competing explanations mentioned in the previous paragraph. To summarize this information, the possible reasons for not attending are classified into eight groups: (i) the individual is currently working, (ii) lack of financial resources, (iii) maternity or household work, (iv) not interested in attending school, (v) no infrastructure, materials, teachers or school available, (vi) finished school, (vii) too old to attend, and (viii) other. Table 1.5 presents the results by restricting the sample to young adults who are 21 years of age, separating individuals belonging to the richest and poorest 10 percent of the population.[25]

---

[24] Cameron and Heckman (1998) estimate a structural model of education choices in the United States and present some evidence against the hypothesis of binding liquidity constraints there. The reality of Latin America is likely to be very different. Cameron and Heckman also discuss the importance of dynamic selection biases.

[25] Similar results are obtained for 12, 15 and 18-year olds.

Table 1.5. Reasons for Not Attending School

(Percent distribution by category)

Category	Bolivia 1995	Costa Rica 1995	Chile 1994	El Salvador 1995	Paraguay 1995	Venezuela 1995	Average
Reasons for not attending school: all 21-year olds							
1 Working	42.1	17.1	32.7	27.8	15.67	38.9	26.4
2 No financial resources	19.9	13.2	10.7	22.3	28.19	9.9	12.7
3 Maternity-household work	10.7	5.1	9.3	14.8	12.55	13.9	9.0
4 Not interested	11.7	22.1	5.0	13.6	10.22	20.2	12.1
5 No infrastructure		6.2	1.9	6.2	0.47	7.4	4.3
6 Finished schooling	1.5			0.4	11.02	1.5	0.9
7 Age	2.7	6.8	28.9	6.9	21.88	1.4	7.8
8 Other	11.2	29.6	11.6	8.1		6.7	13.4
Reasons for not attending in first decile							
1 Working	27.4	9.3	21.6	18.0	9.7	20.8	17.8
2 No financial resources	39.6	22.3	14.0	21.8	33.9	15.8	24.6
3 Maternity-household work	5.7	5.3	11.3	15.6	9.3	13.6	10.1
4 Not interested	9.1	16.0	4.6	14.2	12.0	30.0	14.3
5 No infrastructure		14.5	3.8	9.9		6.8	8.7
6 Finished schooling	1.1			0.5		0.8	0.8
7 Age	3.3	7.7	35.4	11.1	16.4	2.3	12.7
8 Other	13.7	25.0	9.3	9.0	18.7	10.0	14.3
Reasons for not attending school in richest decile							
1 Working	27.6	0.0	42.6	53.3	34.8	49.1	34.6
2 No financial resources	6.2	22.4	4.0	9.8	9.8	2.0	9.0
3 Maternity-household work	11.3	8.2	4.9	13.4		8.1	9.2
4 Not interested	39.2	8.1	2.3	13.2	16.7	23.2	17.1
5 No infrastructure		16.3	2.5	0.8	7.2	9.0	7.2
6 Finished schooling	7.2				0.9	3.0	3.7
7 Age			23.4	2.0	6.0	1.5	8.3
8 Other	8.3	45.0	20.4	7.5	24.6	4.1	18.3

Source: Authors' calculations based on household survey data.

There are interesting differences between rich and poor. For instance, according to these results, around 25 percent of the 21-year olds from the first decile who are not enrolled in school respond that they do not attend because they lack the necessary financial resources, while 17.8 percent do not attend because they are working. Around 15 percent say they are not interested (which could be due to the low quality of the education to which they have access), while 12.7 percent say they do not attend because of their age (which normally reflects high repetition rates). Less than 9 percent say the reason is lack of infrastructure, teachers, materials, etc. In the case of the 21-year olds belonging to the richest quintile, the main reasons are work (34.6 percent), lack of interest (17.1 percent), maternity or household work (9.2 percent), and infrastructure (7.2 percent); only 9 percent respond that the reason is that they lack financial resources.

Apart from the fact that the answers vary, it should be noted that an apparently similar response to the same question does not necessarily mean that the reasons for not attending are identical. For instance, in the case of work, the response by the poor might be associated mostly with financial constraints faced by the family, which cannot afford having a young adult in school instead of generating income in the labor market. However, in the case of a person of the same age but at the top of the income distribution, the situation might be totally different. As illustrated in Figure 1.5, typically a 21-year old in the richest 20 percent has almost four more years more of schooling than one in the bottom 20 percent. Therefore, in the case of the rich, lack of enrollment due to work is more likely to reflect the attractiveness of the opportunities in the labor market for relatively well educated young adults.

One interesting conclusion from these responses is that a rather low proportion of the population seems to be constrained by the supply of public education. In fact, the only country for which more than 10 percent of the sample declares that they are not enrolled in school due to infrastructure limitations is Costa Rica, which is one of the Latin American countries with the best public education services. For the poor, clearly the lack of means to finance the investment is the key restriction for not continuing to accumulate human capital.

A naive interpretation of these results could be that to provide incentives for the accumulation of human capital among the poor, one should offer income transfers to eliminate the income constraint. However, recalling the results in Table 1.4, the problem seems to be more complex. Individuals born in families with low human capital are to some extent predetermined to acquire less education than those born in better conditions. The importance of family background is an indication that the problems are much deeper. Such variables could indicate that capital markets are imperfect and insurance mechanisms are incomplete, so individuals cannot just invest with long-term objectives depending on their preferences. They could also indicate that poor children do not receive the same quantity of educational inputs from their families. In the first case, a possible policy implication would be the relaxation of credit constraints, while in the second case, it would be programs that target very young poor children to substitute for the missing inputs from their families. The reason the "income constraint" is binding for the poor is because there are other constraints on the accumulation of human capital. Loosening the income constraint at least temporarily may facilitate schooling progress, but the family background effect and the forces behind it will continue to inhibit the accumulation of this income-earning asset. The estimation of a structural model of human capital acquisition might be required to consider all these connections adequately.

Results from Country Studies

The country studies in this book on Brazil, Bolivia, Chile, Colombia, Costa Rica and Peru rely heavily on household survey data, but in many cases they combine several other sources. For Brazil, the annual household survey is combined with monthly employment data and a survey on consumer finances. For Bolivia, existing household surveys were used, but a small survey to collect information on social capital was also carried out specifically for this project. The study on Chile uses household surveys and adds information on the quality of education services through the national system of test scores. The Colombia chapter combines several household surveys. The chapter on Costa Rica relies on available household surveys, but also uses a survey on microenterprises carried out specifically for this project. Finally, the chapter on Peru mainly relies on available household surveys.

All six country studies follow a common structure. They first examine the evolution of poverty for the longest possible period of time, decompose the changes in poverty into the effect of economic growth and income redistribution, and present a poverty profile for recent years. Second, each study presents an analysis of the distribution of the income-earning assets. While some studies look at various types of assets—Brazil and Bolivia examine measures of "social capital"—the emphasis is on human capital and in particular on schooling. Most of the studies look into the "utilization" of assets (again, mainly human capital), and some carry out a detailed examination of this issue. Third, with the exception of Chile, the country studies present either logit or probit estimations attempting to quantify the extent to which poverty and assets are linked. It should be stressed that this evidence should be interpreted as illustrating some useful correlation patterns, rather than identifying the "causes" of poverty.

Apart from following this common structure, each study examines a specific aspect of the relationship between poverty and assets. In Brazil, the emphasis is on determining whether income-earning assets play an important role in cushioning the consumption of poor families from unexpected shocks. This study also emphasizes the importance of measuring physical capital assets. The Bolivian study is the only one whose main focus is on the effects of social capital. A survey carried out in the city of El Alto attempts to measure social capital and its link to poverty. The chapter on Colombia emphasizes the measurement of physical capital and performs some simulations to estimate the effect on poverty of widening access to credit. The Chilean study exploits high quality data on student achievement to look into the process of accumulation of human capital. It provides evidence on both the quantity and quality of human capital that the poor are able to accumulate. For Costa Rica, the authors perform an analysis of the access to capital and credit. They make an effort to identify the restrictions that the poor face in accumulating human and physical capital, and stress the role played by the returns to assets (which are determined largely by market forces) on the standard of living of the poor. Finally, the chapter on Peru focuses on the role of assets in a dynamic context. This study exploits the fact that the Peruvian surveys have a (relatively long) panel dimension.[26] Specifically, it determines whether having access to assets increases the probability of escaping poverty.

---

[26] Some of the labor force surveys used in the Brazilian study also have a short panel dimension.

The Evolution of Poverty

To examine the long-term determinants of poverty, it is useful to have some information on the historical trends followed by this variable. Table 1.6 summarizes the evidence provided in each case. It should be stressed that the estimates are comparable within each country, but the levels are neither comparable across countries nor with the evidence presented in Figure 1.1, since the methodology employed in each country and the characteristics of the surveys are not necessarily the same. Note also that the period encompassed in each case varies.

In five of the six cases, the proportion of poor declined between the first and last survey available to the authors.[27] The only case in which poverty increased was Peru. It should be stressed, however, that the sample period includes, in the case of Peru, the dramatic crisis at the beginning of the 1990s, when private aggregate consumption declined by around 25 percent in real terms. For Brazil, the estimates use moderate and extreme poverty lines, and interestingly, while moderate poverty declined, extreme poverty increased between 1985 and 1995.

Table 1.6 also presents the result from a decomposition of the change in poverty into three components: a growth effect, a redistribution component, and a residual.[28] In the case of Brazil (for extreme poverty), Bolivia, Colombia and Costa Rica, the changes in poverty registered in each period were due exclusively to growth. Income distribution deteriorated in these cases, and if this had been the only shift taking place, poverty would have actually increased. In the case of Chile, inequality had a slight poverty-reducing effect, but most of the poverty reduction is still attributable to growth. Peru is the only country where an improvement in income distribution played an important role in poverty reduction, but even here the growth effect was

---

[27] Each country study also reports the evolution of the poverty gap and the squared poverty gap. These estimates are not included for simplicity, but the conclusions derived from them are very similar to the evidence in Table 1.6.

[28] To carry out the decomposition, the authors use the methodology of Datt and Ravallion (1992). The decomposition simulates the change in poverty that would have been observed had average income changed as it actually did, but the distribution had remained constant (the growth effect). The redistribution component is obtained by simulating the change in poverty that would have occurred had average income remained constant but the distribution shifted as it actually did.

Table 1.6. Changes in Poverty and Decomposition of Growth and Redistribution Effects

Country	Period	Poverty line	Initial poverty rate	Change (points)	% Change due to growth	% Change due to redistribution	% Change due to residual
Brazil	(1985-95)	Extreme	10.03	1.02	-0.40	1.45	-0.05
	(1985-95)	Moderate	30.42	-2.4	-0.40	-0.70	0.10
Bolivia	(1990-95)	Moderate	52.4	-5.3	-1.47	0.44	0.03
Chile	(1987-96)	Moderate	45.1	-21.9	-0.85	-0.07	-0.08
Colombia	(1991-95)	Moderate	58.5	-0.04	-1.03	0.06	-0.03
Costa Rica	(1986-95)	Moderate	29.4	-3.8	-1.17	0.17	-0.02
Peru	(1985-96)	Moderate	43.1	7.4	0.99	-0.27	0.28

Source: Calculated from country studies in this book.

larger and of the opposite sign. Thus, wherever there has been poverty reduction, the decline has been mainly associated with growth and not with improvements in the distribution of income.

Distribution, Use and Returns of Assets

Table 1.7 summarizes the range of topics covered by each country study in this book. All six chapters look at the distribution of years of schooling. The data presented are in line with the evidence presented above and confirm that the distribution of human capital has a strong connection with the distribution of income and poverty. In Brazil, Colombia, Costa Rica and Peru, there is an attempt to measure some aspects of physical capital and its distribution. While there are differences in the detail each study is able to achieve, they all confirm that physical capital assets in the economy are very highly concentrated among a small group of the population.

In Bolivia, Colombia and Costa Rica, information on access to credit is also available. As would be expected, the evidence shows a very unequal distribution of access to credit. For Colombia, a static simulation (which admittedly neglects the issue of reverse causation) suggests that if the poor had the same access to credit as the non-poor, poverty might be reduced

Table 1.7. Use of and Access and Returns to Income-Earning Assets

Country	Measurement of stocks			Analysis of use			Estimation of returns			
	Human capital	Physical capital	Social capital	Human capital	Physical capital	Social capital	Human capital	Physical capital	Social capital	Crossed returns
Brazil	x	x	x							
Bolivia	x		x	x		x				x
Chile	x			x			x			
Colombia	x	x		x						
Costa Rica	x	x		x	x		x	x		x
Peru	x	x								x

Source: Information from country studies in this book.

considerably. With regard to social capital, Brazil and Bolivia are the only countries where information allowed for some measurement of magnitude and distribution.

In terms of the use of income-earning assets, the chapters on Bolivia, Chile, Colombia and Costa Rica perform detailed analyses of the determinants of labor force participation (the rate of use of human capital). They show very strong differences between the poor and rich in female participation in the labor force. When the incentives to use the available human capital in market-related activities are high enough, females participate more. However, when the pattern of return to skill is characterized by very low wages for the unskilled, there are very low rates of female participation.

The analysis of the use of physical capital in Costa Rica shows that the accumulation of assets is not necessarily a requirement for increasing income-earning capacity. Having access to some kinds of capital (through credit markets for instance) is an advantage as powerful as owning the asset itself. The policy implication is that poverty alleviation measures aimed at providing not necessarily ownership of investment and capital goods but simply more access to them could have considerable potential for poverty reduction. The country study for Bolivia documents access to several types of social capital assets and shows which are less likely to be associated with poverty.

Four of the country studies provide evidence on the differential returns of either human or physical capital, and in three countries there is evidence that the combination of different types of assets can yield greater incomes than their independent use. Evidence on the crossed returns to social and human capital is presented for Bolivia, and the chapters on Costa Rica and Peru show that human and physical capital, when combined, may yield greater returns than when used separately. A detailed analysis of the returns to human capital in Chile and Costa Rica confirms that the returns to education are non-linear. The poor not only have smaller stocks of human capital, but the scarce assets they have are those that are least rewarded by the labor market. The study for Costa Rica also shows the differences in the returns that the poor and rich receive for similar assets, with emphasis on several kinds of physical capital.

Connections between Poverty and Assets

To examine the relationship between poverty and assets, five of the six country studies estimated probit or logit regressions for the probability of being below the poverty line as a function of the ownership of or access to human, physical and social capital. This kind of analysis is illustrative of the associations between poverty and assets, but since the variables are clearly endogenous, the results can only be taken as evidence about the correlation between the variables without causality implied. Almost by definition, poor people have few assets, so there will be a strong connection between ownership of and access to assets and poverty.

Even so, the results from the probit and logit estimations are illustrative. A summary of the main findings is presented in Table 1.8. To indicate that the study found a significant negative relation between poverty and one of the assets, a (-) sign is included in the relevant cell. A zero is included when the relation was estimated but the resulting coefficient was not statistically significant. In all cases where the estimation was performed, a strong inverse relationship was found between years of schooling and the probability of being poor. In Costa Rica and Peru, there is also evidence that having more labor market experience is associated with a negative probability of falling below the poverty line. Wherever information was available, the correlation between physical capital assets and poverty was also estimated. With the sole exception of owning a business in Bolivia and owning a house in

Table 1.8. Analysis of the Relationship between Assets and Poverty: Effect of Each Type of Asset on the Probability of Being Poor
(Sign and Significance of Coefficients from Logit and Probit Estimations)

Variable	Brazil	Bolivia	Chile	Colombia	Costa Rica	Peru
Human capital						
Years of schooling	x	x		x	x	x
Labor market experience					x	x
Physical capital						
Housing ownership					x	0
Access to credit		x		x	x	
Owns business		0				
Other financial assets						x
Capital for investment					x	
Land					x	x
Household appliances and durables	x					x
Social capital in						
Membership in union	x					
Political party membership	x					
Affiliation with community		x			x	x
Family affiliations		x			x	

Source: Information from country studies in this book.

Peru, the rest of the associations have the expected negative significant coefficient, indicating that greater access to physical capital is associated with a lower probability of being poor.

In Brazil, Bolivia, Costa Rica and Peru some information on access to social capital is available. All estimations report that the relation between social capital and poverty is inverse. As mentioned above, the country study for Bolivia looks into these connections in greater detail, finding that some forms of social capital have a much stronger correlation than others.

Table 1.9. Restrictions on Asset Accumulation

Country	Income constraint	Access to credit	Uncertainty
Brazil	x		x
Bolivia			
Chile	x		
Colombia	x	x	
Costa Rica	x	x	
Peru			

Source: Information from country studies in this book.

Restrictions on Accumulation

The chapters on Brazil, Chile, Colombia and Costa Rica identify some of the restrictions that the poor face in accumulating income-earning assets (see Table 1.9).[29] In all four countries, there is evidence of an income constraint for acquiring human capital. The chapter on Brazil also argues that, since the poor have few assets, they are not able to insure against income risk. Therefore, they need to build up buffer stocks to face unexpected income fluctuations, but since they are continuously exposed to shocks they are only able to have high frequency saving, not the long-term accumulation that is necessary to build up an asset stock. Being subject to high uncertainty in the absence of adequate insurance mechanisms becomes a restriction to acquiring more assets.

The chapters on Colombia and Costa Rica identify the role of capital market restrictions on poverty by examining the role of access to credit. For microenterprises in Costa Rica and for the poor in general in Colombia, access to credit is a major constraint to escaping poverty and gaining access to productive assets to increase incomes.

One of the most interesting cases is that of Peru, for which the authors exploited the panel structure of their data to perform a dynamic analysis.

---

[29] It should be noted that the authors of each of the country studies followed a different strategy for their analysis, as is explained in each chapter.

Specifically, they estimated a model of transitions into and out of poverty conditional on several variables, including the number of assets. Their analysis could be profitably extended in the future to consider the relationship between the ownership of different assets in the initial period and the probability of leaving poverty.

What Do We Learn from Each Study?

From the study on Brazil, we mainly learn two things. The first is that one of the most important roles of assets is that they are strong determinants of the capacity to absorb unexpected shocks to income. The second, which is related, is that in a context of high uncertainty, assets will continuously be used as buffer stock, so the capacity to build up stocks will be limited by the instability of the environment. Even if uncertainty induces precautionary savings, and therefore encourages accumulation, it still leads to depletion rather than accumulation of assets, because uncertainty induces investment in relatively unproductive (but liquid) assets such as cash holdings, instead of human capital. Insurance mechanisms or a stable environment will therefore act in favor of a more equitable distribution of assets.

The main conclusion from the Bolivia study is that social capital also matters for the capacity to escape poverty. Furthermore, when combined with human capital, it may yield greater returns in terms of income. However, as the authors themselves point out, social capital is the most difficult asset to quantify. This study has taken some first steps toward determining its importance in terms of poverty, but there is still scope for obtaining more evidence on its value and distribution.

Perhaps the main conclusion from the study on Chile is that both the quantity and quality of the stock matter. In the specific case of human capital, even though in Chile the difference between the average schooling of children at the top and bottom of the distribution is apparently not that large at young ages, education can be of totally different value because of its quality. Children from poorer families tend to access schools with the lowest scores in terms of student achievement, while the rich mostly attend the best scoring schools. This shows that the effects of family background on attainment may feed through various mechanisms, and that to be able to accumulate more human capital, restrictions other than income must be overcome.

The Colombian study supports the view that providing access to credit and improving financial markets could have great potential to reduce poverty. Improving the distribution of human capital could certainly have a positive effect on poverty, but the effect would be much larger if combined with loosening up liquidity constraints.

One of the main lessons from the Costa Rican study is that, while the distribution and use of assets are important, returns to those assets, which are not fully under the control of households or policy, may be an even more important determinant of poverty. Simulations of the effect on poverty of increasing the rate of use of human capital to non-poor levels reveal that differences in labor market participation account for some of the differences between individuals below and above the poverty line. However, assuming that the poor receive the returns that the rich obtain for the same asset would dramatically reduce poverty. Therefore, while policies aimed at temporarily increasing the incomes of the poor through transfers could be adequate, any policy action of this type will be swimming against the tide if the price structure is permanently acting against the poor. Changing the price structure may not be a realistic policy objective, but if these forces are identified and quantified, it is likely that the policy approach would be different. In addition, enhancing the accumulation of income-earning assets is not the only way to produce a long-term effect on poverty. Providing access to assets through the market may be as effective and perhaps is a more attainable policy goal, at least in the case of some physical capital assets.

Finally, the case of Peru confirms that the productivity of assets may be significantly enhanced if more than one type of asset is owned. Specifically, owning physical capital in the form of land has much higher returns when the asset is combined with human capital. Assets play a crucial role in the probability of exiting poverty. A much better distribution of assets is associated with higher social mobility and better prospects for wider sectors of the population.

Conclusions

This chapter has outlined an asset-based approach to the analysis of poverty in Latin America. Such an approach, rather than focusing only on household income and its distribution, is based on the analysis of the ownership of, access to, and use of income-generating assets and their accumulation. The basic idea is that household income comes from the return on the various assets owned and used in a productive fashion by the household members. These include human capital as well as physical and financial assets and access to what has been labeled "social capital." The focus on assets and their accumulation makes the proposed analysis intrinsically dynamic.

The six studies in this book constitute a first step towards implementation of the proposed approach. It should be stressed that the analysis presented here is far from being complete. Two important limitations need to be mentioned. First, even though the studies use a variety of data sources, data in Latin America and other regions are still limited, especially in measuring the stock of different kinds of assets available to households. As new data sources become available, this constraint is likely to be progressively overcome in the future. It is important to integrate the analysis of human capital accumulation with the availability of and access to other assets, ranging from financial assets to insurance programs and credit. Similar considerations apply to the analysis of small enterprises and, in the case of rural households, to the analysis of production choices.

Second, while this book stresses the importance of the obstacles that households face in the process of asset accumulation and investment, one cannot rely only on simple descriptive analyses to understand fully the effects of incentives, constraints and availability of different assets and their interaction. In the future, it will be necessary to develop and estimate models that recognize the incentives and opportunities available to each individual household. These models would allow the identification of the main determinants of the process of accumulation of different productive assets (especially human capital), and would give policymakers an invaluable instrument to evaluate different policy proposals.

A number of other considerations are also important for the proper formulation of policies that aim to reduce poverty by promoting the accumulation of income-generating assets. One consideration should be the general equilibrium effects of such policies, either on asset returns or on the functioning of private interactions. Moreover, the estimation of dynamic models and the need to identify different types of dynamic effects is likely to require longitudinal data that are often missing. There is a case to be made for the collection of high quality surveys that include a panel component.

In addition to proposing an asset-based approach to the analysis of poverty, this book also reports on recent poverty trends in Latin America. Since much of the focus is on human capital, the book also presents up-to-date information on average levels and distribution of schooling in the region. The evidence makes it quite clear that the process of forming human capital, and to a certain extent using it, is crucial to the development of Latin America and to the progressive elimination of poverty.

References

Attanasio, O., and V. Ríos-Rull. 2001. Consumption Smoothing and Extended Families: The Role of Government-Sponsored Insurance. In N. Lustig (ed.), *Shielding the Poor: Social Protection in the Developing World*. Washington, DC: Inter-American Development Bank/Brookings Institution.

Behrman, J. 1999. Education, Health and Demography in Latin America around the End of the Century: What Do We Know? What Questions Should Be Explored? Inter-American Development Bank Research Department, Washington, DC. Mimeo.

Birdsall, N., and J. L. Londoño. 1997. Asset Inequality Matters: An Assessment of the World Bank's Approach to Poverty Reduction. *American Economic Review* 87(2): 32-7.

Birdsall, N., T. C. Pinckney, and R. H. Sabot. 1999. *Equity, Savings, and Growth*. Working Paper No. 8. Brookings Institution, Center on Social and Economic Dynamics, Washington, DC.

Cameron, S. V., and J. J. Heckman. 1998. Life Cycle Schooling and Dynamic Selection Bias: Models and Evidence for Five Cohorts of American Males. *Journal of Political Economy* 106(2): 262-333.

Coleman, J. 1990. *Foundations of Social Theory*. Cambridge, MA: Harvard University Press.

Cossa, R., J. J. Heckman, and L. Lochner. 1999. Wage Subsidies and Skill Formation: A Study of the Earned Income Tax Credit. University of Chicago. Mimeo.

Datt, G., and M. Ravallion. 1992. Growth and Redistribution Components of Changes in Poverty Measures: A Decomposition with Applications to Brazil and India in the 1980s. *Journal of Development Economics* 38(3): 275-95.

Galor, O., and J. Zeira. 1993. Income Distribution and Macroeconomics. *Review of Economic Studies* 60(1): 35-52.

Heckman, J. J., L. Lochner, and C. Taber. 1998. Explaining Rising Wage Inequality: Exploration with a Dynamic General Equilibrium Model of Labor Earnings with Heterogeneous Agents. *Review of Economic Dynamics* 1(1): 1-58.

Inter-American Development Bank (IDB). 1998. *Facing up to Inequality: 1998 Report on Economic and Social Progress in Latin America.* Washington, DC: Inter-American Development Bank.

Londoño, J. L., and M. Székely. 1997. Persistent Poverty and Excess Inequality: Latin America 1970-1995. Inter-American Development Bank Research Department Working Paper 357, Washington, DC.

Putnam, R. 1993. *Making Democracy Work: Civic Traditions in Modern Italy.* Princeton: Princeton University Press.

Székely, M. 1998. *The Economics of Poverty, Inequality and Wealth Accumulation in Mexico.* London: Macmillan.

Székely, M., and M. Hilgert. 1999. The 1990s in Latin America: Another Decade of Persistent Inequality. Inter-American Development Bank Research Department Working Paper No. 410, Washington, DC.

Székely, M., N. Lustig, M. Cumpa, and J. A. Mejía. 2000. Do We Know How Much Poverty There Is? Inter-American Development Bank Research Department Working Paper No. 437, Washington, DC.

CHAPTER TWO

Poverty and Assets in Bolivia: What Role Does Social Capital Play?

George Gray-Molina
Wilson Jiménez
Ernesto Pérez de Rada
Ernesto Yáñez[1]

Recent analyses of poverty in Bolivia show that, despite a slight decline over the past decade in the proportion of the population living in poverty, the absolute number of poor households continued to rise.[2] The low level of income growth in the poorest households suggests that sustained efforts to maintain moderate levels of economic growth and raise the efficiency of public spending and investment have not been sufficient to reverse the country's chronic poverty.

The analytical approaches that have underpinned growth policies and protection networks in Bolivia and throughout Latin America are also going through a period of questioning and reformulation. Models that emphasize the measurement of poverty by insufficiency of income or basic needs[3] are being called into question by new models that analyze patterns of causality between poverty and access to asset markets for human, physical (public and private) and social capital.[4] This chapter contributes to the analysis of poverty from the standpoint of resources and assets, and describes the approaches used in Bolivia.

The first section of the chapter examines the basic model discussed by Birdsall and Londoño (1997b), which emphasizes the role played by social

---

[1] The authors are research economists affiliated with the Fundación Diálogo of La Paz, Bolivia.
[2] See Jiménez and Yáñez (1997a and 1997b); Vos, Lee and Mejía (1997); World Bank (1996).
[3] See Lipton and van der Gaag (1993); Boltvinik (1992).
[4] See Birdsall and Londoño (1997a and 1997b); Moser (1998); Collier (1998).

capital in intermediation with other asset markets. Factors examined include the persistence of poverty in terms of barriers to access to assets of human capital (education and health), physical capital (housing, private and public physical assets) and social capital (both family social networks and those outside the family). The patterns of access of the poor to asset markets reveal three conditioning factors. First, access tends to be highly inequitable, particularly in the asset markets characterized by market failings that restrict the access of the poorest sectors.[5] Second, differentiated access to asset markets depends on the behavior of the economic agents that access them, which in the case of the poor is characterized by the use of risk-smoothing strategies to mitigate chronic risk conditions in consumption and income.[6] Third, under certain circumstances, social capital provides institutional solutions to some of the market's failings and restrictions on behavior described in the first two points. Social capital may thus be conceptualized as a productive social resource that can help overcome dilemmas of collective action in access to physical and human assets.[7] Similar results are found for the longitudinal and cross-section analysis of poverty in Bolivia. The longitudinal analysis of urban households suggests three patterns for the 1990-95 period. First, there is a markedly inequitable distribution of access to human and physical assets, which does not vary during the reference period. Second, the endowment and uses of human capital best explain the persistence of low incomes in urban households, particularly when they are associated with the migrant condition of heads of households (rural) and patterns of residence in secondary cities (outside Bolivia's central belt). Third, the heads of households who have stable wage-earning access to the labor market report higher income than those who participate in the non-wage-earning sector. The results of the longitudinal analysis agree to a large extent with previous studies, which explain differences in urban incomes in terms of the variables of human capital and ethnicity—particularly for inhabitants of urban areas.[8] The paucity of information on assets of physical and

---

[5] See Birdsall and Londoño (1997b); Londoño and Székely (1997).
[6] See Székely (1997); Morduch (1995); Deaton (1997).
[7] See Coleman (1990); Putnam (1993).
[8] See Wood and Patrinos (1994); Fields, et al. (1997); Pérez de Rada (1997); Jiménez and Yáñez (1997b).

social capital is clear from an analysis of existing sources, and it suggests the importance of reconsidering the results in light of the inclusion of new explanatory variables.

The cross-section analysis incorporates variables of social and physical capital into the analysis of the determinants of poverty and reveals important results. The variables that best explain household income growth include educational level, ethnicity, migrant condition and type of labor market access. Social capital endowment, measured by the number of social affiliations, is negatively associated with the probability of falling into conditions of poverty. No evidence was found to suggest that the type of social capital, associated with credit markets or jobs, is important in the generation of income. Finally, the introduction of variables of interaction between social and human capital is significant for individuals with the highest and lowest educational achievement, but not for the rest. Although the results of this analysis are only valid for one city, social capital resources are significantly associated with the probability of leaving poverty.

Changes in Poverty[9]

The sources used in this study to examine trends in urban poverty are the Integrated Household Surveys (IHS) conducted by the National Statistics Institute (known by its Spanish acronym, INE) since 1989. The cities included in the INE sample account for approximately 80 percent of urban Bolivia, which in turn represents approximately 62 percent of the total population. Despite exclusively urban coverage of the surveys, the follow-up to changes in poverty derived from them permits an analysis of the interrelationship between urban and rural poverty in terms of the migratory flow to cities and the dynamics of urban poverty. The analysis begins with two conditioning developments that explain the concentration of the assets linked to changes in poverty: first, the rapid growth of the provincial capitals, which resulted in an expansion of urban settlements; and second, the labor market, characterized by an expanding informal sector, greater weight of tertiary activities, and the incorporation of women.

---

[9] For an explanation of the methodology used to measure poverty, see the working paper version of this chapter (Gray-Molina, et al., 1999).

Table 2.1. Poverty in Principal Bolivian Cities, 1990-95

Indicators	1990	1991	1992	1993	1994	1995
Sample						
Households in sample[1]	6,353	6,104	5,898	4,297	6,268	5,678
Population						
Total population ('000s)	2,599	2,738	2,855	2,964	3,091	3,189
Poor population[2]	1,527	1,406	1,584	1,602	1,599	1,724
Households						
Estimated ('000s)	555.7	597.6	632.6	635.0	693.0	692.4
Poor	296.3	292.7	323.8	311.6	312.6	331.2
Indigent	145.6	126.3	152.0	141.6	124.7	143.8
Poverty Measurements						
FGTo (moderate)	53.3	49.0	51.2	49.1	45.1	47.8
FGTo (extreme)	26.2	21.1	24.0	22.3	18.0	20.8
FGT1 (gap)	2.46	2.02	2.21	2.09	1.78	1.98
FGT2 (severe)	1.47	1.12	1.25	1.17	0.93	1.10
Gini Index	**0.52**	**0.52**	**0.53**	**0.56**	**0.53**	**0.55**

Note: Relates to provincial capitals and El Alto.

[1] Sample in data base.

[2] Population in private households with family incomes per person lower than the poverty line.

Source: UDAPSO, based on household surveys conducted by the National Statistics Institute (INE).

Trends in Poverty

Between 1990 and 1995, about half of urban households had family incomes that were lower than the price of a basket of basic goods (poverty line), a situation that reflects extreme conditions of poverty. The percentage of poor households fell during the period from 53.3 percent in 1990 to 47.8 percent in 1995, although in 1992 and 1995 the number of poor households increased in absolute terms, evidence of the persistence of the phenomenon (see Table 2.1). The percentage of households in extreme poverty fell throughout the period from 26.2 percent to 20.8 percent.

As can be seen, however, this downward trend was not sufficient to halt the steady increase in the total number of poor during this period. Urban poverty between 1990 and 1995 is associated with trends in macroeconomic determinants (principally growth) and other variables that affect income distribution (inflation rate and open unemployment), along with the variables that characterize households (size, number of employed, education of family members), which are structural determinants of poverty. During this period, Bolivia's economy grew by less than 4 percent annually,[10] a rate insufficient to produce an effective and sustained increase in per capita income. It should be noted, though, that two-digit inflation predominated in four of the six years under consideration. (The exceptions were 1993 and 1994,when inflation was 9.3 percent and 8.5 percent, respectively.) Unlike the late 1980s, however, inflation in the 1990s was maintained at reasonable levels, calming expectations of volatility.

Inequality and growth played major roles in the changes in poverty, particularly growth. Table 2.2 presents the decomposition of the change in successive years, using the Datt-Ravallion (1992) technique.

The evidence for 1990-95 suggests that economic growth was closely related to the process of reducing poverty and that it was more effective when not counteracted by the effects of greater income concentration. In fact, income concentration not only contributed to more poverty but also annulled the effects of income growth.

Socioeconomic Characteristics of Poor Households

Bolivia's accelerated process of urbanization over the last two decades has led to important changes in the composition of households. The decline in household size, the increase in simple nuclear family unions and the fall in the percentage of compound families are a response to new patterns of family organization, which are linked to labor market changes and lower fertility in urban areas in the mid-1990s (ECLAC, 1993). In 1995, over half the heads of households[11] were between 25 and 44 years old, and 32 percent between 45 and 64. Most of the remainder were younger, with another less significant number over 65. Women headed 18 percent of households, a relatively stable percentage since 1990 (see Table 2.3).

---

[10] Estimated as a geometric average of the rates observed in the six years under consideration.
[11] The head of household is the person recognized as such by members of the household at the time of the survey.

Table 2.2. Growth Effect and Redistribution in Measurements of Poverty, 1990-95

Indicators	1990-91	1991-92	1992-93	1993-94	1994-95
Incidence of poverty					
Percentage change	(10.8)	7.7	(4.6)	(5.7)	4.0
Growth effect	(11.2)	6.2	(10.3)	0.7	(0.1)
Redistribution effect	0.4	1.5	5.4	(6.5)	4.1
Residual	(0.0)	0.0	0.3	(0.0)	(0.0)
Poverty gap					
Percentage change	(15.4)	11.1	(5.0)	(10.4)	9.0
Growth effect	(19.9)	8.8	(14.2)	1.0	0.1
Redistribution effect	(0.0)	(3.3)	9.5	(11.5)	9.1
Residual	4.4	5.6	(0.4)	(0.0)	(0.0)
Gap squared					
Percentage change	(18.7)	13.5	(5.4)	(13.6)	12.7
Growth effect	(23.0)	10.6	(16.6)	1.2	(0.1)
Redistribution effect	(0.8)	(3.8)	11.9	(14.8)	12.8
Residual	5.1	6.7	(0.7)	(0.1)	(0.0)

Note: The brackets denote negative changes in the reference period.
Source: UDAPSO, based on household surveys conducted by the National Statistics Institute (INE).

The highest incidence of poverty was in households whose heads were between 25 and 44 (53.4 percent in 1995) and the lowest in households whose heads were aged under 24 (41.6 percent) or over 65 (40.7 percent). The differences in the incidence of poverty by gender of the head are not significant. The largest households (over six members) accounted for 18 percent of total urban households, with an incidence of poverty of 65 percent in 1995, while 15 percent of households with one or two members had an incidence of poverty of 27.4 percent. In contrast, most households (67 percent) had from three to six members, with a level of poverty of 48.4 percent. The largest reduction in the incidence of poverty between 1990 and 1995 was in households with over six members (from 73 percent to 66 percent). So de-
~te this group's low representation, it contributed to the reduction in pov-

Table 2.3. Incidence of Poverty by Characteristics of the Head of Household, 1990–95

Characteristics of household and head	1990		1995	
	% of households	Incidence of poverty	% of households	Incidence of poverty
Gender of head of household	100.0	53.3	100.0	47.8
- Men	82.6	53.1	81.8	48.6
- Women	17.4	54.0	18.2	44.8
Age of head	100.0	53.3	100.0	47.8
- Under 24	6.7	54.1	6.3	41.6
- 25 to 44	54.4	56.5	51.5	53.4
- 45 to 64	30.3	48.8	31.7	42.5
- 65 and over	8.6	48.6	10.6	40.7
Size of household	100.0	53.3	100.0	47.8
- 1 to 2 members	15.3	30.8	15.1	27.4
- 3 to 6	67.9	53.4	67.0	48.4
- Over 6	16.8	73.2	17.9	66.9
Type of household	100.0	53.3	100.0	47.8
- Single person	5.0	24.4	7.6	21.7
- Simple nuclear no children	5.2	30.3	5.4	24.7
- Simple single parent	10.3	53.5	10.2	47.6
- Simple nuclear with children	56.1	58.6	53.6	53.7
- Extended	20.8	54.0	18.7	49.2
- Compound	0.2	28.1	0.1	-
- Others	2.3	35.7	4.3	-
Language spoken[1]	100.0	53.3	100.0	45.1
- Only Spanish	57.1	46.3	57.6	37.1
- Spanish - native	41.2	62.1	41.8	55.9
- Only native	1.7	75.7	0.6	67.0
Educational level	100.0	53.3	100.0	47.8
- None	7.8	69.7	5.2	58.0
- Primary	41.5	62.7	41.3	57.7
- Secondary	30.8	51.2	30.1	49.6
- Higher, technical and university	19.6	29.8	23.3	35.9
- Don't know/No answer	0.4	69.0	0.1	12.8
Condition of activity	100.0	53.3	100.0	47.8
- Worked	83.1	51.2	83.0	46.9
- Looked for work	3.8	81.8	2.7	82.1
- Economically inactive	13.1	58.6	14.3	46.6

[1] The eighth round of the household surveys (1995) did not collect information on language in the household. The replies shown here are from the seventh round (1994), collected the previous year.

Source: Authors' calculations based on household surveys conducted by the National Statistics Institute (INE).

erty. This could be explained by the presence of a higher proportion of people who generate income in large households, as many members of these households are self-employed or do unpaid family work.

In 1995, 53.6 percent of households were of the simple nuclear form with children, a slightly lower percentage than in 1990. Extended households represented almost 19 percent, a downward trend. Single-person households and other groups that do not constitute households grew considerably, while at the same time their incidence of poverty was lower. In synthesis, the largest fall in the incidence of poverty took place in extended households, childless nuclear households and others, a development attributable to a greater presence in the labor force.

Ethnic characteristics of households are important indicators of poverty in Bolivia, and the languages that the head knows or speaks are an approximation for identifying ethnic condition. In 1994, about 58 percent of heads of household spoke only Spanish, 42 percent spoke native languages combined with Spanish, and an unrepresentative fraction (0.6 percent) spoke only native languages. Significant inequality is observed in the incidence of poverty of the heads of households who only speak Spanish (37.1 percent) and those who speak native languages (67 percent). Accepting the hypothesis of the relationship between ethnic condition (monolingual or bilingual) with established or recent migratory status, it can be concluded that households headed by speakers of native languages have a lower probability of leaving poverty, bearing in mind their disadvantaged access to the labor market linked to discrimination and a lower level of human capital endowment. During the period of analysis, the incidence of poverty fell by 6.2 percent in households with bilingual heads, proportionally less than the reduction in households with heads who spoke only Spanish (9.3 percent). For heads of households who only spoke native languages, the reduction was 8.8 points.

Perhaps the most important determinant of poverty is related to the education of the head of the household. In 1995, 5.2 percent of heads had no education, 41 percent had completed primary, 30 percent secondary and 20 percent higher or technical level. Fifty-eight percent of households headed by people with no education were classified as poor. The corresponding figures for households headed by people who completed primary or secondary school were 57.7 percent and 49.6 percent, respectively. In contrast, 35.9 percent of the heads of household who had reached the university or technical level were living in poverty. The largest decline in poverty took place in households headed by people who had higher education, demonstrating that these households have better opportunities for profiting from economic growth. The reduction in the relative weight of households whose heads have low levels of education and the increase in the number of heads with higher or technical education represent promising trends for long-term poverty reduction.

Urban poverty in Bolivia tends to be concentrated in larger households in an intermediate life cycle, especially when their heads have low levels of education, are of native origin and, most critically, are unemployed. These groups have had more capacity to generate income in recent years, though, and were able to reduce the incidence of poverty to a greater extent. Additionally, some traditionally vulnerable groups such as indigenous or inactive people reduced their rates of poverty, but to a lesser extent than the urban population as a whole.

Labor Characteristics of Poor Households

Occupational access differs between poor and non-poor households, expressing the inequality of employment opportunities and the conditions of family labor supply. Several studies in the last decade mention that the degree of global participation grew because the poor needed to supplement their income, which increased pressure on the supply of labor. In turn, their condition of poverty forced the unemployed into the informal sector.

The data presented in Table 2.4 reflect the results of this process. The highest rates of participation are observed among the non-poor, and consequently they were successful in the strategy of leaving poverty. In both years, the rates of participation of the poor are 10 points below the non-poor.

The second hypothesis suggests that although the poor cannot be without work for prolonged periods, they are a group with fewer opportunities for obtaining employment. This situation is reflected in the rates of open unemployment that, in both years, are significantly lower in the non-poor active population. The rates of open unemployment have fallen in general in all segments, which confirms that the non-poor population has practically overcome problems of absolute unemployment.

The problems associated with the quality of employment affect even the non-poor, making them vulnerable. To examine trends in the relation-

Table 2.4. Labor Indicators by Condition of Poverty, 1990 and 1994

(In percent)

	Non-poor	Poor	Total
Global rate of participation			
1990	56.8	46.9	51.2
1994	58.9	48.2	53.8
Rate of open unemployment			
1990	3.7	10.6	7.2
1994	1.8	5.2	3.2

Source: Based on household surveys conducted by the National Statistics Institute (INE).

ship between unemployment and poverty, rates of poverty were estimated by groupings of occupational categories. First, the changes in the structure of employment between 1990 and 1994 raised the participation of employers and professionals and reduced that of self-employed workers (see Table 2.5). Second, the incidence of poverty fell in almost all employed groups, with the exception of employers and individual professionals. Among the latter, the incidence and intensity of poverty increased significantly. In 1990, wage earners recorded the widest poverty gap, which changed in 1994 when they presented the lowest rates of intensity of poverty. Despite signs of improvement in poverty over the period of analysis, a significant proportion of employed groups generated income that was not sufficient to cover their basic needs. Again, the phenomenon of poverty is largely associated with qualifications and human capital endowment.

Assets of the Poor

Table 2.1 shows that the levels of inequality in income distribution in Bolivia deteriorated in the last decade, exceeding even the average rate of regional concentration (World Bank, 1996). The trend in inequality in income distribution has been attributed to the inability of low-income groups to reap the benefits of economic growth stemming from the macroeconomic

Table 2.5. Poverty Rates by Occupational Category, 1990 and 1994
(In percent)

	Structure	Incidence of poverty	Poverty gap
1990			
Wage earners	50.0	52.8	21.5
Employer or independent professional	4.2	13.4	4.1
Self-employed or unpaid family	38.9	46.2	18.1
Domestic employees	6.9	67.3	18.2
1994			
Wage earners	49.1	42.7	15.6
Employer or independent professional	8.5	20.3	6.3
Self-employed or unpaid family	34.4	44.1	16.6
Domestic employees	6.9	67.3	18.2
	8.1	47.9	19.1

Source. Based on household surveys conducted by the National Statistics Institute (INE).

reforms of recent years. However, underlying the profile of impoverishment is the lack of access to assets and the question of why the poor accumulate so few of them.

Physical Assets

The physical capital of urban households is defined as ownership of a home, durable goods (automobile), assets that generate income (agricultural property), shares or other forms of saving in deposits or loans, including payment of antichresis (transfer of the right to the income from real property). The most important physical asset for families residing in urban areas is the home.[12] For city dwellers, this asset is as important as land ownership in

---

[12] In addition to its social use as shelter, this asset can also perform several economic roles: location for small businesses, collateral for access to credit, and a potential source of income through rental or sale.

rural areas. According to data from the 1992 Population and Housing Census, 50.3 percent of households in urban areas live in their own homes. However, the quality of these homes—with respect to construction material, overcrowding, and access to water and basic sewage services—is far from adequate in most cases. Table 2.6 shows a clear negative relationship in Bolivia between income levels and home ownership, reflecting another problem of rural poverty. While in the lower quintiles the accumulation of home ownership apparently declines, in the higher quintiles it increases.[13] If the ratio between the fifth and first quintiles is taken as a proxy for inequality of access, there is a clear process of concentration in access to housing. Access to physical assets such as housing is increasingly restricted. The picture is even more disquieting if the breakdown is by the quality of the home.[14]

Other physical assets help to provide a more complete picture of differences between poor and non-poor households. Automobiles are reported as an asset by 12 percent of households, as reported in the statement of maintenance expenses, with a certain difference in the possession of durable goods between poor and non-poor households. Poor households tend to consume their labor income and do not generally invest in an automobile. It seems reasonable to suppose that a large number of households that own an automobile do not fall into poverty.

Finally, business ownership shows some degree of significance, although it is insufficient to reflect its scope and impact on family income. The proportion of those who own some type of business is substantially greater in non-poor homes, which generally have small productive and/or family units generating income, which may allow them to leave poverty. (However, this group also includes large and small establishments, whose business incomes are not comparable.) The economic recovery helped urban households establish small- and medium-sized businesses, which are options for obtaining income and sometimes strengthen production by using unpaid family members.

---

[13] The qualitative deficiencies decline as incomes increase.

[14] An analysis of the highly skewed distribution of durable goods, agricultural property and savings can be found in Gray-Molina, et al. (1999).

Table 2.6. Home Ownership by Quintile of Household Income
(In percent)

	1990	1992	1994
1st quintile	15.3	14.0	14.7
3rd quintile	19.3	17.3	20.0
5th quintile	25.8	30.0	42.7
5th/1st quintile	1.68	2.14	2.9
Avg schooling	7.34	7.62	7.5
Avg schooling			
head	8.56	8.99	9.18
Avg schooling			
employed persons	8.66	9.06	9.1
1st quintile	7.3	9.7	9.8
3rd quintile	8.0	9.8	10.3
5th quintile	9.3	10.8	10.4
1st quintile	7.5	10.1	10.4
3rd quintile	8.9	9.9	10.5
5th quintile	9.9	11.6	11.9
1st quintile	6.6	4.8	5.3
3rd quintile	7.4	6.2	6.3
5th quintile	9.7	11.1	11.2

Financial Assets

The savings that generate regular income, under the modalities of interest from loans or deposits and even antichretic deposits, constitute a contingency reserve for poor households. The distribution of these assets is important because one-quarter of all households and one-fifth of poor households reported that they had liquid assets. Restrictions on savings, though, are largely conditioned by income. The figures give some indications of the organization of the family budget, which includes savings and their use as a means of avoiding poverty.

Human Capital

The role of education in the generation of income by increasing productivity has been widely demonstrated. However, the evidence shows that even over 1990-94, the improvement in education indicators was limited. Taking the average years of schooling as a proxy, Table 2.7 shows little change in the stock of human capital.[15] Education, therefore, has little effect on socioeconomic outcomes such as income generation and levels of health, fertility and productivity. Further, these effects can be nonexistent if it is considered that in many cases the effect of education is not linear, but requires compliance with specific segments of schooling to have significant effects.

A disaggregated analysis gives a better idea of the effect of the low accumulation of human capital. Table 2.7 shows that average schooling in the early age groups is very much above the average in the same quintiles for the 45-50 age group, particularly in the first income quintiles. This trend reflects to some extent the structural character of the educational problem discussed earlier, as well as trends in the intergenerational transmission of poverty. Opportunities for access to education have deteriorated, as shown by the increase in the standard deviation of years of schooling. This decline affects levels of poverty, basically by concentrating income in the higher income quintiles. It also reduces the possible benefits of structural reforms in terms of distribution, since it is expected that only workers with more education can benefit from the reforms (Londoño and Székely, 1997).

Summarizing, urban areas of Bolivia have low levels of human capital accumulation as well as great inequality in access to education, which evidently contributes to unequal distribution of income and has repercussions on levels of poverty. This is a concern because it is the lowest stratum that has the lowest levels of accumulation of human capital and apparently fewer opportunities for access to education. The distribution of human capital in households shows the same trend as that noted in the profile of household poverty: a general average of 8.6 years of schooling among adults, about 10 years in non-poor households and 7.4 years in poor households. Consequently, the long-term trend suggests a need to increase levels of education,

---

[15] See Barro and Lee (1993). It is true that using average schooling as proxy for human capital has several problems, such as assuming perfect substitution between different levels of schooling. However, its use is justified for the purposes of the study.

Table 2.7. Average Years of Schooling by Age Group and Income Level

Age	Income level	1990	1992	1994
18-20 years	1st quintile	7.3	9.7	9.8
	3rd quintile	8.0	9.8	10.3
	5th quintile	9.3	10.8	10.4
21-24 years	1st quintile	7.5	10.1	10.4
	3rd quintile	8.9	9.9	10.5
	5th quintile	9.9	11.6	11.9
45-50 years	1st quintile	6.6	4.8	5.3
	3rd quintile	7.4	6.2	6.3
	5th quintile	9.7	11.1	11.2

especially in poor households, even in urban areas. Inequality in human capital creates an obstacle to overcoming poverty.

Determinants of Household Income

Table 2.8 shows three specifications for three rounds of the Integrated Household Survey (1990, 1992 and 1994). The key variables include age, education of the head of household and the head's spouse, labor market access, and a "shock" variable that controls for the effect of an unexpected illness on the household's labor behavior. Geographical dummies are also included to reflect local effects by city of residence.

Consistent with previous studies, the present results indicate that the head and spouse's human capital endowment are central determinants of household income. There was not, however, evidence to suggest that the returns on human capital have varied significantly from one period to another. Perhaps this is due to the short reference period (five years), when no significant changes were observed in educational endowment. The age of the head of the household also shows the expected signs (positive and then negative), and a coefficient equivalent to the variables of education.

The two variables of labor market access suggest a revealing pattern. The coefficients of employment in the household are greater by one order

Table 2.8. Determinants of Family Income

Variable	1990 Coef.	1990 P>|t|	1992 Coef.	1992 P>|t|	1994 Coef.	1994 P>|t|
Age of head of household	10.61	0.000	7.56	0.019	10.56	0.001
Age^2 head of household	-0.07	0.001	-0.02	0.495	-0.04	0.205
Schooling of head of household	10.76	0.000	10.76	0.000	24.32	0.000
Schooling of spouse of head of household	10.74	0.000	16.90	0.000	14.87	0.000
Percentage of employed members of household	514.31	0.000	680.45	0.000	514.16	0.000
Number of non-wage-earning members of household	-76.64	0.000	-41.70	0.000	-34.20	0.000
Number of persons who did not fall ill during year	5.47	0.057	3.09	0.634	18.26	0.002
Dummy - Sucre	-25.28	0.248	58.03	0.012	0.45	0.980
Dummy - La Paz	36.46	0.084	132.08	0.065	130.17	0.000
Dummy - Cochabamba	-12.99	0.572	85.00	0.433	24.66	0.287
Dummy - Oruro	-89.04	0.000	-42.94	0.000	-43.32	0.173
Dummy - Potosí	-68.76	0.002	-56.57	0.003	10.96	0.735
Dummy - Tarija	-29.83	0.202	40.09	0.349	31.88	0.320
Dummy - Santa Cruz	44.40	0.048	312.88	0.000	228.20	0.000
Dummy - Trinidad	96.31	0.000	110.76	0.000	71.20	0.052
Constant	-380.86	0.000	-426.016	0.000	-504.68	0.000
Number of observations	4,728		4,250		4,553	
F (x, observations-x)	59.33		97.22		96.58	
Prob>F	0.000		0.000		0.000	
R^2 Adjusted	0.156		0.168		0.254	

Source: Authors' calculations based on household survey data for 1990, 1992 and 1994.

of magnitude than those of education and age. The decision whether to participate in the labor market has direct implications for the income expectations of the household. The second variable of labor market access— the number of non-wage earning members in the household—is also significant and has an inverse relationship with income generation.

The geographical variables suggest a fixed pattern. Living in La Paz and Santa Cruz provides greater opportunities for income generation, while living in the Andean area (Oruro and Potosí) significantly limits these opportunities. This comparison coincides with similar studies of Bolivia, in which variables such as education and ethnic origin appear as principal determinants of poverty.[16] Evidently, structural factors condition poverty in urban areas of the country. Education appears to be one of these factors, and policies to reduce poverty should take this into account, especially since the education variable is very susceptible to public policy action.

Determinants of Poverty: The Case of El Alto

This section looks at physical, human and social assets in order to analyze the probable effects of social capital on the generation of income in poor households in El Alto. Three questions are analyzed relating to the endowment and use of social capital. First, what effect does the *magnitude* of the social networks of a household have on the probability of falling into poverty? Do more community affiliations mean a higher generation of income? A second question is the effect of this *type* of social network on the probability of leaving poverty. Are social networks linked to the credit and employment markets more important than community networks? A third issue is the interaction between social and human capital. Does social capital have a differentiated effect for groups with different educational achievements? The asset approach requires differentiating the *generating* role of income received from different types of assets from the *risk-smoothing* role of patterns of consumption and income. The use of social capital can help explain the second role in the context of the imperfect risk-smoothing markets.

---

[16] See Fields, et al. (1997); Pérez de Rada (1997); Jiménez and Yáñez (1997a and 1997b).

Social Capital and Poverty

This chapter adopts a conventional definition of social capital based on Putnam (1993, p. 167), who states: "Social capital refers to features of social organization, such as trust, norms and networks that can improve the efficiency of society by facilitating coordinated actions."

The concept is further developed by Coleman (1990, p. 302): "Social capital is defined by its function...Like other forms of capital, [it is] productive, making possible the achievement of certain ends that would not be attainable in its absence. Like physical capital and human capital it is not completely fungible, but is fungible with respect to specific activities...Unlike other forms of capital, social capital inheres in the structure of relations between persons and among persons. It is lodged neither in individuals nor in physical implements of production."

This definition is put into operation by identifying generic community social networks (sports and cultural clubs, neighborhood organizations) and social networks specific to credit and job markets (informal credit and job networks). The central dilemma of the analysis in this context is the treatment of the endogenous relationship between social capital and poverty. The incorporation of variables that represent social norms and networks into a decision-making model of households comes up against an insurmountable problem: both the existence and the probable effects of social capital are endogenous to the decisions of households. As Coleman argues, households do not "possess" social capital in the way they possess human or physical capital, because social capital—by definition—arises from relationships *between* households. The search for instrumental variables of social capital that are exogenous to household decisions is, in this context, a contradiction.

However, the presumption of an endogenous relationship between social capital and poverty is not completely hermetic. Much of the literature on risk-smoothing assumes that the existence of an informal institution responds to a need for the function that it performs. From this point of view, the use of social capital by poor households is explained by the need of the poorest sectors to provide (risk-smoothing) institutional solutions in the context of imperfect markets or in their total absence.[17] Bates (1989), Ostrom

---

[17] See Morduch (1995 and 1997); Townsend (1995); Besley (1993).

(1990) and Granovetter (1992) argue that this presumption is not always correct. Although poor households tend to be particularly in need of systems to smooth the risk of consumption and income shocks, this "need" only explains *demand* for institutional solutions, but not *supply*. Explaining supply involves considering not only those who use these solutions, but also how they are provided (which frequently involves the dilemma of collective action of second order). Ostrom argues that social capital can play an important role in the working of an informal institution (by facilitating compliance with norms), but he does not explain how it is provided.

In general, not all use of social capital by poor households is intended to ensure their patterns of consumption and income, and not every act of risk-smoothing depends on the use of social capital. For example, the existence of football teams and religious or cultural groups is not explained by the need to insure against risk, although they can sometimes fulfill that role. Some uses of social capital are genuinely intended to stimulate sport, culture or religious worship. In a complementary way, not all the risk-smoothing institutions depend on the use of the social capital of the poor. Some of these institutions exist because of considerations exogenous to social confidence. The institutional links between borrowers and lenders, for example, arise because of *lack of confidence* between principals and agents due to asymmetric information.[18] The central subject of this study is precisely the use that poor households make of social capital and the return they obtain from it in the context of incomplete markets.

How can social capital be measured? This study analyzes two aspects of the assets of social capital: endowment and use. Endowment is measured by identifying the most visible proxies for social networks: the extended family (siblings, cousins, uncles and aunts) and, outside the family, the most intimate networks (kinship) and most important affiliations (membership of sports, cultural, religious groups, etc.). For the examination of social capital, the analysis is limited to informal credit and job markets. These include forms of informal credit that make use of social networks (loans from family members and friends, moneylenders, stores and local businesses, and rotating credit associations called *pasanakus*), and job search techniques that use them. For the analysis of endowment and use, a distinction is made between the behavior of the head of household and the spouse.

---

[18] See Hoff, Braverman and Stiglitz (1993); Bardhan (1989); Stiglitz (1989).

Data

This section is based on a survey of homes made in El Alto in December 1997 and January 1998.[19] A poverty line is employed based on income, constructed on a basic food basket of 1990.[20] El Alto provides a case study sui generis for analyzing the resources and assets of the poor. The city can be characterized as a poor urban conglomerate with high rates of rural/urban migration that generate significant demographic growth, and a visible presence of social networks that operate the informal credit and job markets. Formerly a marginal neighborhood of La Paz, El Alto today has almost one million inhabitants, mostly working in informal commerce, construction, transport and small-scale activities. El Alto also has strong community links, in many cases transferred from the places of origin of the migrant population, generally Aymara, which mean that kinship relations and membership of community groups influence most economic activities. The continuous formation of new social networks and the dissolution of old ones is conducive to the analysis of social capital and poverty.

Table 2.9 shows that the language spoken and the educational level are the most evident contrasts between poor and non-poor households in El Alto. While 86 percent of heads of poor households speak Aymara and Spanish regularly, only 75.3 percent of the non-poor consider themselves bilingual. Of the heads of non-poor households, 10.5 percent also stated that they are taking university studies (completed or uncompleted), in comparison with 3.3 percent of the poor. Similarly, there are marked differences between the two groups in relation to access to physical and financial assets. While 16 percent of heads of non-poor households have access to bank,

---

[19] The survey contains 3,311 observations of 687 households. The sample was chosen on the basis of an updated sampling framework. Its design is stratified by segment, which establishes an error of 3.7 percent and a level of reliability of 95 percent. The selection of the design is single-stage with simple random sampling. Data collection was carried out by the firm Encuestas & Estudios.

[20] The poverty line was prepared on the basis of a Basic Food Basket (CBA) specific to El Alto, with data from the 1990 Family Budget Survey. The CBA collects the structure of food consumption from a reference stratum in El Alto, which covers average energy needs (2,150 Kcal and 57.6 grams of protein per person per day). The quantities adjusted to average needs have been valued in terms of the average prices in the consumer price index. The cost of the CBA was divided among the proportion of food expense of the reference stratum (Engel coefficient = 0.61) to obtain the poverty line.

Table 2.9. Descriptive Characteristics of Heads of Household, El Alto

		% of poor homes		% of non-poor homes	
	Incidence of poverty	Mean	Standard deviation	Mean	Standard deviation
Total	52.0				
Human capital					
Education					
None	50.0	5.0	2.1	5.5	2.2
Primary incomplete	59.8	34.1	47.3	25.3	43.2
Primary complete	52.6	11.4	21.7	11.4	21.6
Secondary complete	53.8	18.1	38.0	17.6	38.4
Secondary incomplete	53.3	23.2	42.1	21.9	41.3
University incomplete	32.1	2.5	10.5	5.9	10.9
University complete	16.6	0.8	9.0	4.6	16.5
Other	50.0	4.9	18.4	7.8	24.8
Language					
Only Spanish	38.5	14.0	34.5	24.7	43.0
Spanish and Aymara	55.8	86.0	198.0	75.3	186.7
Migration					
Established urban migrant	52.3	9.5	29.2	9.6	29.3
Established rural migrant	54.1	57.5	145.6	54.0	139.4
New urban migrant	36.4	1.1	9.7	2.2	14.8
New rural migrant	59.0	6.4	24.4	4.9	21.6
Head of household					
Female	55.4	13.2	33.3	11.0	31.7
Branch of activity					
Industry	54.6	14.8	26.5	12.8	24.4
Commerce	48.2	21.5	56.8	23.6	58.7
Transport	50.0	9.1	17.6	9.5	17.9
Construction	58.1	13.5	23.8	9.7	19.3
Services	47.5	33.4	68.9	38.4	76.0
Others	s.d.	7.7	23.1	1.6	9.6
Physical capital					
Formal credit					
Account: bank/mutual/coop.	30.2	3.6	4.3	9.2	10.9
Credit: credit/mutual/coop.	36.1	8.4	16.5	16.3	24.1
Physical assets					
Premises outside the home	39.3	3.0	12.8	5.2	18.6
Premises inside the home	52.4	6.0	21.0	6.1	22.9
Fixed site	31.8	1.9	8.3	4.6	28.4
Mobile site	56.0	3.9	15.6	3.4	14.8
Other	39.2	4.9	21.9	3.4	17.5
Social capital					
Social affiliations					
No affiliation	56.0	34.9	54.2	30.4	48.3
Between 1 and 3	53.9	47.9	88.4	45.4	82.8
Over 3	43.9	17.2	38.6	24.2	41.7
Extended family					
Under 10 family members	47.3	20.7	44.1	23.1	68.5
Between 10 and 25 family members	51.4	49.6	56.3	47.0	52.0
Over 25 family members	52.5	29.7	36.7	29.9	44.8
Kinship relations					
None	54.2	8.9	24.0	8.3	22.6
Between 1 and 5	51.1	45.4	64.6	48.1	68.9
Over 5	52.3	45.7	69.2	43.6	62.1
Social Capital – Credit					
Credit from family members, friends	56.0	20.9	52.9	18.2	44.7
Credit from local moneylender	30.7	1.1	9.4	2.8	16.7
Credit from local store or business	51.6	4.5	20.6	4.6	21.8
Pasanaku	50.0	10.5	20.0	11.7	21.5
Social Capital – Job					
Obtained last job alone	49.6	63.4	66.9	71.2	78.5
Obtained last job from family members	51.8	10.8	16.8	12.8	19.3
Obtained last job from friends	66.1	10.8	18.4	6.3	15.1

Source: Authors' calculations based on Survey of Resources and Assets of the Poor (INE, 1998).

mutual or cooperative credit, only 8 percent of the heads of poor house-holds have such access. Similarly, 9.2 percent of non-poor households have savings accounts, in contrast to 3.6 percent of the poor.

Twenty-six percent of all heads of household have had access to infor-mal credit in the last year, and an additional 10.6 percent had participated in a rotating savings and loan association *(pasanaku)*. The differences in access to informal credit by poor and non-poor are not significant, but there are differences in the use of credit. While most heads of non-poor households say they used the *pasanaku* draw to purchase a durable good or as working capital, most heads of poor households bought consumer goods. Generally, households with access to credit from family members or neighborhood stores used the informal credit to purchase consumer goods regardless of their economic status. In the sample, 8.6 percent stated they had no kinship links, with an incidence of poverty of 54 percent (two points above the aver-age). Lastly, 33 percent of the sample state they had no community affilia-tions, with an incidence of poverty of 56 percent (4 points above average).

Extended Families

What types of households have the most extensive family networks? Table 2.10 shows the average size of extended families crossed by level of educa-tion, migrant condition, language spoken and poverty. For the purposes of this chapter, the extended family is defined in terms of the number of sib-lings, aunts and uncles and first cousins reported by the head of household and spouse. With this restrictive definition, the probable network of family assistance available to the head and spouse is represented. The table suggests some unforeseen characteristics: the most extended families tend to be more educated than the less extended, and have more Spanish speakers and non-migrants. What causes this pattern? One possible explanation is the social composition of the majority of households in El Alto. Over two-thirds of the sample are either established or recent migrants, which probably reflects the composition of their urban families, rather than their rural ones. Simi-larly the differences between heads of household and spouses are not very significant, except in education, where the family/level of education ratio tends to be inverse for spouses.

Table 2.10.   Characteristics of Social Capital, Extended Family

	Head			Spouse		
	No. obs.	Mean	St. dev.	No. obs.	Mean	St. dev.
Education	**511**	**20.0**	**14.4**	**447**	**21.0**	**15.5**
None	28	12.7	9.35	47	12.5	9.4
Primary incomplete	149	18.2	14.6	178	20.4	13.1
Primary complete	58	19.1	10.3	49	18.9	11.8
Secondary complete	114	21.7	15.8	88	26.5	22.6
Secondary incomplete	89	20.9	12.6	49	23.7	14.6
University incomplete	20	16.5	13.7	8	17.4	6.9
University complete	20	26.5	19.4	11	23.3	14.0
Normal	21	25.1	16.4	9	21.8	10.5
Technical	12	27.6	16.9	8	19.7	13.7
Language	**511**	**20.0**	**14.4**	**447**	**21.0**	**15.5**
Only Spanish	92	20.5	14.6	88	21.2	15.0
Spanish and Aymara	419	19.9	13.7	359	20.9	15.6
Migration	**511**	**20.0**	**14.4**	**447**	**21.0**	**15.5**
Non-migrant	134			144		
Established migrant	340	19.3	13.3	272	20.2	13.8
New migrant	37	17.7	11.2	31	20.1	14.2
Poverty	**511**	**20.0**	**14.4**	**447**	**21.0**	**15.5**
Poor household	256	19.6	13.5	232	20.9	14.9
Non-poor household	255	20.4	15.3	215	21.1	16.1
No reply	**176**			**219**		
Total	**687**			**666**		

Source: Authors' calculations, based on the Survey of Resources and Assets of the Poor (INE, 1998).

Kinship Networks

Kinship networks include both horizontal-type links (godparents with parents) and vertical (godparents with godchildren). Kinship relations are associated with the social responsibilities of mutual help and intergenerational solidarity. The naming of godparents is commonly associated with recognition of maturity and prestige ("alternate" parents). The existence then of larger kinship networks between relatively prosperous (or at least non-poor) households is not surprising. Table 2.11 shows the average kinship relations of heads of household and spouses, crossed by level of education, language spoken, migrant condition and poverty. The households with the highest number of kinship relations are characterized by low and high levels of education (primary completed and university), by speaking Spanish, and by being established or non-migrants. Spouses report having more kinship relations than heads of household, while new migrants have the least.

Community Affiliations

Community affiliations have received the most attention in the literature on social capital. In the El Alto survey, information was collected on 14 types of affiliation. Table 2.12 shows the frequency of replies by heads of household and spouses. The differences in community affiliation between poor and non-poor households are small and statistically insignificant. This result is especially interesting in relation to the analysis of determinants of poverty, since it suggests that the presumption of high levels of social capital among poor populations must be open to the evidence of the case study. It also suggests that the discussion of social capital in El Alto should highlight the differentiated use of relatively homogeneous networks. The detailed differences shown below are relative. The most pronounced differences between poor and non-poor households are observed in membership in cultural groups, trade unions and political parties. The affiliations that revealed no differences are school boards, and folkloric and religious groups. Poor households participate most in self-help groups, frequently linked to food programs and communal work.

According to their statements, 32 percent of heads of households are not affiliated with any community association (49 percent for spouses), while 46 percent have one or two affiliations (38 percent for spouses) and 22 per-

Table 2.11. Characteristics of Social Capital, Kinship Networks

	Head			Spouse		
	No. obs.	Mean	St. dev.	No. obs.	Mean	St. dev.
Education	**642**	**4.4**	**3.7**	**534**	**4.7**	**3.9**
None	36	4.4	3.5	62	5.5	4.5
Primary incomplete	191	4.4	3.5	210	4.5	3.8
Primary complete	70	5.3	4.8	58	4.8	3.8
Secondary complete	141	4.4	3.8	103	4.7	3.7
Secondary incomplete	116	4.2	3.6	61	4.3	4.1
University incomplete	22	4.9	3.3	9	4.6	2.6
University complete	21	5.0	5.1	12	5.1	3.7
Normal	27	4.0	2.6	11	5.6	3.0
Technical	18	4.8	3.6	8	4.7	3.4
Language	**642**	**4.4**	**3.7**	**534**	**4.7**	**3.9**
Only Spanish	124	4.5	4.2	109	4.8	4.2
Spanish and Aymara	518	4.4	3.6	425	4.7	3.8
Migration	**642**	**4.4**	**3.7**	**534**	**4.7**	**3.9**
Non-migrant	180			163		
Established migrant	416	4.6	3.8	333	4.7	3.8
New migrant	46	3.3	2.5	38	4.4	3.9
Poverty	**642**	**4.4**	**3.7**	**534**	**4.7**	**3.9**
Poor household	333	4.4	3.7	282	4.6	3.6
Non-poor household	309	4.5	3.8	252	4.8	4.1
No reply	**45**			**132**		
Total	**687**			**666**		

Source: Authors' calculations based on the Survey of Resources and Assets of the Poor (INE, 1998).

Table 2.12. Characteristics of Social Capital, Community Affiliations
(In percent)

	Head of household			Spouse		
	Total	Poor	Non-poor	Total	Poor	Non-poor
Trade union	21.4	18.3	24.8	7.9	6.2	10.0
Religious group	19.6	19.4	19.9	19.4	19.1	19.7
Sports group	21.7	20.8	22.7	2.8	2.2	3.5
Cultural group	3.2	1.7	4.9	3.0	1.4	4.8
School board	20.5	20.2	20.8	16.5	14.3	19
Mothers' club	1.2	1.1	1.2	7.5	6.7	8.4
Territorially based organization	18.5	17.2	19.9	10.4	7.9	13.2
Self-help group	3.2	2.8	3.7	1.8	1.4	2.2
Folklore group	10.6	10.5	10.7	8.2	7.9	8.7
Political party	7.9	6.6	9.2	5.4	3.9	7.1
Rural organization	5.7	5.0	6.4	5.4	4.8	6.1
Market or trade group	7	5.8	8.3	10.2	8.1	12.6
NGO	1	1.1	0.9	0.7	0.6	1.0
Other	0.6	0.3	0.9	0.3	0.3	0.3
No reply	0	0	0	0	0	
Total no. of observations	687	361	326	666	356	310

Source: Authors' calculations based on the Survey of Resources and Assets of the Poor (INE, 1998).

cent, three or more (13 percent for spouses). The differences between the poor and non-poor are marked among heads of household. While only 17 percent of the poor are affiliated with three or more associations, 25 percent of the non-poor are. Similarly, 35 percent of heads of poor households report no affiliation, compared with 30 percent of the non-poor.

Analysis of Poverty from the Perspective of Assets

Estimates were run under five different specifications in which the dependent variable is dichotomous and assumes the value of 1 when the person belongs to a poor household and 0 when non-poor. The basic model includes the variables of human capital, demographic conditions, ethnicity, migratory condition and labor characteristics in order to give a first approximation of the determinants of poverty (see Table 2.13). The second specification includes variables of physical capital, while the third, fourth and fifth specifications include variables of social capital.

Models 1 and 2: Human and Physical Capital

The first specification shows the results of a basic model of human capital. The level of schooling indicates that for the first two educational levels (PRIMARY, SECONDARY), there is a decreasing probability of being poor as the level of education rises. Normal school and university studies (NORMAL, UNIVERSITY) have a significant negative effect on the probability of being poor. More years of labor experience suggest that the probability of being poor diminishes, but the probability becomes positive after a threshold (EXPERIENCE and EXPERIENCE_2). Although both variables show the expected signs, they are not statistically significant. The migratory condition of the head of household reveals that the probability of falling into poverty diminishes if the head of household is an established migrant but increases for recent arrivals (ESTABLISHED MIGRANT, RECENT MIGRANT). Both are statistically significant at 5 percent.

The regular language spoken was used as a proxy for ethnicity (SPANISH), reflecting the households that do not speak native languages. The results show that if the head of household speaks only Spanish, the probability of falling into poverty declines. Despite showing the expected sign, the gender of the head of household is not statistically significant (MALE HEAD). Among the variables of labor market access, the fact that the household has a higher proportion of workers in the informal sector (INFORMAL) reduces the probability of being poor.[21] The sign of the variable is the expected 1, although this could seem counterintuitive, because in El Alto the average income of self-employed workers is notably higher than that of laborers and employees in the formal sector, denoting the precarious labor

---

[21] The formal sector is composed of a set of developed economic activities both in the state and private business spheres, where the working population functions in typical relationships of employer-worker dependence, and where there is a clear distinction between the ownership of capital and labor. Independent professionals also form part of the formal sector (Casanovas and de Pabón, 1988).

Table 2.13. Models of Probability of Falling into Poverty

(Dependent variable: 1 = poor, 0 = non-poor)

Variable	(1) Coef.	P>|z|	(2) Coef.	P>|z|	(3) Coef.	P>|z|	(4) Coef.	P>|z|	(5) Coef.	P>|z|
PRIMARY	0.625	0.00	0.818	0.00	0.825	0.00	0.820	0.00	0.929	0.00
SECONDARY	0.253	0.14	0.370	0.02	0.386	0.02	0.369	0.03	0.357	0.05
NORMAL	-1.141	0.00	-1.014	0.00	-0.997	0.00	-1.027	0.00	-1.414	0.01
UNIVERSITY INCOMPLETE	-0.852	0.01	-0.664	0.04	-0.633	0.04	-0.674	0.03	-0.804	0.05
UNIVERSITY COMPLETE	-1.832	0.00	-1.537	0.00	-1.560	0.00	-1.583	0.00	-0.449	0.48
EXPERIENCE	-0.002	0.95	-0.003	0.53	0.001	0.74	-0.001	0.76	0.001	0.97
EXPERIENCE_2	0.000	0.71	0.000	0.38	0.000	0.98	0.000	0.95	0.000	0.82
SPEAKS ONLY SPANISH	-0.314	0.00	-0.330	0.00	-0.354	0.00	-0.356	0.00	-0.351	0.00
MALE HEAD	-0.024	0.78	-0.044	0.71	-0.094	0.32	-0.100	0.29	-0.117	0.22
ESTABLISHED MIGRANT	-0.145	0.02	-0.117	0.36	-1.075	0.10	-0.108	0.09	-0.104	0.11
RECENT MIGRANT	0.272	0.02	0.198	0.22	0.181	0.12	0.199	0.09	0.186	0.12
INFORMAL	-0.759	0.00	-0.679	0.00	-0.645	0.00	-0.641	0.00	-0.638	0.00
DEPENDENTS	0.260	0.00	0.334	0.00	0.345	0.00	0.343	0.00	0.341	0.00
FIXED SITE			-0.099	0.00	-0.099	0.00	-0.100	0.00	-0.092	0.01
MOBILE SITE			1.051	0.00	1.048	0.00	1.038	0.00	1.077	0.00
AFFILIATIONS (ks1)					-0.057	0.02	-0.059	0.02	-0.041	0.02
FAMILY AFFILIATIONS (ks2)					-0.002	0.05	-0.002	0.04	-0.001	0.05
FAMILY CREDIT (ks3)							-0.022	0.72	-0.021	0.74
STORE CREDIT (ks4)							-0.085	0.23	-0.084	0.24
PASANAKU (ks5)							0.063	0.32	0.069	0.28
JOB HELP (ks6)							-0.001	0.96	0.000	0.81
Ks1*PRIMARY (ks7a)									-0.053	0.06
Ks1*SECONDARY (ks7b)									0.006	0.86
Ks1*NORMAL (ks7c)									0.215	0.26
Ks1*UNI INCOMPLETE (ks7d)									0.067	0.59
Ks1*UNI COMPLETE (ks7e)									-2.063	0.00
CONSTANT	0.729	0.00	0.649	0.00	0.655	0.00	0.658	0.112	0.639	0.00
Number of observations	686		686		686		686		686	
Chi2(x)	530.32		630.5		640.1		642.6		669.5	
Prob>chi2	0.00		0.00		0.00		0.00		0.00	
Pseudo R2	0.155		0.184		0.187		0.188		0.196	

Source: Authors' calculations based on the Survey of Resources and Assets of the Poor (INE, 1998).
Note: The variables included are: for schooling, PRIMARY, primary studies completed (head of household); SECONDARY, secondary studies completed (head of household); NORMAL, studies in normal school; UNIVERSITY COMPLETED and INCOMPLETE, university studies (head of household) (category omitted: no cycle completed). The labor variables are: EXPERIENCE and EXPERIENCE_2, labor experience; INFORMAL, proportion of self-employed people in the household; DEPENDENTS, proportion of the economically inactive people in the household. For demographic variables: ESTABLISHED MIGRANT, if the head of household has been a migrant for over five years; RECENT MIGRANT, if the head of household has been a migrant for under five years; MALE HEAD, if head of household is male; SPEAKS ONLY SPANISH, if the head does not speak any native language. For the variables of physical capital: FIXED SITE, if the head has a permanent

market access of the latter. Finally, the higher the number of economically inactive people in the household (DEPENDENTS), the higher the probability of falling into poverty.

The second specification shows that possession of a fixed site for labor activities (kiosk, shop, workshop, home-workshop) increases the probability that the household can leave poverty (FIXED SITE). An inverse relationship is observed for people who work from a movable service point (MOBILE SITE). Both results support the hypothesis that the more physical assets possessed, the greater the capacity to generate income and the lower the vulnerability to falling into conditions of poverty. In the evaluation of the contributions of physical assets, the variables of access to formal credit and the holding of a savings account are omitted; they are assumed to be endogenous.

Models 3 and 4: Human, Physical and Social Capital

Two hypotheses related to social capital are analyzed. First, does the *magnitude* of the social networks have any effect on the probability of falling into poverty? Second, does the *type* of social networks (generic or specific to the credit and job markets) have any effect? The first hypothesis—social capital endowment as measured by the number of community and extended-family affiliations of the head and spouse (AFFILIATIONS, FAMILY AFFILIATIONS)—has a negative correlation with the probability of being poor. Both variables show a statistical significance of 5 percent. Controlling for characteristics of human and physical capital, the results suggest that the higher the social capital endowment, the lower the probability of falling into poverty. This result is particularly interesting in light of the distribution of social capital observed in Tables 2.10, 2.11 and 2.12. In the case of El Alto, the difference between the number of associations that poor households report

---

work location; MOBILE SITE if the head has a mobile location. For social capital: AFFILIATIONS, number of memberships of community associations described in Table 2.4; FAMILY AFFILIATIONS, number of family members of head of household, siblings, uncles and aunts and first cousins; FAMILY CREDIT, if the household has had a family loan in the last year; STORE CREDIT, if the household obtained credit from a store in the last year; PASANAKU if the head or spouse participated in a *pasanaku* in the last year; JOB HELP, if someone in the household obtained his or her last job with the help of relatives, friends and/or social networks. Ks1* LEVELS OF EDUCATION are terms of interaction between COMMUNITY AFFILIATIONS and EDUCATION.

is not statistically different from that of non-poor households. This is an unexpected result, considering the presumption of the literature that the poorest households create institutional mechanisms to fill "gaps" in absent markets.

To analyze the second hypothesis, three variables are introduced for the use of social capital in the credit markets (FAMILY LOAN, STORE LOAN and PASANAKU) and one for employment (JOB ASSISTANCE). The effect of access to social capital networks on the credit market was researched first. Of particular interest was measuring the probable effect of membership in a rotating credit association (PASANAKU), given the attention accorded to this variant in the literature on poverty.[22] In El Alto the *pasanaku* is a regular practice that covers approximately 11 percent of poor households and 12 percent of non-poor households. About 10 people participate in a "typical" *pasanaku*, which holds a weekly draw of contributions. The winners of previous draws are excluded, until each contributor has won once. Despite the relative social importance of the *pasanaku*, there is no conclusive evidence of its effect on the probability of falling into poverty. The PASANAKU variable is not statistically significant in the case of the survey. Neither are the other variables of social capital linked to the credit market, including loans from families, friends and the local store (FAMILY LOAN, STORE LOAN). Excluded from this specification is the variable "informal lender," which is assumed to be endogenous.

Research then focused on the question of whether the existence of social networks linked to the job market had an effect on the probability of falling into conditions of poverty. Of particular interest were the results of the literature that emphasize the "strength of the weakest links," in reference to the use of non-family social networks, as applied to the case study (Granovetter, 1973 and 1992). Variables were constructed to represent the use of family and non-family networks to obtain employment (JOB HELP). There is no evidence, however, to support or reject the results of the literature. The variables of social capital linked to employment are not statistically significant in this study. Generally, there is no evidence to suggest that the *type* of social capital has a significant effect on the probability of falling into poverty in El Alto.

---

[22] See Calomiris and Rajaraman (1998); Besley, Choate and Loury (1993).

Model 5: Interactions between Social and Human Capital

The final hypothesis analyzed is the interaction between social and human capital, with an emphasis on whether social capital has differentiated effects for different groups of educational achievement. Do individuals with certain educational achievements obtain a higher return? In the fifth specification, there is statistical significance for two variables (Ks1*PRIMARY and Ks1*UNIVERSITY COMPLETE) that measure the interaction between the number of community affiliations and educational level. The surprising aspect of this result is the distribution of the interaction. The inverted "U" between poverty and the terms of interaction suggests that social capital has a higher return for the highest and lowest levels of educational achievement, but not for the intermediate group. The significance of this interaction is particularly important in urban areas, where the expansion of opportunities for income generation results from the extensive use of social networks for both the formal and informal sectors, irrespective of other differential characteristics.

Generally, the results of the analysis of determinants of poverty presented above reinforce the findings of earlier works in which the role of education is the determining factor in explaining income growth, and thus in the reduction of poverty.[23] It is also noteworthy that ethnic condition and labor status, along with possession of and access to physical capital, have a marked incidence on levels of poverty. The new finding of this work is the effect that social capital can have on the probability of leaving poverty. Three hypotheses were analyzed, two of which suggest the importance of social networks for poor households and the interaction of these networks with human capital endowment. No statistical significance was found for the evaluation of different types of social capital used by poor households. In the case of El Alto, the results of the survey suggest an instrumental use of family and extra-family networks in smoothing the risk of patterns of consumption and income.

---

[23] See Jiménez and Yáñez (1997); Fields, et al. (1997); and World Bank (1996).

Conclusions

This chapter has analyzed the relationship between assets and poverty for longitudinal and cross-section samples of urban households in Bolivia. While limitations on information have not permitted an analysis of rural areas, this study considers the interrelationships between the processes of urban-marginal and rural impoverishment. In particular, the analysis of social capital suggests the importance of evaluating the effect of the dissolution and recomposition of the social networks of the poorest urban households. In addition, the incorporation of variables of social capital into the basic model of determinants of poverty helps to explain income in the absence of insurance markets.

The longitudinal analysis suggests the weight of variables of human capital in explaining the persistence of urban poverty. There is also a significant relationship between migration, ethnicity and labor market access on the one hand and poverty on the other. The households that enter the labor market through family and semi-business units have more possibilities of generating income than their business counterparts (which include employers, employees and workers). The cross-section analysis suggests, in addition to the importance of human capital, the significance of variables of physical and social capital. Access to productive infrastructure implies a lower probability of finding poverty.

There is also a significant relationship between the measurement of social capital and the probability of escaping poverty. Of the three hypotheses analyzed, two—related to the size of social networks and their interaction with levels of human capital—suggest that social capital has a significant effect on the probability of escaping poverty.

There is no evidence, however, to evaluate the third hypothesis, which would explain this correlation in terms of the linkage to specific markets (credit and job). The study also suggests that the transmission belt between social capital and generation of income is not at all clear. It is probable that the social networks play an indirect role in generating income through the inter-period risk-smoothing of patterns of consumption and income among poorer households.

The findings of this chapter have empirical implications for the poor in Bolivia. First, social capital is susceptible to measurement and analysis in a model of household decision-making. The formulation of a specific survey on these problems reveals some of the difficulties of collecting information on interrelationships between households and highlights the contextual importance of the analysis of social capital. Some of the most idiosyncratic aspects of measurement (such as capture of the differentiated use of social networks) are, in fact, some of the most important, since they show the instrumental use of household decisions. It is also probable that in this study the cross-section observation of social capital underestimates the measurement of its impact on the generation of income. Multiple observations of social capital, consumption and incomes, if available, would probably make the linkages between social networks, risk-smoothing and generation of income more apparent. In any event, the analytical challenge of measuring social capital continues to be important for the empirical progress of the study of human, physical and social assets in the future.

Second, the analysis of social capital and poverty prompts new questions on the causality of the determinants of poverty. Can it be inferred that the presence of resources of social capital reduces the probability of falling into poverty? Or vice versa, that poverty favors the production of social capital to reverse imperfections in access to asset markets? In the case of El Alto, the expected signs were observed of a model in which social capital acts as an explanatory variable (on the right side of the equation). In fact, the higher the social capital endowment, the lower was the probability of falling into poverty. The same result could be explained by the inverse cause (more poverty, more social capital). In fact this assumption is anchored in the literature on risk-smoothing, where institutional solutions arise to counteract imperfections in the asset markets. A priori at the start of the study was that the differentiated treatment of the social capital endowment and use could shed some light on this dilemma. There was not, however, evidence to evaluate the impact of different types of social capital. The analysis of probable mechanisms of transmission between social capital and generation of income, therefore, remains on a future agenda of empirical work.

Third, the analysis of poverty by resources and assets suggests the importance of analyzing the interaction between the different types of assets. In this study, the interaction between social and human capital raises questions regarding the returns on social capital for poor households. If individuals with high and low educational achievement profit most from access to social networks, the presumption of the use of social networks by the poorest sectors to resolve problems of access to asset markets is called into question. Further, the observation that poor and non-poor households make equal use of social networks calls into question the presumption that the poor are the sole users of social capital. Future analyses need to look at differentiating the effect of the use of social networks on the returns of human and physical capital. Social capital plays a decisive role because of its special nature, namely that it is created by interrelationships between individuals and households.

There are also policy implications that can be drawn from this chapter. The importance of social capital for improving access to labor markets may be indicative of the lack of formal information mechanisms on labor market conditions and needs, and of barriers to entry to certain occupations. Similarly, the role that social capital plays in protecting people from unexpected income shocks suggests that formal income-smoothing mechanisms, such as unemployment insurance, are not available. So, the importance of social capital may be due to its capacity to substitute for certain types of institutions. If such institutions were in place, social capital might not be as crucial for escaping poverty as it apparently is in Bolivia.

Finally, examining poverty from the perspective of human, physical and social assets provides a broader analytical matrix. This chapter has applied the assets-based approach to a very ethnically and socially heterogeneous country, finding that the emphasis on the endowment and use of the three types of assets provides new instruments for evaluating urban poverty. The study of the distribution of assets and their return will continue to be an ambitious agenda for analyzing the determinants of household poverty. Given the exploratory characteristics of this approach, future contributions will help build bridges for formulating public policies that are more relevant for generating income and protecting disequilibria in patterns of consumption and income. In addition, a renewed emphasis on the factors influencing the distribution and use of assets will provide better analytical instruments for evaluating gaps in the individual and collective risk-smoothing mechanisms of the poorest populations.

References

Barro, J. J., and J. W. Lee. 1993. *International Comparisons of Educational Attainment*. NBER Working Paper 4349. National Bureau of Economic Research, Cambridge, MA.

Bardhan, P. 1992. *Land, Labor and Rural Poverty: Essays in Development Economics*. New York: Oxford University Press.

_____. 1989. Alternative Approaches to the Theory of Institutions in Economic Development. In P. Bardhan (ed.), *The Economic Theory of Agrarian Institutions*. Oxford, UK: Oxford University Press.

Bates, R. 1989. Contra Contractarianism: Some Reflections on the New Institutionalism. *Politics and Society* 16: 387-401.

Beccaria, L., and O. Fresneda. 1991. La pobreza en América Latina. In *El reto de la pobreza*. Bogota: UNDP.

Besley, T. 1995. Non-Market Institutions for Credit and Risk Sharing in Low-Income Countries. *Journal of Economic Perspectives* 9(3): 115-27.

_____. 1993. *Savings, Credit and Insurance*. Discussion Paper # 167, Woodrow Wilson School of Public and International Affairs, Research Program in Development Studies, Princeton, NJ.

Besley, T., S. Choate, and G. Loury. 1993. The Economics of Rotating Savings and Credit Associations. *American Economic Review* 83(4): 792-810.

Birdsall, N., and J.L. Londoño. 1997a. Asset Inequality Does Matter: An Assessment of the World Bank's Approach to Poverty Reduction. Inter-American Development Bank Research Department Working Paper 344, Washington, DC.

_____. 1997b. Asset Inequality Matters. *American Economic Review* 87(2): 32-7.

Boix, C., and D. Posner. 1996. *Making Social Capital Work: A Review of Robert Putnam's Making Democracy Work: Civic Traditions in Modern Italy*. Paper No. 96-4, Harvard Academy for International Area Studies, Harvard University Center for International Affairs, Cambridge, MA.

Boltvinik, J. 1992. Conceptos y mediciones de la pobreza predominantes en Latinoamérica. Evaluación crítica. In L. Beccaria, et al. (eds.), *América Latina: el reto de la pobreza*. Bogota: UNDP.

Browning, M., and A. Lusardi. 1996. Household Savings: Micro Theories and Macro Facts. *Journal of Economic Literature* 34(4): 1797-855.

Calomiris, C., and I. Rajaraman. 1998. The Role of ROSCAS: Lumpy Durables or Event Insurance? *Journal of Development Economics* 56(1): 207-16.

Casanovas, R., and S. de Pabón. 1988. *Los trabajadores por cuenta propia en La Paz. Funcionamiento de las unidades económicas, situación laboral e ingresos.* La Paz: Centro de Estudios para el Desarrollo Laboral y Agrario.

Coleman, J. 1990. *Foundations of Social Theory.* Cambridge, MA: Harvard University Press.

Collier, P. 1998. Social Capital and Poverty. World Bank, Washington, DC. Unpublished.

Datt, G., and M. Ravallion. 1992. Growth and Redistribution Components of Changes in Poverty Measures. *Journal of Development Economics* 38(3): 275-95.

Deaton, A. 1997. *The Analysis of Household Surveys: Microeconometric Analysis for Development Policy.* Baltimore, MD: Johns Hopkins University Press.

————. 1992a. *Understanding Consumption.* Oxford, UK: Clarendon Press.

————. 1992b. Saving and Income Smoothing in Cote d'Ivoire. Discussion Paper 156. Woodrow Wilson School of Public and International Affairs, Research Program in Development Studies, Princeton, NJ.

————. 1985. Panel Data from Time Series of Cross Sections. *Journal of Econometrics* 30: 109-26.

Economic Commission for Latin America and the Caribbean (ECLAC). 1994. *Panorama social de América Latina 1994 y 1996.* Santiago: United Nations.

————. 1993. *Cambios en el perfil de las familias.* Santiago: United Nations.

————. 1991. *Magnitud de la pobreza en América Latina en los años ochenta.* ECLAC Studies and Reports No. 81, United Nations, Santiago.

Economic Commission for Latin America and the Caribbean (ECLAC) and Unidad de Análisis de Políticas Sociales (UDAPSO). 1995. *Metodología de construcción de la canasta básica de alimentos.* Cuadernos de Desarrollo Humano No. 2, Human Development Ministry, United Nations/Unidad de Análisis de Política Social, La Paz.

Fields, G., J. Leary, L.F. López Calva, and E. Pérez de Rada. 1997. *Descomposición de la desigualdad del ingreso laboral en las ciudades principales de Bolivia.* La Paz: Unidad de Análisis de Políticas Sociales (UDAPSO).

Fiszbein, A., and G. Psacharopoulos. 1995. Income Inequality Trends in Latin America in the 1980s. In N. Lustig (ed.), *Coping with Austerity.* Washington, DC: Brookings Institution.

Foster, J., J. Greer, and E. Thorbecke. 1984. A Class of Decomposable Poverty Measures. *Econometrica* 52(3): 761-66.

Granovetter, M. 1992. Economic Institutions as Social Constructions: A Framework for Analysis. *Acta Sociológica* 35: 3-11.

_____. 1973. The Strength of Weak Ties. *American Journal of Sociology* 78: 1360-80.

Gray-Molina, G., W. Jiménez, E. Pérez de Rada, and E. Yáñez. 1999. *Pobreza y activos en Bolivia: ¿Qué rol juega el capital social?* Documento de Trabajo de la Red de Centros R-356. Inter-American Development Bank Research Department, Washington, DC.

Hoff, K., A. Braverman, and J. Stiglitz. 1993. *The Economics of Rural Organization: Theory, Practice and Policy.* Oxford, UK: Oxford University Press/ World Bank.

Instituto Nacional de Estadística (INE). 1998. Survey of Resources and Assets of the Poor (Encuesta de los recursos y activos de los pobres). La Paz: Instituto Nacional de Estadística.

_____. 1996. *Cuentas Nacionales 1988-1992.* La Paz: Finance Ministry/Instituto Nacional de Estadística.

_____. 1993. *Encuesta Integrada de Hogares.* La Paz: Ministry of Planning and Coordination/Instituto Nacional de Estadística.

Jiménez, W., and E. Yáñez. 1997a. *Pobreza en las ciudades de Bolivia: Análisis de la heterogeneidad de la pobreza a partir de las EIH 1990-1995.* Working Paper, Unidad de Análisis de Políticas Sociales (UDAPSO), La Paz.

_____. 1997b. *Ingresos familiares en un contexto de crecimiento.* Working Paper, Unidad de Análisis de Políticas Sociales, La Paz.

Larrañaga, O. 1994. Pobreza, crecimiento y desigualdad: Chile 1987-92. Research paper, Postgraduate Program in Economics, Instituto Latinoamericano de Doctrina y Estudios Sociales/Georgetown University, Santiago.

Lipton, M., and J. van der Gaag (eds.). 1993. *Including the Poor. Proceedings of a Symposium Organized by the World Bank and the International Policy Research Institute.* Washington, DC: World Bank.

Londoño, J. L., and M. Székely. 1997. Sorpresas distributivas después de una década de reformas: América Latina en los noventa. Inter-American Development Bank Research Department Working Paper 352, Washington, DC.

Lustig, N., and A. Mitchell. 1995. Poverty in Mexico: The Effects of Adjusting Survey Data for Under-Reporting. *Estudios Económicos* 10(1).

Montaño, G., and M. Padilla. 1994. *El empleo urbano en Bolivia: tendencias y lineamientos de políticas.* La Paz: Unidad de Análisis de Políticas Sociales.

Morduch, J. 1997. *Between the Market and State: Can Informal Insurance Patch the Safety Net?* Harvard Institute for International Development Working Paper, Harvard University, Cambridge, MA.

———. 1995. Income and Consumption Smoothing. *Journal of Economic Perspectives* 9(3): 103-14.

Moser, C. 1998. The Asset Vulnerability Framework: Reassessing Urban Poverty Reduction Strategies. *World Development* 26(1): 1-19.

Ostrom, E. 1990. *Governing the Commons: The Evolution of Institutions for Collective Action.* Cambridge, MA: Cambridge University Press.

Pérez de Rada, E. 1997. *Discriminación por género y etnia en el mercado laboral urbano de Bolivia.* La Paz: Unidad de Análisis de Políticas Sociales.

Psacharopoulos, G., and H. Patrinos (eds.). 1994. *Indigenous People and Poverty in Latin America: An Empirical Analysis.* Washington, D.C.: World Bank.

Putnam, R. 1993. *Making Democracy Work: Civic Traditions in Modern Italy.* Princeton, NJ: Princeton University Press.

Raczynski, D. 1994. Estrategias para combatir la pobreza en América Latina, diagnóstico y lecciones de política. Informe comparativo nacional. Inter-American Development Bank, Department of Economic and Social Development Working Paper No. 193, Washington, DC.

Ravallion, M., and G. Datt. 1992. Growth and Redistribution Components of Changes in Poverty Measures: A Decomposition with Applications to Brazil and India in the 80s. World Bank Working Paper 83, Washington, DC.

Stiglitz, J. 1989. Rational Peasants, Efficient Institutions, and a Theory of Rural Organization: Methodological Remarks for Development Economics. In P. Bardhan (ed.), *The Economic Theory of Agrarian Institutions.* Oxford, UK: Oxford University Press.

Székely, M. 1997. Household Savings and Income Distribution in a Developing Economy. Office of the Chief Economist, Inter-American Development Bank. Mimeo.

_____. 1996. El ahorro de los hogares en México. Series of Economic and Sectoral Studies No. 1, Inter-American Development Bank Operations Department, Region II, Washington, DC.

Townsend, R. 1995. Consumption Insurance: An Evaluation of Risk-Bearing Systems in Low-Income Economies. *Journal of Economic Perspectives.* 9(3): 83-102.

Unidad de Análisis de Políticas Sociales (UDAPSO). 1997. Carpeta de Indicadores Laborales. Serie Estadísticas Sociales No. 1, UDAPSO, La Paz.

_____. 1993. *Mapa de pobreza: Una guía para la acción social.* La Paz: UDAPSO.

United Nations Development Programme (UNDP). 1995. Erradicar la pobreza: marco general para la elaboración de estrategias nacionales. Documento de políticas generales, UNDP, New York.

Urquiola, M. 1994. Participando en el crecimiento: expansión económica, distribución del ingreso y pobreza en el área urbana de Bolivia 1989-1992 y proyecciones. Cuadernos de Investigación No. 2, Unidad de Análisis de Políticas Sociales, La Paz.

Van Ginneken, W. 1980. Some Methods of Poverty Analysis: An Application to Iranian Data, 1975-1976. *World Development* 8(9): 639-46.

Verbeek, M., and T. Nijman. 1992. Can Cohort Data be Treated as Genuine Panel Data? *Empirical Economics* 17: 9-23.

Vos, R., H. Lee, and J. Mejía. 1997. Structural Adjustment and Poverty in Bolivia. IDB Working Paper Series I-3, Washington, DC.

Wood, B., and H. Patrinos. 1994. Urban Bolivia. In G. Psacharopoulos and H. Patrinos (eds.), *Indigenous People and Poverty in Latin America: An Empirical Analysis.* Washington, DC: World Bank.

World Bank. 1996. *Bolivia: Poverty, Equity and Income: Selected Policies for Expanding Earning Opportunities for the Poor.* Washington, DC: World Bank.

CHAPTER THREE

Assets, Markets and Poverty in Brazil

Marcelo Côrtes Neri
Edward Joaquim Amadeo
Alexandre Pinto Carvalho[1]

Brazil's relatively high per capita GDP, combined with its very high degree of income inequality, generate favorable conditions for the design of redistributive policies. The country's inequality and poverty indices are particularly sensitive to changes in certain policy instruments, such as changes in the minimum wage and inflation rates. On the other hand, perhaps due to its history of instability, Brazil has not advanced much in implementing structural poverty alleviation policies that could enhance the asset portfolio of the poor.

Increasing asset holdings of the poor can have three effects on social welfare. First, people extract greater direct utility from owning more assets. This implies a need to expand social welfare measures to include the possession of different kinds of assets. This point is especially relevant in Latin America, given its long-established tradition of using income-based poverty measures.

The second effect is that higher asset levels can increase the income-generating potential of the poor, leading to a reduction in standard poverty measures. In terms of poverty alleviation policies, compensatory income transfer schemes (e.g., negative income tax programs and unemployment

[1] Marcelo Côrtes Neri and Alexandre Pinto Carvalho are economists with the Center for Social Policies at the Getúlio Vargas Foundation in Brazil. Edward Joaquim Amadeo is a professor of economics at the Pontifícia Universidade Católica do Rio de Janeiro. The authors wish to thank Mabel Cristina Nascimento, Manoel Flávio Daltrino and Flávia Dias Rangel of the Instituto de Pesquisa Econômica Aplicada (IPEA) for their contributions to this chapter.

insurance) should be separated from those that attempt to increase permanent per capita income by transferring productive capital (e.g., public provision of education, micro-credit policies, agrarian reform). The assessment of the rates of return and utilization of different assets can help the design of capital-enhancing policies to alleviate poverty.

The last effect of increasing asset holdings is to improve the ability of poor people to deal with adverse income shocks. The role played by the consumption-smoothing properties of assets depends on how significant the shocks and how developed the capital markets are (i.e., asset, credit and insurance segments). Therefore, assessment of this last effect requires an analysis of the dynamic properties of income processes of the poor and an evaluation of institutions that constrain their financial behavior.

This chapter establishes a basis for research on the relationship between poverty, resource distribution and asset markets in Brazil. The strategy is to analyze the three different types of impacts that increasing the assets of the poor may have on social welfare. Accordingly, the chapter has three parts. The first evaluates the possession of different types of capital along the income distribution scale. As a point of departure, this part assesses standard poverty measures, their temporal evolution, and their cross-sectional composition. The aim is to augment standard poverty measures by incorporating the direct effect of asset holdings on social welfare. The lack of certain assets may imply unsatisfied basic needs.

The second part describes the income-generating impact that asset holdings may have on poverty. Using logistic regressions, it examines how the accumulation of different types of capital affects income-based poverty outcomes.

Finally, the chapter studies the dynamic aspects of poverty, taking into consideration different time horizons. Long-run issues are related to the study of low-frequency income fluctuations, life-cycle assets holdings, and intergenerational transmission of wealth. Short-run issues are related to assessing behavior of the poor and the welfare losses in dealing with high frequency gaps between income and desired consumption.

Data Issues

Three basic data sources are used:

- *Pesquisa Nacional por Amostra de Domicílios* - PNAD: an annual national household survey covering 1976, 1981, 1985, 1990, 1993, 1995 and 1996.

- *Pesquisa Mensal do Emprego* - PME: a monthly employment survey with a rotating panel characteristic covering 1980-97.

- *Pesquisa de Comportamentos Financeiros da Associação Brasileira de Crédito e Poupança* - ABECIP: a survey on consumer finances used as a secondary source for 1987.

The empirical analysis focuses on two geographical dimensions: the national level, and six main metropolitan areas (labeled here as "Metropolitan Brazil"). In moving from the national level to metropolitan Brazil, data availability increases, especially in terms of the possession of different types of capital. This is probably explained by the spatial distribution of the Brazilian population, as 81 percent live in non-rural areas and there is a lower cost of information collection in more densely populated regions. The empirical and institutional analysis will rely heavily on metropolitan segments, which hold about one-half of the urban population. Another strategic advantage of the metropolitan focus is that there are recently calculated poverty lines available (Rocha, 1993).

Poverty Assessment

This section describes the temporal evolution of poverty and its close determinants in Brazil, and then traces a poverty profile based on the characteristics of households and heads of households. These poverty profiles will provide initial hints as to which assets (e.g., human capital) are the most important to examine.

The analysis of poverty at the national level begins using PNAD data, from which the three poverty indices (P0, P1 and P2) are constructed. Each

Table 3.1. Poverty in Brazil: Level and Changes, 1985–95

Poverty indices	P0	P0	P0	P1	P1	P1	P2	P2	P2
Poverty line (multiples)	0.5	1	1.5	0.5	1	1.5	0.5	1	1.5
Reference period	(%)	(%)	(%)	(%)	(%)	(%)	(%)	(%)	(%)
Poverty level 1985	10.03	30.42	47.01	3.85	11.97	21.01	2.36	6.68	12.32
Poverty level 1995	11.05	27.68	42.71	5.73	12.45	20.10	4.42	8.07	12.78
Total poverty change* 1985 to 1995	1.02	-2.74	-4.31	1.88	0.48	-0.91	2.05	1.40	0.46
Growth component* 1985 to 1995	-0.41	-0.97	-0.87	-0.12	-0.38	-0.54	-0.06	-0.22	-0.36
Inequality component* 1985 to 1995	1.48	-1.67	-3.60	2.00	0.80	-0.44	2.11	1.58	0.77

*Adjusted to National Accounts.

index is calculated according to three poverty lines corresponding to 0.5, 1 and 1.5 of the values of the basic poverty line used, adjusted for cost of living differences between regions (using estimates by Rocha, 1993). The analysis of these nine poverty measures will be centered on the proportion of poor according to the basic poverty line. The second column of Table 3.1 shows that in 1995, 41.8 million people, or 27.7 percent of Brazil's total population of 151 million, were living below the poverty line.

Poverty Changes

Table 3.1 also shows the percentile differences between the 1985 and 1995 poverty profiles, adjusted for the rather small rate of per capita GDP growth (2.09 percent) during the period. Using the basic poverty line, the proportion of poor fell by 2.74 percentage points, which is equivalent to 9 percent in relative terms. Given the shift in income distribution over the period, when higher weights are given to the poorest segments, poverty indices actually rose in the last decade. For the basic poverty line, the poverty gap (P1) rose 0.48 percent, while the average squared poverty gap (P2) rose 1.4 percentage points.

Similarly, all poverty indices present either greater declines or smaller increases when higher poverty lines are used. For the low poverty line, the head-count ratio rose 1.02 percentage points. But that ratio fell 4.31 percentage points when the highest poverty line was used. The respective statistics are 1.88 and -0.91 for the average poverty gap (P1) and 2.05 and 0.46 for the average squared poverty gap (P2). Taken together, these results imply that the pattern of unbalanced growth across different segments of the Brazilian economy generated different results depending on the binomial poverty measure-poverty line used. This lack of robustness to poverty changes is also influenced by the low per capita GDP growth rate during the period (average 0.2 percent annually).

Decomposition of Poverty Changes

This section applies the Datt and Ravallion (1992) decomposition of changes in poverty over 1985-95. This decomposition sheds light on what is driving the changes in poverty discussed above. These changes can be better understood in terms of three close determinants: mean per capita income, the degree of inequality of per capita income, and a residual term that captures the interaction between these two terms (not presented here). This simple decomposition between a balanced growth component that affects all agents and a redistributive component allows quite general comparisons of poverty changes across different societies and time periods.

The growth-inequality decomposition, when applied to the 1985 and 1995 PNADs, reveals that growth explains a small part of the changes of the different poverty measures calculated (Table 3.1). For the head-count ratio, using the basic poverty line, the growth component explains less than one percent of the decline in poverty. The inequality component of poverty change responds to twice the effect of growth for the basic poverty measure. Nevertheless, this is not a robust result. The poverty alleviation effect of the inequality component tends to increase poverty the lower the poverty line used and the more weight is attributed to the very poor (i.e., P1 and especially P2).

Poverty Profile

A poverty profile can be developed using national 1995 PNAD data on the main attributes of heads of households, such as gender, age, schooling, race, sectors of activity, type of work, population density and region. Table 3.2

Table 3.2. Decomposition of Poverty Indices according to Household Characteristics, 1995

Sample: All households

Head of the household	P0	P1	P2	Total population	Contribution to total poverty		
					P0	P1	P2
Total	**27.68**	**12.45**	**8.07**	**100**	-	-	-
Gender							
Male	26.53	11.40	7.09	82.79	79.35	75.84	72.69
Female	33.22	17.47	12.81	17.21	20.65	24.16	27.32
Age							
Less than 15 years	36.99	31.40	29.63	0.02	0.03	0.06	0.09
15 to 25 years	42.95	24.71	19.49	5.73	8.89	11.38	13.84
25 to 45 years	31.71	14.49	9.38	51.24	58.70	59.66	59.55
45 to 65 years	23.88	10.02	6.08	27.87	24.04	22.43	21.00
More than 65 years	15.25	5.32	2.95	15.13	8.33	6.47	5.53
Years of schooling							
0 years	43.06	19.18	11.84	21.04	32.74	32.43	30.86
0 to 4 years	36.16	16.19	10.20	21.56	28.17	28.05	27.25
4 to 8 years	25.09	10.96	7.23	31.13	28.21	27.40	27.88
8 to 12 years	14.10	6.71	4.86	19.51	9.94	10.52	11.75
More than 12 years	3.85	2.94	2.72	6.76	0.94	1.60	2.27
Race							
Indigenous	53.17	27.64	18.23	0.11	0.22	0.25	0.26
White	18.07	7.89	5.26	53.03	34.62	33.63	34.58
Black	38.82	17.68	11.29	46.31	64.94	65.80	64.76
Oriental	10.86	7.24	5.99	0.54	0.21	0.31	0.40
Sector of activity							
Agriculture	39.81	17.99	11.20	24.69	35.51	35.68	34.27
Industry	21.25	7.83	4.26	15.89	12.20	10.00	8.39
Construction	27.36	9.75	5.17	9.96	9.85	7.81	6.38
Public Sector	15.80	5.85	3.09	10.18	5.81	4.79	3.90
Service	21.38	8.17	4.49	39.28	30.33	25.80	21.86
Working class							
Unemployed	74.02	53.43	46.14	3.18	8.50	13.64	18.16
Inactive	28.42	15.45	11.90	17.17	17.64	21.32	25.32
Employees (w/card)	19.74	6.36	3.11	27.16	19.37	13.87	10.46
Employees (no card)	40.09	15.57	8.30	15.43	22.35	19.30	15.87
Self-employed	30.75	13.40	8.05	31.12	34.57	33.50	31.02
Employer	5.37	2.73	2.03	5.95	1.15	1.30	1.49
Public servant	15.44	5.81	3.10	10.04	5.60	4.68	3.86
Unpaid	38.20	25.61	21.60	2.27	3.13	4.66	6.07
Population density							
Rural	33.70	15.61	10.23	21.10	25.70	26.47	26.74
Urban	25.36	11.36	7.26	49.25	45.12	44.94	44.32
Metropolitan	27.24	12.00	7.88	29.65	29.18	28.59	28.94
Region							
North	44.23	20.67	12.96	4.47	7.14	7.42	7.18
Northeast	43.12	20.32	13.01	29.56	46.06	48.26	47.66
Southeast	20.94	8.94	5.87	43.39	32.82	31.18	31.53
South	13.49	5.80	3.92	15.16	7.39	7.07	7.37
Center-West	24.61	10.19	6.82	7.41	6.59	6.07	6.27

Source: The PNAD conducted by the Instituto Brasileiro de Geografia e Estatística (IBGE).

presents the three Foster-Greer-Thorbecke (FGT) poverty indexes for the proposed basic poverty line. Once again, the analysis will be centered on the head-count ratio for the basic poverty line.

The overall proportion of poor (P0) during 1995 was 27.7 percent. As expected, the groups with higher head-count ratios were headed by females (33 percent), young families from 15 to 25 years old (43 percent), the illiterate (43 percent), non-whites (indigenous, 53 percent and black, 38 percent), inhabitants of rural areas (34 percent), inhabitants of the regions of the North (44 percent) and Northeast (43 percent), those working in agriculture (40 percent) or construction (27 percent), the unemployed (74 percent) and informal employees (40 percent).

The three last columns of Table 3.2 show how each of these cells forms a part of aggregate poverty indices. Since the poorest groups are often minorities, race is not always the greatest contributing factor to poverty outcomes. The categories with the highest levels of poverty are female-headed households, families headed by people under the age of 25, families headed by the unemployed or indigenous, and people living in rural areas or in the North.

Distribution of Assets

The assessment of resources possessed will be structured under three headings:

- Physical capital (financial assets, durable goods, housing, land, public services and transportation);

- Human capital (schooling, technical education, age, experience and learning by doing);

- Social capital (employment, membership in associations or trade unions, political participation and family structure).

The availability of new sources of data opens new opportunities for tracing an asset profile of Brazil's poor. Adding different household surveys opens the way for a broad picture of the possession of assets in 1996. The strategy is to compare access of the poor and the non-poor to different assets.

Physical Capital

Housing and Land

As summarized in Table 3.3, the 1996 PNAD shows that financing that the poor use for dwellings is divided approximately as follows: 71 percent live in their own housing that is already paid for; 5 percent live in their own housing for which they are still paying; 10 percent rent; and 22 percent live in ceded housing.[2] The same statistics for the non-poor population are: 68 percent live in their own housing that is already paid for, 8 percent live in their own housing for which they are still paying, 17 percent live in rented places and 24 percent live in ceded housing. The comparison between the poor and the non-poor population indicates that the former live more often than the latter in their own housing that is already paid for, or in ceded housing.[3] These statistics show that renting, or continuing to pay for your own housing while you are still living in it, are essentially luxury forms of housing financing.

A complementary line of inquiry compares housing quality in both segments: 95 percent of the poor (99 percent of the non-poor) have access to solid wall construction; 92 percent of the poor (98 percent of the non-poor) have access to bathrooms inside their houses; the average density per bedroom is 0.58 among the poor (0.37 for the non-poor); and the average density of family members per dwelling room is 1.43 among the poor (1.04 for the non-poor). The difference between these last two statistics can be explained by the fact that the poor have larger families than the non-poor— 4.1 and 3 members, respectively. That is, the density of bedrooms and dwellings is approximately proportional to the number of people living in the house. In other words, the house size in terms of the number of rooms or bedrooms is similar, but more people live in poor households.

---

[2] Ceded housing refers to properties inhabited by squatters or by people without a formal land title, such as residents of favelas.
[3] When the attribute for the type of housing financing is combined with land ownership, 62 percent of the poor live in their own housing with land that is already paid for, while that figure increases to 63 percent for the non-poor population. This reversal is explained by the fact that the poor are more likely not to own the land on which their houses are built (15 percent of the poor and 8 percent of the non-poor, respectively).

Table 3.3. Asset Possession Profile of the Poor and Non-Poor: Housing, Durable Goods, Public Services and Transportation

Access to housing	Poor		Non-Poor	
Access to rented or ceded housing	21.72	0.01%	23.74	0.01%
Access to rented housing	9.91	0.01%	17.21	0.01%
Access to own house, already paid for	71.07	0.02%	67.71	0.01%
Access to own house, still paying	5.23	0.01	7.79	0.00%
Housing quality	**Poor**		**Non-Poor**	
Access to construction	95.62	0.01%	99.19	0.00%
Interior bathroom	92.14	0.01%	97.98	0.00%
Number of people in dwelling	4.05	0.01%	3.03	0.00%
Bedroom density	0.58	0.00%	0.37	0.00%
Dwelling density	1.43	0.00%	1.04	0.00%
Access to durable goods	**Poor**		**Non-Poor**	
Stove	99.65	0.00%	99.91	0.00%
Filter	57.42	0.02%	71.44	0.01%
Refrigerator	84.97	0.01%	97.56	0.00%
Telephone	13.04	0.01%	39.08	0.01%
Radio	92.80	0.01%	97.71	0.00%
Color TV	72.88	0.02%	93.96	0.00%
TV	92.17	0.01%	98.19	0.00%
Freezer	9.12	0.01%	26.93	0.01%
Washing machine	22.71	0.01%	56.69	0.01%
Access to public services	**Poor**		**Non-Poor**	
Water	90.24	0.01%	97.76	0.00%
Sewage	73.65	0.02%	89.33	0.01%
Electricity	99.49	0.00%	99.89	0.00%
Garbage	80.20	0.01%	94.12	0.00%
Commuting time (in minutes)	**Poor**		**Non-Poor**	
Heads – average time	38.60	0.02%	42.07	0.01%
Spouses – average time	35.89	0.02%	32.79	0.01%
Heads – more than 30 minutes	50.70	0.02%	50.95	0.01%
Spouses – more than 30 minutes	41.13	0.02%	38.79	0.01%
Human capital	**Poor**		**Non-Poor**	
Avg. years of schooling – head	4.70	0.01%	7.16	0.00%
Avg. years of schooling – spouse	4.59	0.01%	7.05	0.00%
Age average – head	41.47	0.02%	44.91	0.01%
Age average – spouse	37.87	0.02%	40.52	0.01%

Source: PNAD.

Durable Goods

According to the 1996 PNAD, access rates of poor families to durable goods in Metropolitan Brazil are as follows:

- Basic goods: stove (99.6 percent), water filter (57 percent), refrigerator (85 percent), radio (93 percent), TV (92 percent);

- Luxury goods: telephone (13 percent), color TV (73 percent), freezer (9 percent) and washing machine (23 percent).

These access rates are, in general, higher when the sample of non-poor individuals is used: (a) basic goods: stove (99.9 percent), water filter (71 percent), refrigerator (98 percent), radio (98 percent), TV (98 percent) and color TV (94 percent); (b) luxury goods: telephone (39 percent), freezer (27 percent) and washing machine (57 percent).

Public Services

Access to basic public goods and services such as water, sewage, electricity, communications, and public transportation is easy to measure using standard household surveys. According to the 1996 PNAD, access to public services is more pronounced among the non-poor population: 98 percent had access to running water, 89 percent to sewage, 100 percent to electricity and 94 percent to garbage collection. Access rates for the poor were 90 percent to running water, 74 percent to sewage, 99 percent to electricity and 80 percent to garbage collection. There is a monotone increase of all these indices of access to public services from the first to the last tenth of per capita income distribution. The increase in non-access rates from the first to the tenth decile for each of these public services is 73 percent to 99 percent for running water, 73 percent to 98 percent for sewage, 99.5 percent to 100 percent for electricity and 80 percent to 99 percent for garbage collection.

Transportation Infrastructure

The question used in the PNAD to capture the quality of transportation was: "How long does it take for you to get to work?"[4] This information can be used to assess the transportation cost evaluated at the individual hourly wage rate. Nevertheless, it is not possible to know the exact combination between public and private transportation infrastructure that has led to that outcome. The differences between the poor and the non-poor are not significant: 50 percent of both spend less than 30 minutes commuting.

Human Capital

Completed Years of Schooling

The relationship between completed years of schooling and poverty is clear from the evidence presented in the previous sections. As shown in Table 3.3, the average number of completed years of schooling of the household head for the poor and the non-poor is 4.7 and 7.2 years, respectively. Similarly, the spouses of poor families also present on average two years less schooling than spouses in the non-poor population: 4.6 and 7 years, respectively. This point is noteworthy, since completed years of schooling is probably the best approximation to permanent earnings found in Brazilian household surveys.

Age and Experience

The common approximation to experience used in household surveys is age, the effects of which on poverty play a central role in this study. This is basically an attempt to capture the life-cycle pattern, if any, of poverty. According to the 1996 PNAD, the average ages of the household head and spouse in poor families are 41 and 38 years, respectively, while the same variables in the non-poor population are 45 and 41 years, respectively. This two to three-year difference may indicate a slight downward trend of poverty incidence measured by the head-count ratio across the life cycle. That is, as family

---

[4] Data were computed only for those who reported going straight to work. These data correspond to 96 percent of household heads and 97 percent of spouses in the sample.

heads acquire more experience, or accumulate other sorts of capital, the probability of escaping poverty increases.

Social Capital

Social capital can be understood in a broad sense by a variety of types of coordination mechanisms (or institutions) that affect the social and private returns of public and private assets. The complementarity between this type of capital and other types of capital is essential in understanding the concept of social capital. For example, the organization of production factors will be a key determinant of the returns obtained from a given amount of accumulated physical and human capital.

Association and Trade Union Membership

A first set of social capital indicators, shown in Table 3.4, is related to enrollment rates in trade unions and non-community association activities. There is an inverse relationship between membership rates in such organizations and poverty (18 percent for poor household heads and 33 percent for non-poor ones). Consistent with this result is the fact that household heads with higher levels of formal education have higher probabilities of being members of those organizations. The universe of those who are not members of trade unions or noncommunity associations today but were members in the last five years is much closer (15 percent for poor household heads and 16 percent for non-poor ones). The rates of effective current participation in these activities are much lower in both groups. Only 2.9 percent of poor household heads attend at least one meeting per year, compared to 6.5 percent among the non-poor.

Membership rates in community associations are much lower (12 percent for poor household heads and 15 percent for non-poor ones) and more uniformly distributed along the income distribution scale than the rates for trade unions and noncommunity associations mentioned above. Nevertheless, the proportion of people who attend at least one meeting per year is higher for community associations than for the other associations analyzed. Note that the discrepancy in membership rates between poor and non-poor household heads (especially controlled for intensity) is also smaller for community associations.

Table 3.4. Asset Possession Profile of the Poor and Non-Poor: Schooling, Memberships and Political Activities

		Human capital			
Schooling strictly greater than		**Poor**		**Non-Poor**	
Head	Father	36.03	0.23%	42.19	0.22%
	Mother	38.10	0.24%	45.50	0.23%
Spouse	Father	34.84	0.23%	43.88	0.23%
	Mother	37.84	0.24%	46.26	0.23%
Specific human capital		**Poor**		**Non-Poor**	
Completed vocational technical training equivalent		8.26	0.13%	17.23	0.17%
Expect to work in the same occupation in the next 5 years					
	91	57.61	0.24%	67.29	0.21%
	96	78.45	0.20%	83.44	0.17%
Find it difficult to adapt to new equipment					
	91	17.12	0.18%	16.59	0.17%
	96	17.13	0.18%	16.70	0.17%
Trade union and noncommunity association membership		**Poor**		**Non-Poor**	
% Trade union and association membership					
	Total	18.17	0.19%	32.62	0.21%
	Occupied	23.63	0.21%	38.26	0.22%
% Attends at least one meeting per year		2.85	0.08%	6.51	0.11%
% Attends at least four meetings per year		1.94	0.07%	4.57	0.09%
% Is not a member today, but was in the last 5 years		14.92	0.17%	16.51	0.17%
Community associations		**Poor**		**Non-Poor**	
% Membership		11.61	0.16%	14.64	0.16%
% Attends at least one meeting per year		9.32	0.14%	11.28	0.14%
% of those who are members of neighborhood associations		39.49	0.24%	25.86	0.20%
Religious associations		36.62	0.24%	34.10	0.22%
% Atheist		5.83	0.11%	6.54	0.11%
Political activities		**Poor**		**Non-Poor**	
% Members of political parties		3.33	0.09%	5.55	0.10%
% Participants in political party activities		43.54	0.24%	37.20	0.22%
% with link to political parties		19.10	0.19%	24.76	0.20%
Does not use any source of information to decide voting		41.46	0.24%	33.37	0.21%
Of those that use source of information:					
% that use TV to decide voting		61.72	0.24%	66.58	0.21%
Knows the correct name of president		76.59	0.21%	89.61	0.14%
Knows the correct name of mayor, governor and president		62.15	0.24%	78.50	0.19%

Analysis of the composition of community associations revealed a greater importance among the poor of neighborhood associations (39 percent for poor household heads and 26 percent for non-poor ones) and religious associations (37 percent for poor and 34 percent for non-poor).

Political Activities

As indicated in Table 3.4, rates of formal affiliation with political parties are quite low (3.3 percent for poor household heads and 5.5 percent for non-poor ones), especially in light of the fact that the analysis is restricted to the six main Brazilian metropolitan regions. The rate of participation of those who are members of political parties is relatively high, especially among the poor (44 percent for poor household heads and 37 percent for non-poor ones). The low affiliation rates can be a result of pressures to actively participate that result from political affiliation.

Given the low rate of formal affiliation with political parties, a less stringent measure is to sympathize with a political party (19 percent of poor household heads and 25 percent of non-poor ones). The qualitative results yielded by the two concepts are similar, including their relative constancy along the income distribution. One final set of questions on political literacy shows that 77 percent of poor household heads (90 percent of non-poor ones) knew the correct name of the Brazilian President (Fernando Henrique Cardoso). When the more stringent condition was imposed—that the household head know the names of the respective governor and mayors as well—these statistics fell to 62 percent and 79 percent, respectively.

Poverty and the Income-Generating Impact of Assets

A decisive step in studying the role played by capital accumulation in the income-generating potential of the poor is to look at the relationship between the possession of different assets and poverty outcomes. The previous section analyzed access to different types of capital among the poor and non-poor. This section turns to the possible impact of these assets on poverty, considered jointly and controlling for demographics. The aim is to help determine the type of capital-enhancing policies that should be implemented.

The impact of human capital and physical assets on poverty will be studied together using the 1996 PNAD at the national level, while the effects of social capital will be examined using the special supplement of the monthly employment survey (PME) from 1996.

Physical and Human Capital and Poverty

This subsection summarizes the relationship between the probability of being poor with demographic variables and various aspects of physical and human capital. Table 3.5 presents the basic logistic regression estimates.

Omitted here is the analysis of demographic and regional control variables. The analysis moves directly to the dummy variables representing access to different types of physical capital. These variables include both durable goods and housing as well as access to public services. The relationship between poverty and access rates to physical assets suffers from severe simultaneity problems. Nevertheless, a logistic regression may shed some light on the existing relationship (no causality implied in this case) between the possession of each type of asset and poverty outcomes.

Almost all physical capital parameter estimates in the final model were statistically significant at 95 percent confidence levels and present expected signs, in the sense that having access to a given asset, in general, implies a lower probability of being poor. The exception is access to electricity, with a negative sign. Higher coefficients are found for luxury durable goods and public services such as urban garbage collection (-0.39), a telephone (-0.67) and a washing machine (-0.65).

The relationship between poverty and human capital accumulation is less likely to be affected by simultaneity problems, since the former variable is largely accumulated before people enter the labor market. This means that one can interpret the relationship between poverty and school attainment in a casual manner.[5] Coefficients for years of schooling of household heads and spouses were around 0.1 and precisely estimated.

Variables referring to the educational status of the fathers of household heads and spouses were also included in the model in order to capture

---

[5] For example, families with literate household heads and spouses have 56 percent and 36 percent less chance of being poor, respectively, when compared with families with illiterate household heads.

Table 3.5. Logit Model of Poverty and Human and Physical Capital: Analysis of Parameter Estimates

Variables	Observations	Estimate		t-Statistic	Deviance
HEAD COLOR	White	-0.4298	**	-14.9756	48142.33
HEAD EXPERIENCE	Age	0.1055	**	18.1897	48064.62
HEAD EXPERIENCE	Age squared	-0.0014	**	-14.0000	48053.14
HEAD SCHOOLING	Completed years of schooling	-0.1046	**	-19.3704	39801.87
SPOUSE SCHOOLING	Completed years of schooling	-0.0948	**	-17.8868	38234.22
HEAD FATHER SCHOOLING	Completed years of schooling	-0.0269	**	-3.4935	38130.38
SPOUSE FATHER SCHOOLING	Completed years of schooling	-0.0354	**	-4.5974	38026.76
HEAD EMPLOYED	Yes	-1.4012	**	-32.0641	37283.03
SPOUSE EMPLOYED	Yes	-0.7315	**	-25.2241	36954.01
HEAD MIGRANT	Yes	-0.1645	**	-5.6336	36710.34
METROPOLITAN CORE[1]		0.1660	**	3.3468	36645.68
LARGE URBAN[1]	Between 100,000 and metropolitan	-0.0163		-0.3247	36483.95
MEDIUM URBAN[1]	Between 20,000 and 100,000	-0.0684		-1.3333	36323.87
SMALL URBAN[1]	Less than 20,000 inhabitants	0.1033	**	1.9981	36304.32
RURAL[1]		0.1424	**	2.6273	35902.12
ELECTRICITY	Has access to	0.2471	**	3.5351	35742.54
WATER SUPPLY	Has access to	-0.2979	**	-6.3518	35347.83
URBAN SEWAGE	Has access to	-0.2342	**	-6.9086	35125.55
URBAN GARBAGE COLLECTION	Has access to	-0.3916	**	-10.9081	34879.08
TELEPHONE	Has access to	-0.6713	**	-15.0854	34347.90
REFRIGERATOR	Has access to	-0.6343	**	-14.0022	33892.99
WASHING MACHINE	Has access to	-0.6470	**	-17.3458	33512.85
COLOR TV	Has access to	-0.6015	**	-16.7083	33224.13
RADIO	Has access to	-0.1490	**	-2.9681	33214.95
APARTMENT	Has access to	-0.4506	**	-5.3643	33183.20
SOLID WALLS	Has access to	-0.0724	*	-1.9462	33179.42

	Value	DF	Value/DF
Number of observations: 38,698;			
Log likelihood: -16680.8932;			
Pearson Chi-Square:	42416.600	39000	1.097

*At 90% confidence level. **At 95% confidence level.

[1] The omitted category is the metropolitan periphery.

household educational background. The coefficients of these variables were between one-third and one-fourth the coefficients for the actual educational attainment of household heads and spouses. This points out the relative importance of the intergenerational transmission of human capital.

Experience, a type of human capital proxied by age, presents a poverty reduction effect. Age squared was positive and significant, indicating the occurrence of decreasing returns to experience. Finally, dummies for the employment status of household heads and spouses presented a negative sign. These dummies can be interpreted as a measure of the rate of utilization of accumulated human capital. The life cycle profile of mean earnings and occupation rates will be analyzed below.

Social Capital and Poverty

This subsection summarizes the relationship between the probability of being poor with various sorts of social capital, together with demographic and human capital variables similar to those used in the previous subsection. The difference is that here the 1996 PME supplement is used as a data source to take advantage of the social capital variables included in the questionnaire. It should be pointed out that PME income concept and geographic dimensions are more restrictive than those in the PNAD data used in the logistic regressions. PME income data include only labor earnings in the six main metropolitan regions. On the other hand, a broader sample is used here that also includes single-parent households. The idea is to assess the influences of the presence of spouses on poverty outcomes. In order not to crowd the analysis, the characteristics of spouses were not used as explanatory variables. Table 3.6 presents the logistic model estimated.

All variables were statistically significant and presented the expected sign. An analysis was made of the likelihood ratio of the two states assumed by each dummy variable used. In other words, instead of analyzing the estimated coefficients, the impact of the different variables on the chances of being poor is examined directly. The analysis shows that human capital variables of the household head and his or her parents present the expected signs. Male-headed households present a 20 percent lower chance of being poor than female-headed households. The presence of a spouse in the household reduces the probability of poverty by 23 percent. This result indicates the importance of marriage as a basic unit of social capital. The dependency

Table 3.6. Logit Model of Poverty and Social and Human Capital: Analysis of Parameter Estimates

		Estimate		t-Statistic	Deviance
Head schooling	Illiterate	0.6183	**	14.8273	21228.03
Head schooling	Above 8 complete years	0.6881	**	-16.9483	19965.82
Head father schooling	Illiterate	0.1853	**	2.5314	18312.36
Head father schooling	Above 8 complete years	-0.1223	*	-1.8092	19202.28
Head mother schooling	Above 8 complete years	-0.1780	**	-3.8034	19037.88
Gender	Male	-0.2289	**	-3.3612	18454.91
Is there a spouse in the family?	Yes	-0.2564	**	-2.6190	18607.01
Dependency ratio	Up To 2.5	-2.4522	**	-64.5316	22151.23
Head race	Black or indigenous	0.8305	**	13.2035	18289.87
Working class	Employees (w/card)	-0.9821	**	-21.0300	19429.58
Working class	Public servant	-1.1663	**	-17.1263	18454.91
Working class	Self-employed	-0.6066	**	-12.2298	18269.70
Working class	Employer	-1.7377	**	-33.6112	18948.23
Trade union membership	Yes	-0.4647	**	-8.5896	21274.56
Has link with political parties	Yes	-0.1323	**	-3.1727	21228.03
Knows correct name	Of president	-0.2341	**	-3.5470	21127.46
Knows correct name	Mayor, governor and president	-0.1722	**	-3.1830	21274.56

	DF	Value	Value/DF
Number of observations: 18,308; Log likelihood: -10371.4604; Pearson Chi-Square:	18000.00	18206.932	0.996

* Statistically significant at 90% confidence level.   **Statistically significant at 95% confidence level.

ratio and the race of the household head present the expected signs. Working class status of the household head turns out to have important effects on reducing the probability of being poor: the universe of employees with a union card has a 73 percent lower chance of being poor than those without one. The same statistics for other working classes are public servant, 69 percent, self-employed, 45 percent, and employer, 78 percent.

The analysis of other variables related to social capital reveals that trade union membership reduces by 37 percent the chances of being poor, while links to political parties reduce it by less than 9 percent. Finally, political literacy questions show that knowing the president's name is associated with a 21 percent reduction in the chance of being poor.

Dynamic Aspects of Poverty and Asset Holdings

The last effect of increasing asset holdings is to improve the ability of poor people to deal with adverse changes in income. The role played by the consumption-smoothing properties of assets depends on the significance of these changes and the state of development of financial markets (i.e., asset, credit and insurance segments). Therefore, the assessment of this last effect requires an analysis of the dynamic properties of the income processes of poor people and an evaluation of institutions that constrain their financial behavior.

The dynamics of earnings are an essential determinant of asset holdings and of the level of people located at the lower tail of income distribution. This section assesses three short-run dynamic issues that are inter-connected: (i) the extension of per capita earnings volatility measured at an individual level; (ii) the intensity of movements into and out of earnings-based poverty; and (iii) the impact of the period used to measure income on aggregate poverty measures.

Volatility of Per Capita Earnings of the Poor and Non-Poor

In Brazil, the dynamics of per capita earnings can be measured using longitudinal information from the PME. The PME replicates the U.S. Current Population Survey (CPS) sampling scheme, attempting to collect information on the same dwelling eight times during a period of 16 months. More specifically, PME attempts to collect information on the same dwelling during months t, t+1, t+2, t+3, t+12, t+13, t+14, t+15.

The first aspect to be analyzed here is the extent of per capita short-run volatility in poor and non-poor Brazilian households. Besides mean earnings levels and dispersion, earnings volatility constitutes a key determinant of the level of social welfare. The longitudinal information used in this analysis was obtained by first concatenating observations of the same individuals during four consecutive observations.[6] The average temporal variance of individual log per capita earnings across four consecutive months was then calculated. The inspection of these time series of temporal variability of earnings indicates the presence of bumps in the series that coincided with inflation peaks followed by stabilization plans in 1986, 1990 and 1994. These bumps indicate the influence of inflationary instability on per capita income volatility.

The average temporal variance of log per capita earnings of the poor corresponds to 0.158 over 1983-96. This statistic is more noisy than the corresponding ones found for the non-poor population (0.124). Furthermore, this is a robust result across time, since it holds for all 182 months in which this statistic was calculated. A similar exercise used the median household head's education as the criterion to separate the poor from the non-poor. Families with little human capital presented a variability of per capita earnings equal to 0.139, while the corresponding statistic for the rest of the population was slightly higher, at 0.143.

Poverty Dynamics

A high degree of social mobility is normally viewed as a positive attribute for a society. However, depending on how social mobility is defined and measured, one can end up labeling part of the existing income instability as social mobility.[7] For one thing, if a strictly positive economic variable such as consumption is being measured, higher variance, translated as risk, could be perceived as a positive quality, in the sense that when one can only get better, higher variability enhances the person's chances of moving out of the bad state. This subsection presents unidirectional measures of per capita earnings mobility. In particular, the transition probabilities into and out of

---

[6] For people successfully observed eight times, each block of four consecutive observations was treated separately.

[7] The distinction between circular and structural mobility is key here.

Table 3.7. Transitions into and out of Poverty, 1996-98

Period	Sample Movement	Total population IN	Total population OUT	Low schooling IN	Low schooling OUT	High schooling IN	High schooling OUT
12 months	4 by 4	9.77%	24.84%	13.24%	21.51%	6.30%	28.18%
12 months	1 by 1	8.95%	27.00%	12.48%	23.60%	5.42%	30.40%
1 month	1 by 1	8.21%	25.23%	9.64%	22.56%	6.77%	27.90%

Source: PME.

poverty are estimated according to different horizons.[8] Estimates of these transition probabilities for 1996-98 are presented in Table 3.7.

Given the basic poverty line used, they reveal the following:

(i) When transitions are compared at a four-month period one year apart, the probabilities of entering into and leaving poverty are 9.77 percent and 24.84 percent, respectively;

(ii) When two isolated months are compared one year apart, these probabilities are 8.95 percent and 27 percent, respectively;

(iii) On a month-by-month basis, the entering and exiting probabilities are 8.21 percent and 25.23 percent, respectively.

The magnitude of these transition probabilities reveals a degree of mobility into and out of poverty that is greater than expected.

When the sample is split between poor and non-poor according to the household head's median school level, there are, as expected, higher enter-

---

[8] Formally, $t = P[Y2<L\backslash Y1>L]$ and $s = P[Y2>L\backslash Y1<L]$ where Yi is income in period i and L is the poverty line used. Assuming the environment is time-homogeneous and a steady-state has been reached, these transition probabilities, t and s, measure the proportion of non-poor households becoming poor each month and the proportion of poor households escaping poverty each month, respectively. If a Markovian process is assumed, then these transition probabilities still have this interpretation, even if the steady-state has not yet been reached.

ing probabilities and lower exiting probabilities for families that have little human capital. For example, the probability of entering poverty between 12-month periods, based on four-month period earnings, is 13.24 percent for the poor and 6.3 percent for the non-poor. The corresponding poverty exiting probabilities are 21.51 percent for people with little human capital and 28.18 percent for the remaining population.

Temporal Aggregation

The final exercise compares different poverty measures using two different windows to measure earnings: one-month and four-month periods. To be sure, poverty measures are compared for a period of four consecutive months using average per capita income and the results obtained treating each observation independently. Table 3.8 presents yearly averages of FGT poverty indexes (P0, P1 and P2) over 1985-96.

The difference between the poverty measures using the four-month and the one-month periods is striking, especially as the analysis moves to measures that take into consideration inequality among the poor. During the whole period, the differences amounted to 11 percent for P0, 24 percent for P1 and 32 percent for P2. In certain periods of high economic instability, such as 1989, the difference of the squared poverty gap (P2) reaches an annual average of more than 40 percent.[9]

To evaluate the suitability of different windows of income measurement implicit in poverty measures, it is necessary to make explicit hypotheses about the functioning of capital markets. The reason is because people extract utility from consumption and not from labor income itself. The operation of capital markets allows consumption-smoothing in spite of earnings fluctuations. In a complete market setting, the relevant concept of income would correspond to the permanent income over the planning horizon of the individual. On the other hand, the existence of capital market failures would imply the imposition of restrictions on the period used to measure

---

[9] Similarly, the estimates reveal that poverty, by all three FGT measures, is higher when determined by the distribution of per capita consumption than by the distribution of per capita income. The headcount for São Paulo based on income data is 0.31, whereas the corresponding headcount based on consumption data is 0.42.

Table 3.8. Poverty Measures, Yearly Averages

Poverty Index	P0		P1		P2	
Time Period	4-Month	1-Month (4X)	4-Month	1-Month (4X)	4-Month	1-Month (4X)
85	0.23661	0.26116	0.11577	0.14564	0.08113	0.11261
86	0.15484	0.18218	0.07600	0.10536	0.05448	0.08494
87	0.15918	0.18941	0.07648	0.10621	0.05443	0.08403
88	0.16677	0.19694	0.07845	0.10980	0.05509	0.08724
89	0.15907	0.19528	0.07492	0.11176	0.05336	0.09004
90	0.18763	0.22240	0.08699	0.12264	0.05977	0.09502
91	0.23720	0.26579	0.11157	0.14434	0.07597	0.10982
92	0.31018	0.33694	0.15155	0.18682	0.10356	0.14154
93	0.30660	0.33632	0.15418	0.19305	0.10845	0.15086
94	0.32546	0.35277	0.16398	0.20348	0.11413	0.15775
95	0.25592	0.28541	0.12674	0.16394	0.08921	0.12878
96	0.22835	0.25284	0.11398	0.14860	0.08098	0.11886

Source: PME.

earnings. In other words, capital market failures truncate the horizon in which agents can implement their decisions. In this case, it makes sense to use shorter periods of poverty measurement.

Short-Run Financial Behavior of the Poor

This section examines the effects of the short-run earnings dynamics on the financial behavior and welfare of poor households.

A profile of poor savers begins to take shape according to the ABECIP consumer finance surveys. ABECIP surveys during 1987 show that 47 percent of adults did not possess any financial asset. This statistic rises to 70 percent in the poor segment of the population. These surveys also reveal that the most popular financial assets in Brazil are savings deposits (cadernetas de poupança). Of poor people who held any asset, 95 percent held only savings deposits. This means that little is lost if analysis of the financial holdings of the poor is restricted to savings deposits. In 1987, there were 70 million active savings accounts in Brazil. Of course, each person can hold more than one account, but ABECIP data show that the average number of accounts per user of savings deposits was 1.42.

An initial explanation for the popularity of savings accounts is the minimal requirements imposed on people to open them. The requirements are minimal because of the operational simplicity of the monthly capitalization period of savings accounts. The philosophy adopted when savings deposits were first introduced implied the absence of entry barriers in official institutions, like Caixa Econômica Federal. In 1987, 36 percent of owners of savings accounts had deposits in this institution.

An indication of the easy access to savings accounts is found among the explanations offered by respondents for not having one. The response "opening limit way too high" appears with a null proportion even in the poorest segments of the population. On the other hand, difficult access to other assets besides savings deposits is captured by the fact that no poor adult chose as an explanation for not having a savings account that he or she prefers to use another asset. At the same time, 37 percent of the high-income group presented this justification for not having an account.

As expected, average savings balances of the poorest depositors were lower than those of higher income brackets: 5.1 minimum wages against 21.8 minimum wages. However, the ratio between average balances to income was higher in the group of poor owners of savings accounts: 2.5 as compared to 1.1. If the zero balances of individuals who did not hold savings deposits are computed as well, the ratios between average balances and income between these two income groups become more similar, reaching 0.72 and 0.64, respectively. This result may be attributable to the higher portfolio diversification of higher income groups. At the same time, it reinforces the importance of savings deposits among the poorest segments of the Brazilian population.

The automatic determination of nominal interest rates of savings deposits at 0.5 percent per month plus lagged monetary correction implies that transitions towards higher inflation rates generated real interest rate losses. Similarly, transitions towards lower monthly inflation rates were followed by increases in the real interest rates of savings deposits. For example, the inflation rise observed after the failure of the Cruzado Plan in 1986 (from 3 percent to 20 percent per month in one year) implied an erosion of 14 percent on the real value of savings deposits. This lagged monetary correction mechanism was not always understood by economic actors. According to the 1985 ABECIP survey, 18 percent of people who did not finish primary school agreed with the proposition that the nominal interest rate of savings deposits always surpasses the inflation rate. At the other extreme, only 3 percent of respondents with a university degree agreed with this proposition.[10]

Among the characteristics recognized as important by deposit holders, risk, captured through such phrases as "security" or "warranted by the government," appears in first place among both the poorest and wealthiest segments of the population. Second is "expected return," among 26 percent and 40 percent, respectively. "Liquidity" is third at 5 percent and 6 percent, respectively. The phrase "easy to use" represented 4 percent and 3 percent of answers, respectively.

The poorest segments appear to attribute a higher value to risk. On the other hand, expected return appears to be more important among the wealthiest groups, reflecting the higher margin of substitution between assets observed. The low importance attributed to liquidity is explained by the monthly capitalization period of savings deposits. This low liquidity imposed difficulties in the use of savings deposits as a flight-from-money mechanism in the interval between wage payments.

Most operations with savings deposits presented a high frequency. The average amount of time since the last deposit was 6.9 months for the poorest segment and 3.7 months for the higher income bracket. On the other hand, the average time since the last withdrawal was 4.9 months and 5.2 months, respectively.

The main reasons for not intending to make savings deposits in the next few months were not having any money or having too little (90 percent for the poorest segment and 46 percent for the wealthiest). On the other hand, the main motivation presented for intending to withdraw money from savings deposits in the next few months was to complement the household budget (83 percent for the poorest segment and 36 percent for the wealthi-

---

[10] Anecdotal evidence of the difficulty faced by the poor in dealing with inflationary complexities is that the only asset to which the poor presented higher access rates was bonuses from Baú da Felicidade. These assets were well known for not offering any type of monetary correction.

est). These reasons, combined with the high frequencies of savings deposits and withdrawals, suggest a consumption-smoothing process with respect to short-run fluctuations in family income.

The consumption-smoothing process appears to be more intense among the poorest savings deposits holders. This is consistent with evidence of a high variability of family income at the lower end of the distribution mentioned above. The high frequency and the low duration of poverty spells can be explained by unemployment spells with similar characteristics, like those frequently reported for Brazilian labor markets. Although the response that the person is unemployed explains little about ex-post savings deposit withdrawals, the unemployment motivation can be implicit in more general justifications presented. The most important reasons given for making a withdrawal from savings were to complement the household budget (56 percent for the poorest segment and 26 percent for the wealthiest) and for an emergency (21 percent for the poorest segment and 22 percent for the wealthiest).

Another possible reason for the high variability of family incomes would be the combination of high inflation and infrequent nominal wage adjustments, generating a saw-toothed pattern of real wages. A simple interpretation for the high frequency of deposits and withdrawals—to complement the household budget—would be to smooth the saw-toothed patterned fluctuations in income on the consumption path (see Neri, 1990).

Conclusions

This chapter has attempted to establish a basis for research on the relationship between poverty and asset markets in Brazil. The chapter has combined annual household survey data with monthly employment surveys and a survey on consumer finances. The combination of these sources of information sheds some new light on the nature of poverty and on the connection between assets and poverty, since it makes possible for the first time an assessment of the level and distribution of physical, human and social capital in Brazil. The chapter provides a threefold map of the different effects that the possession of these different assets may have on poverty, and asks whether income-earning assets play an important role in cushioning the consumption of poor families from unexpected shocks.

One of the main conclusions is that the poor have incentives to save because they need to build up buffer stocks to face unexpected income fluctuations. However, since they are continuously exposed to shocks they are only able to have high frequency saving, rather than long-term accumulation necessary to build up an asset stock. The ability to build up these stocks will therefore be limited by instability. In the absence of adequate insurance mechanisms, uncertainty becomes a restriction to acquiring more assets. Moreover, uncertainty induces investment in relatively unproductive (but liquid) assets, such as cash holdings instead of other assets with a longer run return, such as human capital.

Insurance mechanisms or a stable environment will therefore act in favor of a more equitable distribution of assets. Public policies oriented in this direction may have a long-lasting positive effect on the standard of living of the poor.

References

Datt, G., and M. Ravallion. 1992. Growth and Redistribution Components of Changes in Poverty Measures: A Decomposition with Applications to Brazil and India in the 1980s. *Journal of Development Economics* 38(3): 275-95.

Neri, M. 1990. Inflação e Consumo: Modelos Teóricos Aplicados ao Imediato Pós-Cruzado. Rio de Janeiro: Banco Nacional de Desenvolvimento Econômico e Social.

Ravallion, M., and G. Datt. 1995. *Growth and Poverty in Rural India.* World Bank Policy Research Working Paper No. 1405, Washington, DC.

Rocha, S. 1993. Poverty Lines for Brazil: New Estimates from Recent Empirical Evidence. Instituto de Pesquisa Econômica Aplicada, Rio de Janeiro. Mimeo.

CHAPTER FOUR

From Quantity to Quality: Human Capital and Income in Chile

Dante Contreras and Osvaldo Larrañaga[1]

Insufficient income, which constitutes the definition of poverty, is ultimately a response to the lack of income-generating assets, or to the low return on existing assets. The principal asset associated with individual income is human capital; that is, the acquired capacities that permit people to generate wealth by applying their labor. Possession of physical assets can also provide income, either through direct exploitation, as in the case of independent workers, or indirectly from property rights to business assets. Lastly, there are more intangible assets: public capital, which provides benefits for the community as a whole, and social capital related to forms of interaction between people, which can be functional in the generation of income.

This chapter examines the links between the possession of assets and poverty in Chile. The research uses homogeneous household surveys from 1987 to 1996. These surveys make possible a study of the association between human capital and income, though not in relation to physical capital.

Antecedents

Measurements of poverty are relatively new in Chile. The first study was based on a 1968 income survey conducted by the National Institute of Statistics. This survey used a methodology that defines as poor any household whose per capita income is below a threshold or poverty line, calculated as the cost of a basket of goods and services that satisfies a set of basic needs.

---

[1] The authors are members of the faculty of the Department of Economics of the University of Chile.

During the 15 years that followed, isolated measurements of poverty were carried out. Some used the same methodology (Pollack and Uthoff, 1986; Rodríguez, 1985), while others were based on specific unsatisfied thresholds of achievement in areas such as education, nutrition and housing. This latter approach was used to prepare poverty maps based on population censuses.

Consistent and homogeneous measurements of poverty have only been available since 1987, when the National Socioeconomic Survey began. Known by its Spanish acronym CASEN, the survey is carried out approximately every two years and provides national and regional coverage for a subset of the country's municipalities (*comunas*). Its original objective was to estimate the distributive incidence of social programs; in practice, however, the survey has become the official source for measuring poverty and income distribution in Chile.

In order of importance, proximate determinants of poverty at the household level are the following: low levels of labor income among the employed, low household rates of labor participation, high rates of unemployment affecting poor households, and the number of people who live in the representative poor household.[2]

In addition, the dependency rate, defined as the number of people who depend on each employed person, is almost three times higher in poor households than in those with middle incomes. Contrary to expectations, however, household type—whether nuclear, enlarged or extended—has no relationship to poverty. This can be interpreted as an adaptation of household type to the income situation.

With regard to women and poverty, labor participation by female spouses contributes significantly to household income. This introduces an association between paid work by women and the probability that the household is classified as poor. This association, though, has little relevance at the aggregate level because of lower labor participation by women in the middle and lower income strata. It also shows that female-headed households are more likely than others to be poor, particularly households headed by a young woman. The absolute number of households in this condition is nonetheless relatively small, a reflection of their low economic viability.

---

[2] See Raczynski and Larrañaga (1995); World Bank (1997); Contreras and Larrañaga (1998).

These poverty profiles confirm the importance of a life cycle approach that relates the ages of the household head and spouse to the household's per capita income. Thus, it can be deduced that poverty is in part transitory, that is, related to low incomes associated with the early stages of the household. The reference period, however, can be sufficiently long (e.g., between 20 and 39 years of age), for this "transitory" poverty to be a concern of public policy.

Empirical Analysis

This section presents descriptive statistics and a decomposition analysis on poverty in Chile. The material covers both the long term, in the case of Santiago, and the last decade of high economic growth, for which detailed information is available for the whole country.

The Long Term

The construction of a long-term series for Chile is restricted by the availability of only relatively recent information on poverty. The main long-term source is the surveys of employment and unemployment by the Department of Economics of the University of Chile since 1957 in Greater Santiago (representing one-third of the country's population). The survey is quarterly, with an annual income module. It should b‰4borne in mind that the survey is not designed to accurately reflect incomes, so when it is used to construct a poverty series, its results have to be interpreted as general trends.

Figure 4.1 shows an unpublished poverty series constructed from per capita income and the official poverty line currently used in Chile. In general terms, the poverty trend replicates the country's economic history during the last 40 years. Levels of poverty increase significantly in periods of macroeconomic crisis (1973-76 and 1982-86) and decrease during periods of economic boom (1978-81 and 1987-96). The trend also seems to follow periods of a more activist public policy with redistributive objectives (1968-72).

This result should not be surprising, considering that the poverty trend is the result of fluctuations in the level of per capita income and its distribution (in the case of a constant poverty line). A note of caution is necessary regarding the hyperinflationary phenomenon of 1973, however, which could

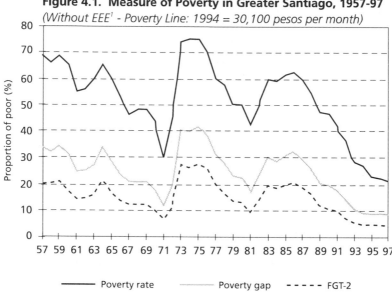

Figure 4.1. Measure of Poverty in Greater Santiago, 1957-97
(Without EEE[1] - Poverty Line: 1994 = 30,100 pesos per month)

———— Poverty rate   ·········· Poverty gap   - - - - - FGT-2

[1] An adult equivalent scale.
Source: Department of Economics, University of Chile.

seriously distort the price deflators used to construct the poverty series. Hence, the subperiods of 1957-71 and 1975-96 are more consistent relative to the period as a whole.

Poverty over 1987-96

In Chile, the decade from 1987-96 was a period of rapid economic growth, with average annual per capita income growth of 5.6 percent. At the same time, the percentage of poor households was cut in half, from 45.1 percent in 1987 to 23.2 percent in 1996. However, the distribution of incomes has remained relatively constant.

Table 4.1 presents poverty measures for 1987, 1992 and 1996. The years selected are reasonably representative of the decade under study, which does not present structural or economic changes that would require a more detailed subdivision. The measures used correspond to the three classic Foster-Greer-Thorbecke (FGT) poverty indices: percentage of poverty, poverty

Table 4.1. Poverty and Income Inequality, Chile, 1987-96

	1987	1990	1992	1994	1996
Poverty rate[1] (%)	45.1	38.6	32.6	27.5	23.2
Quintile 5/Quintile 1 (%)	13.3	12.9	12.2	13.1	13.8
Participation, quintiles 3 & 4 (%)	30.7	30.1	30.3	30.2	30.7
Without EEE[2]	**1987**		**1992**		**1996**
Poverty rate (%)	44.9		29.4		23.1
Poverty gap (%)	19.1		10.4		8.2
FGT-2 (%)	10.7		5.2		4.2
Gini index	0.57		0.56		0.56
With EEE	**1987**		**1992**		**1996**
Poverty rate (%)	36.0		20.1		15.5
Poverty gap (%)	13.5		6.3		5.1
FGT-2 (%)	7.1		3.0		2.6
Gini index	0.56		0.54		0.55
Without EEE (2PPP)[3]	**1987**		**1992**		**1996**
Poverty rate (%)	23.6		12.5		10.1
Poverty gap (%)	8.5		3.8		3.3
FGT-2 (%)	4.4		1.9		1.7
With EEE (2PPP)	**1987**		**1992**		**1996**
Poverty rate (%)	15.5		6.4		5.5
Poverty gap (%)	5.1		2.1		2.0
FGT-2 (%)	2.6		1.1		1.2

[1] The percentage of poor people according to official measurements.
[2] An adult equivalent scale.
[3] Purchasing power parity equivalent to US$2 daily per person.
Source: CASEN Surveys, respective years.

gap, and square of the poverty gap. For each measure, two variants are identified with respect to the poverty line: the official line, which in 1996 was US$94.70 per month according to the exchange rate adjusted by purchasing power parity (PPP),[3] and a line for international comparison of US$60 monthly (US$2 daily) per inhabitant. Two variants were also used for the

---

[3] Only the official poverty line mentioned is used in this work. No distinction is made between urban and rural poverty, as is done by the official measures in the Chilean case. See discussion in World Bank (1997).

equivalent of scale: the official version for the Chilean case, which does not consider adjustments for household per capita income, and an alternative measure that adjusts for the number and composition of the members of the household using the procedure established in Contreras (1996).[4]

All of these measures indicate a strong decline in poverty during the period under consideration. The percentage of poor not adjusted for equivalences of scale falls to practically half (49 percent) of its initial value during the period of analysis. The other two FGT indicators fall even more sharply—the poverty gap by 57 percent and the FGT-2 by 61 percent—indicating that the gains in terms of combating poverty are even more appreciable within the population that remains in this condition.

The alternative measures reflect a similar trend, although the levels differ according to the definition used. The official measure adjusted for equivalences of scale provides values inferior to the official version because children, strongly represented in poor households, have less weight than adults in calculations of consumption requirements. In addition, the downward trend of these poverty indicators over 1987-96 is more pronounced than in the measurement of per capita income. This phenomenon, which is not inherent in the change of definition, is associated with the change in the composition of poor households, particularly the fact that households that leave poverty have a higher proportion of children than those that remain in poverty.

For its part, the measure that uses the poverty line of US$2 per day per person records poverty levels correspondingly lower than those associated with the official line, reflecting the gap of 49 percent between these parameters in 1996. Here again, gains are observed in terms of a more accentuated reduction of poverty relative to the official measurements. This time, the cause could be in the devaluation of the value of the dollar relative to the national currency, which makes the line measured in dollars, although adjusted by PPP, lower in 1996 in relation to the domestic alternative.[5]

---

[4] Income is divided in this case by $N_i = 1.2 + 0.8 (N_{aa} + N_{11-15}) + 0.4 N_{5-10} + 0.3 N_{0-4}$. Where: N_i: number of persons in the household adjusted by EEE (an adult equivalent scale); N_{aa}: number of adults additional to the head of the household; N_{11-15}: number of children aged 11 to 15; N_{5-10}: aged five to ten; N_{0-4}: aged under four.

[5] A poverty profile for different groups classified by age, gender, education, economic sector and geographic location can be found in the larger working paper version of this chapter (Contreras and Larrañaga, 1999).

Table 4.2. Datt-Ravallion Decomposition for Chile
(In percent)

	1987-96	1987-92	1992-96
Rate of poverty			
Change	-17.0	-9.8	-7.2
Growth effect	-14.6	-9.4	-5.8
Distribution effect	-1.2	0.8	-1.7
Residual	-1.3	-1.1	0.2
Poverty gap			
Change	-10.9	-7.3	-3.7
Growth effect	-9.0	-5.9	-3.2
Distribution effect	-1.9	-0.9	-0.6
Residual	0.0	-0.4	0.2

Table 4.2 presents the decomposition of changes in poverty using the Datt-Ravallion (1992) methodology. The results confirmed the trend detected for shorter periods with respect to an approximate incidence of the growth effect of 80 percent, which would explain the reduction in poverty during the period (Larrañaga, 1994). The remaining 20 percent is associated with a slight distribution effect and a residual that is also of lower order.

Poverty and Human Capital

Work is the principal asset of the poor in countries like Chile, where economic development is at the intermediate level and urban economic activity predominates. Human capital represents the productive capacities that people possess and constitutes a principal determinant of the value of the work they do. In this respect, one of the most important statistical regularities of the economy is the relationship between income from work and a set of variables that approximate human capital, such as years of schooling and work experience.

This section examines the relationship between human capital and poverty based on a detailed estimate of the human capital possessed by each household. The procedure is based on the aggregation of the human capital possessed by each member of the family of working age, measured by the wage predicted from equations of income generation corrected by the decision of labor participation. The calculation includes the capital available to members of the household who are not actively participating in the labor market.

The estimates of human capital are used to relate possession of this asset to poverty over 1987-96. There is also an analysis of how opportunities to accumulate new human capital are distributed, as measured through tests of the achievements of educational establishments.

The methodological steps are as follows:

1. Estimate of income generation equations for household members of working age corrected by the decision of labor participation. Three groups are considered: young people, adult men and adult women.

2. Estimate of the value of human capital at market prices for each person of working age. The procedure is based on the equations of human capital estimated in the previous point.

3. Estimates of human capital at the household level, based on the aggregation of human capital estimated for each member of the household.

4. Definition of a threshold level of human capital, associated with the probability of poverty for the household.

5. Classification of households into groups according to the relationship between the human capital variable and poverty based on insufficiency of income. There is also a time analysis of this relationship.

6. Identification of factors that explain differences between the income of the household and its endowment of human capital.

7. Relationship between existing human capital and the accumulation of the asset by the children who reside in the households.

Three groups of the working age population are analyzed. Young people aged 12 to 24, women aged 25 to 65, and men in the same age group. The rationale behind this classification is that it encompasses groups that present different structures of labor-participation decisions and of income generation. The end years of the period under study (1987 and 1996) are also analyzed, considering a single geographical partition of the sample that covers households in the metropolitan region and the rest of the country.[6]

Determinants of Labor Participation

The estimate of the stock of human capital possessed by each individual is based on equations of income generation corrected for selection bias by the Heckman method (see Contreras and Larrañaga, 1999). The equations are specified in traditional form, including the variables of human capital, schooling and experience. The schooling variable is accompanied by qualitative variables which make possible an estimate of differentiated returns by level of education (primary, secondary, tertiary). Dummy variables are also incorporated to consider the effect of the type and place of occupation on labor income, as a means of controlling the impact of possible differentiating factors in the generation of income.

As mentioned earlier, the income equations were corrected by the Heckman procedure, where the secondary equation corresponds to a probit model of participation in the labor market. In this dichotomous model of participation, the dependent variable takes the value one if the person is actively participating in the labor market (employed or unemployed) and zero in the contrary case. The explanatory variables include the following: schooling, age and its square, and schooling by age; access by the household to public services; urban or rural area of residence; number of children in the household in different age groups; access by children to school food programs; and gender and marital status.

In general terms, the specified models provide results consistent with the human capital theory. In particular, longer schooling and experience increase the probability of participation. People who live in urban areas par-

---

[6] See Contreras and Larrañaga (1999) for descriptive statistics for the groups under study in relation to the structure of labor force participation, average income and average years of schooling.

Table 4.3. Rates of Return of the Components of Human Capital

	Men	Women	Young people
Metropolitan region, 1987			
Primary return	0.01 (0.0012)	-0.01 (0.0015)	0.05 (0.0034)
Secondary return	0.13 (0.0009)	0.11 (0.0012)	0.10 (0.0018)
Tertiary return	0.24 (0.0010)	0.17 (0.0008)	0.19 (0.0011)
Experience	0.03 (0.0007)	0.01 (0.0009)	0.10 (0.0048)
Metropolitan region, 1996			
Primary return	0.00 (0.0010)	-0.01 (0.0014)	0.22 (0.0040)
Secondary return	0.09 (0.0008)	0.12 (0.0001)	0.18 (0.0022)
Tertiary return	0.20 (0.0005)	0.17 (0.0007)	0.18 (0.0012)
Experience	0.02 (0.0180)	0.03 (0.0007)	0.27 (0.0059)
Rest of the country, 1987			
Primary return	0.01 (0.0009)	0.01 (0.0016)	0.01 (0.0025)
Secondary return	0.11 (0.0007)	0.09 (0.0013)	0.07 (0.0014)
Tertiary return	0.20 (0.0006)	0.15 (0.0009)	0.18 (0.0012)
Experience	0.02 (0.0008)	0.01 (0.0009)	0.01 (0.0037)
Rest of the country, 1996			
Primary return	0.01 (0.0008)	0.00 (0.0012)	0.07 (0.0025)
Secondary return	0.13 (0.0006)	0.14 (0.0015)	0.10 (0.0012)
Tertiary return	0.18 (0.0005)	0.18 (0.0012)	0.19 (0.0009)
Experience return	0.02 (0.0005)	0.02 (0.0007)	0.09 (0.0036)

Note: All the coefficients are significant at 5% (standard errors are in brackets).

ticipate more than those who live in rural areas, women with a partner participate less than other women, and women with more children reduce their participation rate (irrespective of the children's age). The probability of participation increases if the children are in a school food program, reflecting the substitution between childcare in homes and in schools.

Special attention should be paid to the parameters that represent the returns of years of schooling and experience, which are summarized in Table 4.3.[7] First, they highlight the great difference between the returns on school-

---

[7] The returns correspond to regression coefficients from the Mincer equation (spline regressions) and do not include the cost of education.

ing relative to level of education. In almost all the cases reported, the return on primary education is low or nonexistent and the return on secondary education is intermediate, while the return on tertiary education presents the highest values. It is very possible that this structure of rates of return is affected by selection biases attributable to unobservable variables such as the quality of education and personal ability. In any event, the differences in the rates are sufficiently important to make inadvisable the use of average returns that are not differentiated by level of education.

Second, some special features should be mentioned. The return on schooling for men tends to be higher than for women. By way of illustration, in 1987 the rate of return on tertiary education for men is five to seven points higher than for women. Over the decade that followed, men's rates of return fell moderately, while women's rates seemed to be more stable. This coincided with a strong increase in women's employment rates, which implies a corresponding increase in the demand for women workers (otherwise the returns would have fallen).

Endowment of Human Capital for Households

There are two essential aspects in the estimate of the human capital of households. First, human capital is calculated for each household member of working age, regardless of whether the person participates in the labor market (but controlling for that decision). The rationale for this procedure lies in the concept of human capital as an asset that the family *can* mobilize to generate income. The difference between the total endowment and the capital effectively used to generate income is unused capital, which responds to two different factors. In the first case, it can result from a rational decision in which different members of the household undertake activities consistent with their preferences and income possibilities. Thus, continuation of studies or work in the home can respond to optimum allocations of the time of the people in the household. In the second case, there may be exogenous restrictions that limit the labor participation of household members, as in the case of legislation that prohibits companies from contracting women to work in their own homes (thus, paid work cannot be combined with childcare and other household activities).

The second essential aspect of household human capital is that it is estimated in monetary terms. The value of individual human capital is estimated as the wage predicted by a basic equation of human capital that contains only the variables of schooling and potential experience. This is an attempt to measure the value of human capital incorporated into the person, abstracting market variables that determine a different return on the human capital according to the type of occupation or other variable. However, the parameters utilized come from the estimate of the income-generation function presented in the previous section, which does control for such external effects.[8]

By way of example, some results for women can be cited. Working women outside metropolitan Santiago in 1987 received an average estimated monthly wage in 15,280 pesos, while women who did not work received 9,906 pesos, the equivalent of the value of work in the home. From these estimates, it is possible to calculate the ratio between the value of work in the market and the value of work in the home, which is 1.54.[9] The respective figures for the metropolitan region were 19,182 pesos, 13,373 pesos, and a ratio of 1.43.

In 1996, working women outside the metropolitan region earned an average hourly wage of 359 pesos, while in the home the equivalent wage was 230 pesos, a ratio of 1.56.[10] In the metropolitan region in 1996, the market paid an average hourly wage of 537 pesos, while the equivalent wage in the home was 318 pesos, a ratio of 1.68.

From these figures, it can be concluded that the predicted wages for women are higher in the metropolitan region than in the rest of the country; that the gap between the market and household wages is about 50 percent in the first year; that wages grew more in the metropolitan region over 1987-96; and that the gap between market and household wages grew significantly in the metropolitan area.

---

[8] As a result, the possibility of bias in the estimate of human capital is minimized.

[9] The income reported by the 1987 and 1996 CASEN surveys is in nominal terms, hence the use of this ratio facilitates the interpretation of the results.

[10] In 1987, the database did not include hours. Later, monthly wage was used in the estimate of the wage equation. In 1996, the database did include this variable and it was decided to estimate the model using the hourly wage. Given that the estimates are for the average, this difference in the information does not bias the results.

Relationship between Income and Human Capital

This section presents the results of relating the endowment of human capital to the availability of household income, both variables measured in per capita terms. Households are classified as poor and non-poor according to per capita income and the poverty line. The division of households by level of human capital per capita is somewhat more arbitrary since there is no equivalent to a poverty line to make it possible to divide households into groups similar to the classification by income.

The procedure followed was to establish as a human capital (per capita) threshold for 1987 the level at which the distribution function of the variable results in a percentage of households equal to the percentage of poverty for that year. Hence, the households are arranged according to the value of the variable for human capital per capita. A level is selected as threshold (k*), which presents an accumulated frequency of households equal to the percentage of poor households. Next, the households are divided into three groups according to their endowment of human capital per capita: low (below k*), medium (between k* and 2k*) and high (over 2k*).

For 1996, a similar procedure is followed for the classification of households by level of income and human capital per capita. But the threshold level of capital (k*) is fixed at the level defined in 1987. This makes it possible to analyze the increases in capital relative to a reference point, just as the poverty line provides a reference level with respect to changes in income.

The results of the procedure are shown in Table 4.4. Each horizontal line totals 100.0 because all households are included in the six groups presented in the respective columns. In 1987 in the metropolitan region, 17.6 percent of households were poor with low human capital, 19.5 percent poor with intermediate capital, and 2.4 percent poor with high human capital. Note that the sum of these groups is equivalent to the percentage of poor households (headcount) for this region in the year mentioned, that is, 39.5 percent. The households not classified as poor, which total 61.5 percent, are divided into the three categories mentioned according to their endowment of human capital.

A comparison of changes in the endowment of human capital and in the poverty level between 1987 and 1996 shows that in the metropolitan region, poverty levels generally fell, while possession of human capital in-

Table 4.4. Distribution of Households by Level of Income and Human Capital
(In percent)

	Poor households			Non-poor households		
	Endowment of human capital			Endowment of human capital		
	Low	Medium	High	Low	Medium	High
Metropolitan region						
1987	17.6	19.5	2.4	18.2	23.5	18.9
1996	3.3	10.4	1.4	17.5	34.2	33.3
Rest of the country						
1987	30.2	18.7	1.6	18.3	19.4	11.8
1996	9.6	18.7	1.3	20.4	32.2	17.8

creased. In 1996, over two-thirds of households (67.5 percent) were non-poor with a medium or high endowment of human capital. In contrast, only 42.4 percent of households satisfied this requirement in 1987. A similar trend occurred in the other regions of the country, although poverty levels were higher than in the metropolitan region. In these regions in 1987, 32.2 percent of households were not poor and had intermediate or high levels of capital per capita, but by 1996 this percentage had increased to 50 percent.

A large number of households also show a disassociation between income level and possession of human capital. In the metropolitan region, 21.9 percent of households in 1987 were classified as poor despite having intermediate or high levels of human capital, while 18.2 percent of households were not poor even though they had a low endowment of human capital. This type of result can be generalized for 1996 and for the other regions of the country.

Poor Households and Their Human Capital

The relationship between low levels of human capital and income is well known and forms the basis of policies that aim to combat poverty by increasing this type of asset. The most surprising result is the large set of households with intermediate levels of human capital that generate a low level of income and are thus classified as poor. Why do these intermediate levels of human capital not result in higher income for the households?

Three principal types of factors could explain this asymmetry. First, the return on human capital may vary because of the presence of labor segmentation or the action of equalizing differences in wages. In this case, workers with equal levels of human capital may be paid unequally according to the type or place of occupation. Second, unobservable factors cause errors in the measurement of human capital. Households that have equal endowments of human capital can in reality have unequal endowments, when measured more comprehensively. Third, there may be other income in the household—such as government transfers and the income generated by other types of assets—that explains the difference between the endowment of human capital and total household income.

To determine the incidence of these factors a probit regression was estimated, taking as a sample only households with intermediate human capital, both poor and non-poor. The dependent variable takes the value one if the household is poor and zero if not. The variables on the right include those related to the place and type of occupation, as well as household variables related to the generation of income. The regression analysis thus attempts to identify observable factors that explain the divergences between human capital and household income.

The results are given in Table 4.5. First, the presence of differences of income by economic sector is confirmed. Households with medium levels of human capital whose head works in agriculture, construction or commerce have a greater probability of being classified as poor than those whose heads work in the mining or industrial sector (reference group in the regression). The probability of poverty decreases in families that live in urban areas outside the metropolitan region and in those where the head works in the public sector or armed forces.

Second, the regressions confirm the effect on poverty of decisions taken in the household. Smaller families have less probability of being classified as poor, as do families with a higher participation rate in the labor market. Third, the probability of poverty decreases with possession of other assets, and with the presence of income from other sources in addition to human capital.

Access to Human Capital: Distribution of Educational Achievements

Education is the principal source of accumulation of human capital and explains most of the variance in labor incomes. As a result, in recent dec-

Table 4.5. Probability of Poverty for Households with Medium-Level Human Capital

(Coefficients of probit regression analysis)

	Metropolitan region,1987	Metropolitan region, 1996	Rest of the country, 1987	Rest of the country,1996
Agriculture	0.273	0.751	-0.043	0.355
Mining	-0.714	-0.362	-0.194	-0.133
Construction	0.147	0.265	0.356	0.300
Commerce	-0.373	-0.286	-0.087	-0.001*
Financial sector	0.075	-0.511	0.239	0.056
Personal services	-0.042	0.021	0.106	0.203
Transport and communications	-0.194	-0.025	0.048	0.155
Community services	-0.388	na	0.037	na
Urban sector	0.113	-0.198	-0.126	-0.042
Public sector	-0.675	-0.302	-0.388	-0.166
Armed forces	-0.107	-0.449	-0.999	-0.991
No. of persons in household	-0.075	0.114	0.141	0.101
Rate of labor participation	0.044	-0.449	-0.042	-0.510
Other household income	-0.002	-0.000	-0.002	-0.001
Access to potable water	-0.237	-0.193	-0.035	-0.015
Access to electricity	0.365	-0.818	-0.057	-0.072
Access to sewerage	-0.166	-0.493	-0.226	-0.473

Note: All coefficients are significant at 5%, except those marked with an asterisk.

ades, policies aimed at expanding educational coverage and reinforcing the quality of education have acquired a privileged place in strategies designed to foster economic development and combat poverty.

The level of schooling of the Chilean population is very high in relation to the rest of Latin America. The average schooling of the labor force is around 10 years, and secondary education covers 80 percent of the population. However, the available indicators reveal a very unequal distribution of educational achievements acquired by persons with an equal number of years of schooling. One example is the wide gap in access to higher education among students from different secondary schools. It is also probable that the pronounced inequality of income that characterizes Chilean society is not attributable to the levels and distribution of *years of schooling* found in the population. It is therefore necessary to deepen the analysis and examine

Table 4.6. Human Capital and Educational Results in the Metropolitan Region, 1996

		Distribution of human capital of households				
		Quintile 1	Quintile 2	Quintile 3	Quintile 4	Quintile 5
Distribution	Quintile 1	23.9	22.4	18.2	13.8	6.2
results	Quintile 2	22.7	22.2	21.2	18.8	10.8
in schools	Quintile 3	21.2	20.6	21.8	22.2	15.4
(mathematics)	Quintile 4	18.0	20.2	22.2	23.3	19.5
	Quintile 5	14.2	14.7	16.6	21.8	48.1
	Total	**100.0**	**100.0**	**100.0**	**100.0**	**100.0**
		Distribution of human capital of households				
		Quintile 1	Quintile 2	Quintile 3	Quintile 4	Quintile 5
Distribution	Quintile 1	23.7	22.3	16.9	13.6	6.1
results	Quintile 2	22.6	21.3	21.7	18.8	11.7
in schools	Quintile 3	21.1	20.8	21.3	22.3	17.5
(mathematics)	Quintile 4	17.9	20.6	22.8	23.6	19.5
	Quintile 5	14.8	14.9	17.3	21.6	45.2
	Total	**100.0**	**100.0**	**100.0**	**100.0**	**100.0**

the distribution of *educational achievements* to more precisely determine access by the population to human capital resources.

This section aims to link the distribution of human capital of households with the distribution of opportunities for access to new human capital obtained by the children. To do this, the database of the results of the SIMCE test (system for measuring quality in education) was used. The purpose of the test, which has been implemented in Chile since 1988, is to measure the percentage of achievement of educational objectives. The test has universal coverage, since it is applied in all schools in the fourth and eighth years of basic education in correlative years. This chapter considers the test taken in 1996, although the choice of year is not critical to the conclusions because the distribution of the variable shows very little variation in proximate years.

Table 4.6 shows a classification of households by quintiles of per capita human capital and the quintiles of the scores of the SIMCE tests of the schools attended by school-age family members. Read vertically, these figures show the probability of attending schools of different levels of educational achievement for a child from a household with a particular level of human capital. In this respect, the information approximates a transition matrix of levels of human capital between generations and illustrates the distribution of opportunities.

The table reveals that the distribution of educational opportunities is relatively similar in the first four quintiles of the distribution of human capital. That is, there is no great difference in the average quality of the school attended by students from this type of household. In contrast, there is a more marked association between the higher quintiles of both distributions: between 45 percent and 50 percent of students from the households in the highest quintile of human capital attend schools that are ranked in the highest 20 percent of educational achievement.

For a deeper analysis of the association between the human capital of households and the accumulation of human capital by the new generation, the relationship was controlled by the level of per capita income of households and by place of residence. The analysis was applied to the metropolitan region, which was divided into 12 geographically similar subregions. The choice of school by the family was conditioned by three factors: income or capacity to pay, human capital, and supply of schools in the area of residence. The latter variable measures the possibility of access in relation to the geographical proximity of the household and school, there being no institutional restrictions that limit access by place of residence.

Schools in Chile are of three types: municipal schools, which are former public schools that were transferred to local governments in the early 1980s and which provide free education; subsidized private schools administered by private agents but largely financed by the state; and paid private schools, financed by wealthier families.

Table 4.7 presents the results of the regressions. The observations correspond to all primary students represented in the 1996 CASEN. The human capital variable is expressed in per capita terms and constructed in line with the method described in the preceding sections of the chapter; the per capita income variable corresponds to the total monetary income of the household and includes an allocation for property rent; and the dependent variable corresponds to the score of the 1996 SIMCE test, obtained as an average of the educational establishment attended by each student.

Table 4.7. Determinants of the Choice of Educational Establishment
(OLS regression coefficients)

Dependent variable: average school in SIMCE test	Math test	Spanish test
Per capita income household	0.122	0.114
Human capital per capita household	0.330	0.351
Area of residence of household		
Area 1	-3.91	-4.81
Area 2	0.93*	0.26
Area 3	0.55*	-0.29*
Area 4	-4.05	-4.48*
Area 5	-7.47	-9.35
Area 6	-1.34*	-1.85*
Area 7	-5.64	-7.05
Area 8	-4.11	-5.37
Area 9	-7.47	-9.05
Area 10	-6.45	-8.09
Area 11	-6.89	-6.25
Area 12	-8.51	-8.53
Constant	72.61	74.21
Coefficient determination	0.239	0.239
Number of observations	5390	5390

Notes: (1) All variables are significant at 5%, excluding those marked with an asterisk.
(2) The area of residence represents the differential impact with respect to Santiago.

The results show that families with higher per capita income register their children in schools that obtain better educational results. This result is standard and is reflected fundamentally in the relationship between the quality of education and the volume and quality of educational inputs possessed by the privately financed schools. Second, the level of human capital of the household is directly associated with the quality of the school attended by the children, controlling for the family income variable. Families with equal levels of income differ in the choice of school depending on the level of human capital possessed by the household. The effect could be associated with the greater capacity to make informed choices derived from the endowment of human capital—as well as educational preferences—and points to a recognized effect of transmission of human capital (Behrman and Wolfe, 1991). Lastly, the place of residence is an important factor in the opportunities available to the family in the choice of education for children. This parameter, which is more related to educational supply, is controllable by educational policy.

Conclusions

Six principal conclusions can be drawn from this chapter on the assets of the poor population in Chile. First, the long-term series and the decomposition exercises for the last decade show that the principal force behind the trend in poverty was the performance of the economy, generated by the structural trend in growth and short-term cyclical movements. In fact, the poverty series constructed for Santiago over the last 40 years reveals a strong correlation with the trend in GDP during the period. The Datt-Ravallion technique also shows that most of the reduction in poverty over 1987-96 was due to average growth of income rather than redistribution.

Second, the strong reduction in poverty over 1987-96—a decade marked by growth—has favored all socioeconomic groups, particularly those that had high initial levels of poverty. This finding is shown by the trend in the poverty profile and, more specifically, by the decomposition of the poverty measure based on partitioning the population into subgroups according to degree of socioeconomic vulnerability. Hence, the process of poverty reduction has been widespread rather than selective.

Third, there is an association between human capital and household income. Reduced poverty is associated with increases in the endowment, use and valuation of human capital by households. Over 1987-96, this is revealed by the rise in average years of schooling of the working-age population, the decrease in unemployment rates, the strong rise in the rate of participation of women, and the substantial rise in average income from paid work.

Fourth, the relationship between human capital and household income is measured by different types of factors. Some income is obtained from government transfers and other types of assets. There is also evidence of differentiated returns on the same level of human capital, associated with economic sector or type of work. In this respect, the empirical evidence does not permit discrimination between competitive hypotheses such as structural segmentation and equalizing differences on wages.

Fifth, the entry of the asset of human capital into the labor market differs greatly from household to household depending on women's labor force participation. However, the calculation of shadow prices for work done by women in the home establishes that at least part of this "labor inactivity" reflects the cost-benefit-efficiency criterion. In this respect, the rise in market wages was a driving force behind the increase in work by women over 1987-96 and is likely to remain so over the next few years.

Sixth, there is evidence of the intergenerational transmission of human capital, taking the results of the test of educational achievement at the primary level as a proxy for the asset accumulated by new generations. The human capital of the family influences the new accumulation of the asset through an indirect link—more human capital leads to higher income and more possibilities of acquiring a better education—and through a direct channel that links the human capital of the household with the choice of better schools, controlling for the effect of the level of income.

This last conclusion suggests that not only does the size of the human capital stock matter for generating income, but also that its quality can be even more important. The difference between the average schooling of children at the top and bottom of the income distribution is apparently not that large in Chile at young ages, but education can still be of totally different value in the market because of its quality. Children from poorer families tend to access schools with the lowest scores in terms of student achievement, while the wealthy mostly attend the best scoring schools. This shows that the effects of family background on attainment may feed through various mechanisms, and that to be able to accumulate more human capital, restrictions other than income must be overcome.

The implication of this finding is that policies aimed at increasing the accumulation of assets by the poor can focus either on improving the quality of the existing educational services in low-income areas, or devising income support schemes for families that allow them to send their children to higher quality schools. In any case, an important result is that in Chile the main challenge does *not* seem to be the creation of infrastructure or services to cover all income groups, as is the case in poorer countries. It is a matter of improving the quality of the existing stock.

References

Behrman, J.R., and B.L. Wolfe. 1991. Earnings and Labor Force Participation Functions in a Developing Country: Are There Gender Differentials? In N. Birdsall and R. Sabot (eds.), *Unfair Advantage: Labor Market Discrimination in Developing Countries.* Washington, DC: World Bank.

Contreras, D. 1996. Pobreza y desigualdad en Chile: 1987–1992: Discurso, metodología y evidencia empírica. *Estudios Públicos* 64.

Contreras, D., and O. Larrañaga. 1999. *Los activos y recursos de la población pobre en América Latina: El caso de Chile.* Latin American Research Network Working Paper R-358. Inter-American Development Bank, Research Department, Washington, DC.

———. 1998. Movilidad de ingresos y pobreza en Santiago. University of Chile, Department of Economics, Santiago.

Cowan, K., and J. de Gregorio. 1996. Distribución y pobreza en Chile: ¿Estamos mal? ¿Ha habido progresos? ¿Hemos retrocedido? *Estudios Públicos* 64.

Datt, G., and M. Ravallion. 1992. Growth and Redistribution Components of Changes in Poverty Measures. *Journal of Development Economics* 38(3): 275–95.

Foster, J., J. Greer, and E. Thorbecke. 1984. A Class of Decomposable Poverty Measures. *Econometrica* 52(3): 761-66.

IDB/ECLAC/UNDP. 1995. *Informe de la Comisión Latinoamericana y del Caribe sobre el Desarrollo Social.* Santiago: IDB/ECLAC/UNDP.

Larrañaga, O. 1994. Pobreza, crecimiento y desigualdad: Chile 1987–92. *Revista de Análisis Económico* 9(2).

Lipton, M., and M. Ravallion. 1995. Poverty and Policy. In J. Behrman and T.N. Srinivasan (eds.), *Handbook of Development Economics* Volume 3-B. Amsterdam: Elsevier Science.

Mookherjer, D., and A. Shorrocks. 1982. A Decomposition Analysis of the Trend in UK Income Inequality. *Economic Journal* 92: 886–902.

Pollack, M., and A. Uthoff. 1986. *Pobreza y mercado del trabajo. Gran Santiago 1969–1984.* Documento de Trabajo 299. Santiago: International Labour Organization.

Raczynski, D., and O. Larrañaga. 1995. Características y determinantes de la pobreza y la distribución de ingresos en Chile: diagnóstico y lecciones de política. Santiago: Instituto Latinoamericano de Doctrina y Estudios Sociales/Corporación de Investigaciones Económicas para Latinoamérica.

Rodríguez, J. 1985. La distribución del ingreso y el gasto social en Chile, 1983. Instituto Latinoamericano de Doctrina y Estudios, Santiago. Mimeo.

World Bank.1997. Chile: Poverty and Income Distribution in a High-Growth Economy: 1987–1995. World Bank Country Management Unit, Argentina, Chile and Uruguay, Latin America and the Caribbean Region.

CHAPTER FIVE

The Urban-Rural Poverty Gap in Colombia

José Leibovich
Jairo Núñez[1]

There is a clear consensus among economists that the purpose of the development process should be to achieve a richer and more egalitarian society. This reaffirms the need not only for sustained economic growth but also for more equal opportunities of access to resources for all citizens, combined with a better distribution of assets, which is a condition sine qua non for better distribution of income.

Improved distribution of assets is also a necessary condition for stimulating economic growth. It would generate more equal growth of income which, in turn, would minimize the need for redistribution, generating a virtuous circle of more growth and more equity (Bourguignon, 1996).

Among the countries of Latin America, Colombia has had relatively stable but moderate economic growth for decades, accompanied by very unequal distribution of assets and income. This means that at the dawn of the 21st century, Colombia still has appreciable levels of poverty.

This chapter analyzes the extent to which the poor population in Colombia has certain assets, the lack of which to a large extent is the cause of poverty. These diverse assets are grouped into four major categories: human capital, physical and/or financial capital, public capital and social capital.

The first category includes the amount of formal education, work experience and other forms of classification of manpower[2] that can strengthen the principal asset possessed by the poor, which is their capacity to work.

---

[1] The authors are economists with the Centro de Estudios Sobre Desarrollo Económico at the Universidad de los Andes in Bogotá, Colombia.

[2] The quality of human capital should be included, but unfortunately no information is available on this variable.

The chapter contains an analysis of labor participation, particularly in rela-tion to the poor. The second category includes possession or access to assets such as land, savings and credit, which are directly linked to the generation of income and other assets such as housing and electrical appliances that indicate the degree of a household's material well-being. The third category relates to assets or resources supplied by the state, which range from public services to justice and security. The fourth category of social capital has to do with the organization of individuals around certain values upon which assistance and solidarity networks are built.

Trends in Poverty

Poverty in Colombia as measured by the percentage of poor in the total population has followed a downward trend in recent decades. In the urban sector, the incidence of poverty dropped from 58.9 percent in 1973 to 11.3 percent in 1995. Information on the seven major cities is available from 1986. In that year, the incidence of poverty was 16.8 percent, declining to 14.2 percent in 1995. In the rural sector, the improvement is even greater, falling from 88.4 percent in 1973 to 31.5 percent in 1995.

These measurements reveal great progress in the state's provision of certain goods (public services, education, low-cost housing, etc.).

Table 5.1 presents estimates of poverty taken from studies on Colom-bia. While they all show moderate drops in the national incidence of pov-erty, there are differences in the amount of the reduction and in the initial incidence levels.[3] At the national level, Londoño (1996a) presents the most favorable decline in poverty: from 53 percent in 1971, poverty fell to 32 per-

---

[3] This is because the methodology used varies from study to study. The estimates in Londoño (1996) were based on the poverty line of US$2/person per day of 1985 used in comparative international studies, converted to pesos with purchasing power parity for Colombia. The World Bank (1996) studies used the poverty line estimated by Colombia's Departamento Administrativo Nacional de Estadística (DANE) for the urban and rural sectors, multiplied by two. The line was updated by taking into account inflation of food prices for the low-income urban population. The Nina (1997) estimates used the DANE poverty line for rural and urban sectors, updated for the inflation of food prices for the low-income urban stratum. The esti-mates by Ocampo et al. (1998) were based on the DANE poverty line, updated in line with the price changes of a basket of food and other basic goods.

Table 5.1. Incidence of Poverty in Colombia
(In percent)

	1971	1974	1978	1988	1991	1992	1993	1994	1995
National									
JLL	53	45	34	32				28	
WB			52.5	46.9	44.6	45.7			
EN			58.1	54	56.5	54.6	55.2	53.2	53.8
JAO			57.7		58.5	57	56.4	53.4	52.5
Urban									
EN			48.3	44.3	47.3	45.4	43.6	42.5	42.5
JAO			54.5	51.2	50.2	41.7	39.8	40.1	39.2
7 cities									
WB			38.9	32.4	31.1	32.1			
EN			48.1	46.3	44.4	42.8	27.4	28.8	29.1
JAO				40.4	40.5	40.1	31.6	32.5	31.6
Rural									
WB			69.9	66.3	62.6	64.6			
EN			70.3	62.6	68.4	66.8	70.7	67.4	68.9
JAO			61.8	70.4	68.5	66.4	66.6	65.4	65

Incidence of Extreme Poverty in Colombia
(In percent)

	1978	1988	1991	1992	1993	1994	1995
National							
WB	23.6	18.7	16.9	17.7			
MJP	22.1		22	20.5	17.4		
Urban							
WB				9.9			
MJP	14.5	11.6	11.8	13	8.6		
7 cities							
WB	12.1	8	7.8	8			
MJP		11	9.5	10.5	5.5	6.5	
Rural							
WB	38.4	33.1	29	31.2			
WJP	39	36.3	36.8	37	37.2		

* MJP: Pérez (1995).
** JLL: Londoño (1996a)
*** EN: Nina (1997).
**** WB: World Bank (1996).
***** JAO: Ocampo et al. (1998).

cent in 1988 and to 28 percent in 1993. The World Bank (1996) shows a favorable but more moderate trend, starting from a higher level of incidence of 52.5 percent in 1978 and falling to 45.7 percent in 1992. The Nina (1997) and Ocampo et al. (1998) studies show smaller reductions, down from 58 percent in 1978 to 53 percent in 1995.

Urban versus Rural Poverty

By separating out the urban and rural sectors, these studies lead to the conclusion that the nationwide reduction in poverty is explained overwhelmingly by the decline in urban poverty, particularly in the seven major cities of Bogota, Medellin, Cali, Barranquilla, Bucaramanga, Manizales and Pasto. In contrast, the decline in rural poverty is quite small.

Table 5.1 further shows that the urban poverty rate fell from around 51 percent in 1978 to 41 percent in 1995. For the seven major cities, the World Bank estimates a fall from 39.9 percent in 1978 to 32.1 percent in 1992, while the Nina and Ocampo studies present a decrease from 48.1 percent in 1978 to about 30 percent in 1995. In the rural sector, there was modest improvement: an incidence rate of nearly 70 percent in 1978 fell slowly to 65 percent in 1995.

According to estimates for 1995, approximately 20.4 million people out of a total population of 39.2 million live below the poverty line. Of these, 12 million are urban and 8.4 million rural. The population living in extreme poverty is approximately 7.9 million, (3 million urban and 4.9 million rural). These estimates confirm that, despite improvements, the problems of poverty and extreme poverty remain critical in Colombia, particularly in rural areas.

Several studies corroborate this picture of gradual overall improvement, but with increasing disparities between urban and rural sectors. Londoño (1996) confirms that in the last two decades Colombia has made substantial progress in social and redistributive areas and poverty reduction. These improvements place Colombia above the international standard for countries with its per capita income and higher than many countries in Latin America. Londoño further notes that, measured by any of these indicators, poverty declined more rapidly in the 1990s than in the 1980s.

The World Bank (1996) also recognizes that Colombia has substantially raised the standard of living of its people. However, the World Bank notes that poverty remains critical, with high rates of malnutrition and infant mortality, particularly in rural areas and in specific regions (e.g., the Atlantic, Pacific and eastern regions). Although Colombia fares well in international comparisons, the severity of its rural poverty demands measures to increase rural income and reduce the poverty gap between cities and the countryside.

Ocampo et al. (1998) recognize the decrease in poverty in recent times but stress the deterioration in distribution over the last decade between rural and urban sectors, explained by the crisis in the agricultural sector in 1991 and 1992. The study points out that the 1970s represented the golden era of social improvement and poverty reduction, a result of forces in play for many years: a major reduction in excess manpower in the countryside because of massive migration to cities; a significant accumulation of capital in urban and rural areas; a considerable reduction in urban-rural wage differentials; and the lagged effects of educational policies applied in previous decades that improved human capital in Colombia. Finally, from econometric time series exercises, Ocampo et al. conclude that the incidence of urban poverty as defined by the national poverty line was reduced by economic growth, in spite of the negative effect of growth on income distribution. The real minimum wage also had a positive effect on poverty reduction, as did greater depreciation of the exchange rate. Increases in unemployment, on the other hand, exacerbated poverty.

Examining rural poverty, López and Valdés (1996) find very serious problems in Colombia, particularly among peasant farmers and landless farm workers whose access to basic services of education, health, extension and credit is below international standards. Contrary to conventional wisdom, landless farm workers are in a better situation than peasant farmers with respect to education and access to other services. And workers in non-farm activities have higher incomes and more assets than either of those groups.

López and Valdés conclude that investment in education in the Colombian rural sector produces very modest increases in income. They also find that access to land could have an important impact on income, which would help the poorest groups escape poverty. If this were the only instrument used, however, enormous transfers of land would be required. Finally, workers in nonagricultural activities are much more mobile than peasant farmers and even wage-earning rural workers, suggesting the need for policies designed to stimulate nonagricultural activities in an effort to combat rural poverty.

Changes in Poverty in Relation to Growth and Distribution, 1985-96

Table 5.2 decomposes changes in poverty using the Datt-Ravallion (1992) method. The first exercise for the national total shows that over 1978-95, poverty fell by 18.6 points. This is fully explained by the growth effect (20 points), which neutralized the negative effect of redistribution (3.1 points). A similar pattern is found by subperiods: from 1978 to 1991, the reduction in the incidence is 15.1 points, explained by the growth effect (16.8 points), which neutralized the negative effect of redistribution (2 points). Between 1991 and 1995, the reduction was 3.5 points, fully explained by the growth effect.

In the urban sector, poverty decreased by over 2 points from 1985 to 1996. This decline was fundamentally due to the growth effect (7.6 points), which neutralized the negative effect of income redistribution (7 points). The rest is explained by the residual (1.8 points).

For the rural sector, although the result for the period analyzed (1988-95) shows a decrease in poverty of over three points, the sources of the change were the opposite of the urban case. While the redistribution effect was positive at 11.6 points, the growth effect worked in the opposite direction, contributing to an increase in poverty of 8 points.

While the downward trend in poverty has continued in both urban and rural areas in recent years, the improvement in cities was due to the growth effect, which neutralized the negative effect of redistribution. In rural areas, on the other hand, the trend is fully explained by the positive effect of redistribution, which neutralized the negative effect of growth.

These conclusions confirm the divergence in the pattern of urban and rural development in the 1990s. Ideally, the decline in poverty would represent the combined result of growth in income and progressive redistribution, which is what occurred in the urban sector over 1978-88. Although there has been a decrease in poverty in the rural sector, a pattern based exclusively on redistribution is not sustainable and requires help from growth. On the other hand, the pattern observed in the recent period (1988-96) in the urban sector could feasibly continue, though it is not desirable from a social point of view.

Table 5.2. Points of Incidence of Poverty

Datt-Ravallion Decomposition, Colombia, 1978-95

	1978-91	1991-95	1978-95
Estimated variation	-0.151	-0.035	-0.186
Growth effect	-0.168	-0.036	-0.200
Redistribution effect	0.027	0.002	0.031
Residual	-0.011	-0.001	-0.017

Datt-Ravallion Decomposition, Urban Sector, 1985-96

	1985-87	1987-92	1992-96	1985-96
Estimated variation	-0.069	0.068	-0.022	-0.023
Growth effect	-0.024	-0.022	-0.037	-0.076
Redistribution effect	-0.048	0.098	0.014	0.072
Residual	0.003	-0.008	0.001	-0.018

Datt-Ravallion Decomposition, Rural Sector, 1988-95

	1988-92	1992-95	1988-95
Estimated variation	-0.004	-0.029	-0.033
Growth effect	0.036	0.161	0.080
Redistribution effect	-0.039	-0.076	-0.116
Residual	0	-0.114	0.003

Note: The quadratic parameterization of the Lorenz Curve was used.
Sources: Authors' calculations based on National Household Surveys (ENH); and Departamento Administrativo Nacional de Estadística (DANE).

Assets and Resources of the Poor

The National Socioeconomic Survey (abbreviated as CASEN in Spanish) and the Quality of Life Survey, both for 1993, were used to analyze poverty in Colombia. The analysis was centered on information from the CASEN survey on household spending along with a set of variables related to possession of assets and resources. Some variables from the Quality of Life Sur-

vey were also incorporated (alcoholism or drug addiction, and mistreatment by authorities) assimilable to the social capital of the province (*departamento*). Variables for public capital at the provincial level were also incorporated into the analysis from other sources.

CASEN Survey

Conducted by the National Planning Department in 1993, the CASEN survey is representative for rural and urban levels, as well as for provinces and major cities. Some 27,271 households were interviewed, 22,257 of them urban and 5,014 rural. The survey provides information on access to public services (water supply, sewerage, garbage, telephone, gas, electricity), health (membership in prepaid health schemes or social security, morbidity, medical consultations, etc.) and education (spending, private or state schools and years of education). The survey also contains information on household spending and income, as well as data on home ownership and its costs, rental payments,[4] and possession of household goods (television, car, washing machine, etc.)

For rural households, information is available on some assets, such as land ownership and its use, as well as on the coverage of specific government programs such as credit or infrastructure works (water supply, roads, schools, etc.).

Information from the survey was used to construct variables at the provincial level covering the labor market (unemployment rate, average wage); credit conditions for home ownership (percentage of credit from the public and private sectors); educational level (illiteracy rates, coverage in primary, secondary, university, etc.); health (percentage of members of social security); and infrastructure (construction of waterworks, roads, schools, etc.).

Quality of Life Survey

This survey was carried out in 1993 for 24,882 households, of which 21,213 were in urban areas and 1,669 in rural areas. It is representative for the cities of Bogota, Medellin, Cali, Barranquilla, remaining urban areas and the rural total. This survey used a series of variables at the provincial level of house-

---

[4] The value of rent was imputed to home-owning households.

hold living conditions (kidnappings, abuse by authorities, problems with alcohol or drug addiction, etc.). These variables were combined with the CASEN survey to broaden the analysis of poverty and per capita spending of households.[5]

Comparing the Resources and Assets of the Poor and Non-Poor

Tables 5.3a and 5.3b present the average value of a series of household socio-demographic variables, discriminating between the poor and non-poor. Table 5.3a separates the urban and rural sectors.[6] The analysis extrapolated the survey data to the national level; used the 1985 poverty line of US$2 per capita expressed in 1993 pesos using Colombian PPP; and used household spending per capita to classify the households.

According to this line and imputing the rental value, the incidence of national poverty was 32 percent, with an urban poverty rate of 20.4 percent and a rural poverty rate of 60.4 percent. Based on 1993 census data, the poor urban population is 5.2 million and the poor rural population 7.1 million, the rural poor accounting for 57.7 percent of the total poor population. The data confirm that rural poverty is in relative and absolute terms the most significant.

The urban and rural poor have larger households than the non-poor. In the urban sector, there is an average of 5.75 members in poor households versus 4.14 in non-poor homes, and in the rural sector, an average of 5.5 compared to 3.81. This result is linked to the higher fertility of the poor. The average number of live births in the urban sector is 3.48 among the poor, compared to 2.51 among the non-poor, and 4.34 among the rural poor, as opposed to 3.04 for the non-poor.

Poor households have a higher percentage of female heads: in the urban sector, 29.2 percent of poor households have a female head, compared to 23.5 percent of non-poor households. In the rural sector, the proportion is 18.1 percent (poor) to 15.4 percent (non-poor). This reflects the discrimination suffered by women in the labor market.

---

[5] The variables were "joined" by calculating values by province in the Quality of Life Survey, and that value of the variable was attributed to the CASEN households by province.

[6] In Leibovich and Núñez (1999), the distribution of some of these assets is presented by quintile.

Table 5.3a. Characteristics of the Poor and Non-poor (Urban vs. Rural)

	Urban		Rural	
	Poor	Non-poor	Poor	Non-poor
Number of households	1,095,115	4,267,302	1,269,912	831,338
Percentage	20.42	79.57	60.43	39.56
Average no. of persons in household	5.75	4.14	5.50	3.81
Number of live births	3.48	2.51	4.34	3.04
Households with women head (%)	29.2	23.5	18.1	15.4
Average years of education of head of household	4.02	7.33	2.25	3.92
% of population unable to read	11.77	3.82	24.67	12.02
% of population unable to write	9.35	2.84	19.90	9.20
Hours of attendance per week	25.36	26.19	25.51	26.32
Total spending (monthly)	1,166.85	6,817.21	265.83	1,313.48
Attends public school (%)	80.55	57.77	95.32	68.47
Attends private school (%)	16.21	35.64	3.48	9.36
Attends private religious school (%)	2.46	8.45	0.27	2.80
Attends private cooperative school (%)	0.46	0.88	0.58	1.19
Don't know (%)	0.29	0.24	0.32	0.12
Receive scholarship (%)	5.31	9.68	1.61	7.64
Total participation (%)	54.90	58.86	57.25	62.23
Unemployment rate (%)	9.74	5.61	1.99	2.00
Hours of work	45.13	47.40	42.71	46.51
Government employee (%)	5.01	11.91	2.51	5.72
Private employee (%)	52.63	49.87	38.54	42.17
Domestic employee (%)	8.95	4.69	2.17	3.11
Entrepreneur (%)	1.72	4.43	2.53	7.11
Self-employed worker (%)	27.99	25.01	37.64	32.32
Unpaid family worker (%)	3.67	4.06	16.58	9.55
Working in agriculture (%)	11.29	3.59	71.87	55.68
Working in mining (%)	0.66	0.59	1.53	1.74
Working in industry (%)	16.53	20.69	6.79	6.05
Working in electricity, gas and water (%)	0.50	0.89	0.12	0.24
Working in construction (%)	10.37	5.65	1.75	2.97
Working in commerce (%)	26.05	27.38	8.20	16.47
Working in transport and communications (%)	5.06	6.11	1.43	2.76
Working in financial services (%)	1.56	5.07	0.10	0.38
Working in other services (%)	27.94	29.99	8.17	13.68
Suffered illness* (%)	13.60	16.92	14.26	18.34
Absent from work because of illness* (%)	5.76	7.00	6.80	7.85
Member of social security or health scheme (%)	12.59	37.69	3.16	14.30

* Suffered from a dental or medical problem or an injury during the past month.
* During the past month.
Source: Authors' calculations based on CASEN and Quality of Life Surveys.

Table 5.3b. Characteristics of Poor and Non-Poor (Combined Urban and Rural)
(In percent)

	Poor	Non-poor
Access to credit institutions: Corporación de Ahorro y Vivienda (Savings and Housing Corp.)	5.47	28.53
Access to credit institutions: Fondo Nacional del Ahorro (National Savings Fund)	1.39	6.36
Access to credit institutions: bank	7.76	21.86
Access to credit institutions: other	21.18	18.15
Access to infrastructure: waterworks	7.72	5.46
Access to infrastructure: feeder roads	13.48	14.16
Access to infrastructure: rural electrification	8.30	12.18
Access to infrastructure: school	8.40	9.41
Access to infrastructure: health post	1.09	3.25

Source: Authors' calculations based on CASEN; and Quality of Life Surveys.

Human capital, measured by years of education, is quite different between poor and non-poor. The average number of years of education of urban adult household heads is 4.02 for the poor and 7.33 for the non-poor. In the rural sector, the difference is less pronounced: while the poor have 2.25 years of education, the non-poor have 3.92 years. Illiteracy rates (reading and writing) are higher for the poor than for the non-poor in both urban and rural areas. Obviously, with positive rates of return for education, this variable is fundamental for determining the probability of poverty. The average number of hours of attendance at school is higher for the non-poor. These families spend much more on tuition and other expenses associated with education than poor families. With respect to school transport, the majority of the poor go to school on foot, whereas a large percentage of the non-poor use school or public transport or family vehicles. These aspects can affect the quality of education and the capacity to assimilate, reproducing poverty in the new generation.

The urban and rural poor are largely educated in public schools, while private schools are more important for the non-poor, although not for the majority. This variable could serve as a proxy for the quality of education, since public establishments are associated with lower quality. This is an additional variable of human capital that influences the probability of being poor. A higher percentage of non-poor students receive scholarships in urban and rural sectors, evidence of the regressive character of this type of program.[7] Lastly, a higher percentage of students attending training courses such as the Servicio Nacional de Aprendizaje (SENA) and others, come from the non-poor.

Participation of the poor in the labor market is lower than that of the non-poor (urban sector: 54.9 percent versus 58.86 percent; rural sector: 57.25 percent versus 62.23 percent). The poor also have a higher unemployment rate, at least in the urban sector (9.74 percent against 5.61 percent); the poor and non-poor rates are virtually the same in the rural sector (1.99 percent against 2 percent). The poor also work fewer hours on average than the non-poor (urban sector: 45.13 hours a week versus 47.4; rural sector: 42.7 compared to 46.5).

Classifying heads of household by occupational position, in the urban sector government employees and entrepreneurs predominate among the non-poor. In the rural sector, the non-poor are generally government workers, private employees and entrepreneurs. Based on these results, a hypothesis can be formulated about certain imperfections in the labor market (government employees versus private employees) that could influence the generation of income with consequences for poverty.

Farming and construction predominate among the urban poor. In the rural sector, larger numbers of the poor than the non-poor work in agriculture. However, the percentage of poor households that own land is very similar to that of the non-poor.

In health, a higher percentage of illness and absence from work is found among the non-poor. This could mean that the non-poor have better access to health services than the poor. In fact, social security membership is very high among the non-poor compared with the poor in both rural and urban sectors.

Among the population with access to state family welfare programs (particularly childcare), coverage was greater among the poor, making this one of the few progressive state programs. A second progressive state program—access to credit for home purchase—was detected in the urban sector. State programs for waterworks, roads, electrification, schools and health posts did not discriminate in favor of the poor.

---

[7] The amount of the scholarship was not taken into account in the classification of households in the poor category.

Functions of Per Capita Household Spending

Using information from the surveys and variables obtained from other sources, the first econometric exercise estimated functions of spending per capita nationally and for the urban and rural sectors in terms of a set of socio-demographic variables, including proxy variables for human, public and social capital. Note that some variables in these exercises may in fact be endogenous, even though they are presented as explanatory of per capita spending. These exercises should be interpreted more as correlations than with a strict sense of causality.

Table 5.4 shows the results of the national model. The explanatory variables of per capita spending are socio-demographic relative to the head of the household (educational level, age, gender, migrant status and branch of activity); and to access of the household to public capital (credit, social security membership or a prepaid health scheme, and illiteracy of the head). In the regional context, they are socioeconomic variables of infrastructure and social capital (unemployment rate, home purchase credit, primary coverage, time in school, existence of waterworks and roads, level of alcoholism and level of abuse by the authorities).

For the national model, the percentage of the variance explained is 32 percent, a satisfactory level for cross-section analysis. The level of per capita household spending depends positively on the educational level, age (decreasingly, although not significant) and migrant status of the head.[8] The branch of activity where the head of household works also influences per capita spending, in decreasing order as follows: commerce, financial services, transport and communications, mining and oil, industry, construction, other services, public services and agriculture.

With respect to access to public capital, the variables of access to credit and social security (public or private) have a positive effect on per capita spending, while the illiteracy of the head has a negative impact. Among contextual variables, per capita spending is negatively affected by the unemployment rate in the region, primary health coverage, longer average schooling of children, and waterworks infrastructure. The negative effects of primary health coverage and waterworks infrastructure must be inter-

---

[8] See Leibovich (1996), who explains how migrants to cities do relatively well at assimilating into labor markets.

Table 5.4. Model of Spending Per Capita, Colombia
Dependent variable = Log (spending per capita)

Variable	Model 1	
	Coefficient	t
Socio-demographic characteristics		
Education of head	0.063	48.23*
Gender of head	-0.004	-0.36
Age of head	0.006	3.76*
Age squared of head	-5.48E-06	-0.34
Head migrated last 5 years	0.070	5.34*
Branch of activity of head**		
Agriculture	-0.072	-4.12*
Mining and oil	0.130	3.42*
Industry	0.072	3.82*
Electricity and water	-0.001	-0.01
Construction	0.056	2.52*
Commerce	0.234	15.15*
Transport and communication	0.171	7.69*
Financial services	0.179	5.32*
Other services	0.035	2.18*
Access to public capital		
Credit***	0.323	8.86*
Head member of social security	0.169	15.65*
Head member of prepaid health	0.456	15.37*
Illiterate head	-0.162	-10.36*
Context variables (province)		
Unemployment	-2.057	8.07*
Private credit****	0.187	7.58*
Primary health coverage	-0.306	-2.54*
Time in school	-0.018	-7.32*
Waterworks	-0.203	-2.33*
Road system	0.314	6.22*
Alcohol or drugs	-0.327	-1.15
Abuse	-7.798	-10.03*
Membership in Social Security	1.605	20.29*
Area	-0.041	-1.73
Constant	9.716	73.76*
Number of observations	24,234	
F	409.69	
Prob > F	0.0000	
R²	0.3215	
R² Adjusted	0.3208	

* Coefficient significant at 95%.

**The reference branch is financial services.

***Credit for microenterprises from SENA or agricultural credit from Caja Agraria, Banco Ganadero and/or Banco Cafetero.

**** Percentage of credits for housing granted by private sector.

Source: Authors' calculations based on CASEN and Quality of Life Surveys.

preted as the result of state action in these fields in the most backward regions. Access to private credit, the road system and higher rates of social security membership have a positive effect on per capita spending. In the area of social capital, alcoholism and abuse by the authorities have a negative influence on spending. Finally, per capita spending in rural areas is 4.1 percent lower than in urban areas.

Table 5.5 presents the results of the urban model. The explained percentage of the variance of the dependent variable is 25.7 percent. Note that most of the variables presented in the previous model maintained their significance, and the sign of the effect was similar. Moreover, home ownership is negatively associated with per capita spending, indicating that the poor have a high probability of being owners. Dummy variables for the major cities were also introduced. Their coefficients indicate the differential effect of each one on per capita spending with respect to the rest of the urban sector, finding the positive fixed effect of Medellin on the other cities.

Table 5.6 presents the results of the rural model. In this case, the explained percentage of the variance of the dependent variable is 26.6 percent. The significant variables, with the expected signs, were found among the socio-demographic characteristics of years of education of the head of household (+) and female gender (-). Moreover, a positive effect on per capita spending was found for access to credit for productive activity and land ownership with title, although their elasticity is low. Finally, contextual variables that were significant were the road system (+), illiteracy rate in the region (-), and social security membership (+).

Table 5.7 presents the results of two variants of the model of per capita spending estimated for the group of peasant farmers who own and work land, giving a more detailed analysis of the impact of land, credit and title deeds. First, the following are significant: the education variables of the head (+), female gender (-), road system (+), illiteracy rate in the region (-), alcoholism or drug addiction (-), and social security membership (+). In the first model, land has a positive effect with an elasticity of .025, and credit has a positive effect with a coefficient of .19, whereas the effect of land title deeds is not significant. In the second model, instead of introducing the credit variable, the credit variable multiplied by the logarithm of land is used to measure the joint effect on land ownership and access to credit, obtaining a value of 0.09 for this variable. That is, total elasticity over per capita spending of land and credit is 0.12. In this model, the effect of having a title deed is positive and significant.

Table 5.5. Model of Spending Per Capita, Urban Total
Dependent variable = Log (spending per capita)

Variable	Coefficient	t
Socio-demographic characteristics		
Education of head	0.059	42.99*
Gender of head	-0.008	-0.64
Age of head	0.006	3.55*
Age squared of head	1.20E-06	0.07
Head migrated last 5 years	0.074	5.21*
Homeowner	-0.025	-2.32*
Branch of activity of household head**		
Agriculture	-0.118	-5.65*
Mining and oil	0.101	2.42*
Industry	0.055	2.77*
Electricity and water	-0.019	-0.38
Construction	0.032	1.39
Commerce	0.216	13.43*
Transport and communications	0.157	6.85*
Financial services	0.160	4.73*
Other services	0.019	1.15
Access to public capital		
Credit for microenterprises	0.339	7.85*
Training courses head	0.103	8.19*
Head member of social security	0.155	13.93*
Head member of prepaid health scheme	0.442	14.75*
Illiterate head	-0.191	-10.07*
City		
Bogotá	0.070	1.67*
Cali	0.044	1.12
Medellín	0.131	3.25*
Barranquilla	0.039	1.01
Context variables (province)		
Unemployment	-2.599	-8.51*
Private credit***	0.182	6.29*
Primary coverage	-1.037	-4.42*
Time in school	-0.011	-2.34*
Waterworks	-0.282	-2.51*
Road system	0.316	5.42*
Alcohol or drugs	-0.330	0.84
Abuse	-8.235	-6.13*
Membership in Social Security	1.393	13.60*
Constant	10.370	47.44*
Number of observations	19,757	
F	207.20	
Prob > F	0.0000	
R²	0.2574	
R² Adjusted	0.2562	

* Coefficient significant at 95%.
**The reference branch is financial services.
***Percentage of credits for housing granted by private sector.
Source: Authors' calculations based on CASEN and Quality of Life Surveys.

Table 5.6. Model of Spending Per Capita, Rural Total
Variable dependent = Log (spending per capita)

Variable	Coefficient	t
Socio-demographic characteristics		
Education of head	0.080	10.30*
Gender of head	-0.032	-0.64
Age of head	0.013	1.66
Age squared of head	-0.000	-1.18
Head migrated last 5 years	-0.298	-4.51*
Land and credit		
Credit**	0.243	3.84*
Area land of household by title deed	0.034	10.66*
Context variables (province)		
Road system	2.042	4.41*
Unemployment	1.521	1.21
Writing illiteracy	-2.097	-5.25*
Primary health coverage	0.192	0.88
School building	-1.413	-2.13*
Alcoholism or drug addiction	0.172	0.19
Abuse	-5.400	-1.51
Membership in Social Security	2.241	3.73*
Constant	8.883	31.09*
Number of observations	1,598	
F	38.14	
Prob > F	0.0000	
R^2	0.2656	
R^2 Adjusted	0.2586	

*Coefficient significant at 95%.

**Credits from Caja Agraria, Banco Ganadero and/or Banco Cafetero.

Source: Authors' calculations based on CASEN and Quality of Life Surveys.

Table 5.7. Models of Spending Per Capita, Farmers
Dependent variable = Log (spending per capita)

Variable	Model 1		Model 2	
	Coefficient	t	Coefficient	t
Socio-demographic characteristics				
Education of head	0.080	19.993*	0.079	10.79*
Gender of head	-0.060	-2.083*	-0.003	-0.05
Age of head	0.008	1.871	0.006	0.76
Age squared of head	0.000	-1.383	0.000	-0.41
Head migrated last 5 years	0.045	1.268	-0.242	-3.91*
Land and credit				
Farmcre****	-	-	0.094	3.45*
Credit***	0.194	3.196*	-	-
Log (household land)	0.025	9.263*	0.025	9.56*
Title deed for land	-0.033	-1.224	0.111	2.97*
Context variables (province)				
Road system	0.579	2.403*	0.994	2.52*
Unemployment	1.284	1.859	1.818	1.50
Writing illiteracy	-2.055	-7.977*	-2.132	-4.43*
Primary health coverage	0.218	1.532	0.411	1.98*
School	-0.223	-0.751	-0.219	-0.38
Alcoholism, drug addiction	-1.064	-2.029*	-0.775	-0.88
Abuses	-2.298	-1.483	0.537	1.16
Membership in Social Security	2.106	7.112*	2.623	4.42*
Constant	9.113	59.014*	8.765	33.84*
Number of observations	4,484		1,694	
F	78.15		36.76	
Prob > F	0.0000		0.0000	
R²	0.2187		0.2596	
R² Adjusted	0.2159		0.2526	

*Coefficient significant at 95%.

**D1farmi = (quintile i = 1, quintile i = 0) *log (land per capita).
***Credits from Caja Agraria, Banco Ganadero and/or Banco Cafetero.
****Farmcre = (credit = 1, no credit = 0) *log (land per capita).
*****Difc = D1farmi *(credit = 1, no credit = 0).

Source: Authors' calculations based on CASEN and Quality of Life Surveys.

Logit Functions of Poverty

Logit functions corresponding to the functions of per capita spending were estimated to determine the influence of socio-demographic household variables of infrastructure and public and social capital on the probability of being poor. Using the results of these estimates, a series of policy simulations were formulated to evaluate the quantitative effect of increased access to or possession of resources and assets by the poor on poverty reduction.

Tables 5.8, 5.9 and 5.10 present the results obtained at the national level for the urban and rural sectors. Table 5.11 presents the results of the logit model for peasant farmers in two variants.

On the national model, the pseudo R^2 is .19, and the coefficients of the explanatory variables were significant at 95 percent, with the education, age and immigrant status of the head of household having an impact that reduced the probability of being poor. Those who work in agriculture have the highest probability of being impoverished, while workers in financial services have the lowest probability. In terms of access to public capital, the variables that reduce the probability of being poor are access to credit and social security membership (public or private), while being illiterate increases the probability of being poor. The contextual variables that help to reduce poverty are private home credit, road systems and social security membership, while those that foster poverty are the unemployment rate in the region, children's distance from school, and mistreatment by the police. Finally, living in a city rather than the country reduces the probability of being poor by 20 percent.

In the results of the urban model (Table 5.9), the pseudo R^2 is 0.14 and the significant variables that contribute to decreasing the probability of poverty are education, age and migrant status of the household head, and nonagricultural work. In terms of public capital, access to credit, training courses, and social security membership have a favorable effect on poverty reduction. Finally, the contextual variables that contribute to poverty reduction are access to credit for home purchase, road systems and social security membership. In contrast, the unemployment rate, primary health coverage, and mistreatment by the police contribute to increased poverty.

In the rural model, the effects on the probability of being poor are as follows: education of head of household (-), immigrant status (-), access to credit to finance productive activity (-), size of the land worked with title deed (-), illiteracy in the region (+), and social security membership in the region (-).

Table 5.8. National Logit Model
Dependent variable = In poverty (SI = 1, NO = 0)

Variable	Coefficient	z
Socio-demographic characteristics		
Education of head	-0.173	-31.74*
Gender of head	-0.026	-0.65
Age of head	-0.014	-2.51*
Age squared of head	0.000	0.26
Head migrated last 5 years	-0.174	-3.61*
Branch of activity of household head**		
Agriculture	0.272	4.55*
Mining and oil	-0.468	-3.36*
Industry	-0.166	-2.51*
Electricity and water	0.122	0.68
Construction	-0.122	-1.62
Commerce	-0.612	-11.31*
Transport and communications	-0.528	-6.55*
Financial services	-0.675	-4.05*
Other services	-0.066	-1.18
Access to public capital		
Credit***	-0.746	-5.61*
Head member of Social Security	-0.714	-17.19*
Head member of prepaid health scheme	-1.298	-6.57*
Head illiterate	0.321	5.89*
Context variables (province)		
Unemployment	4.873	5.23*
Private credit****	-0.544	-6.13*
Primary health coverage	0.635	1.49
Time in school	0.035	3.84*
Waterworks	0.349	1.084
Road system	-1.190	-6.57*
Alcohol or drugs	-1.572	-1.53
Abuses	21.010	7.58*
Membership in Social Security	-3.584	-11.87*
Area	0.206	2.51*
Constant	0.8620084	1.852*
Number of observations	24,285	
Chi²	6236.69	
Prob > Chi²	0.0000	
Pseudo R²	0.1947	
Log likelihood	12900.568	

*Coefficient significant at 95%.

**The reference branch is financial services.

***Credit for microenterprises from SENA or agricultural credit from Caja Agraria, Banco Ganadero and/or Banco Cafetero.

****Percentage of credits for housing granted by private sector.

Source: Authors' calculations based on CASEN and Quality of Life Surveys.

Table 5.9. Urban Logit Model
Dependent variable = In poverty (SI = 1, NO = 0)

Variable	Coefficient	z
Characteristics of household		
Education of head	-0.167	-27.86*
Gender of head	-0.021	-0.49
Age of head	-0.017	-2.50*
Age squared of head	2.14E-05	-0.34
Head migrated last 5 years	-0.145	-2.69*
Own home	0.001	0.03
Branch of activity of household head**		
Agriculture	0.382	5.32*
Mining and oil	-0.474	-2.92*
Industry	-0.149	-2.10*
Electricity and water	0.145	0.78
Construction	-0.033	-0.42
Commerce	-0.577	-9.94*
Transport and communications	-0.498	-5.84*
Financial services	-0.643	-3.73*
Other services	-0.036	-0.60
Access to public capital		
Credit for microenterprises	-0.885	-4.67*
Training courses head	-0.281	-5.25*
Head member of social security	-0.674	-15.13*
Head member of prepaid health scheme	-1.297	-5.98*
Head illiterate	0.360	5.65*
City		
Bogotá	-0.093	-0.46
Cali	0.091	0.54
Medellín	-0.235	-1.43*
Barranquilla	0.044	0.31
Context variables (province)		
Unemployment	5.229	4.68*
Private credit***	-0.450	-4.29*
Primary health coverage	3.469	4.02*
Time in school	9.71E-05	0.01
Waterworks	0.955	2.24*
Road system	-1.538	-7.11*
Alcohol or drugs	-3.848	-2.63*
Abuses	29.308	5.99*
Membership in Social Security	-3.103	-7.73*
Constant	-1.240	-1.56
Number of observations	19,784	
Chi²	3588.63	
Prob > Chi²	0.0000	
Pseudo R²	0.1477	
Log likelihood	-0.524	

*Coefficient significant at 95%.

**The reference branch is financial services.

***Percentage of housing credits granted by the private sector.

Source: Authors' calculations based on CASEN and Quality of Life Surveys.

Table 5.10. Total Rural Logit Model
Dependent variable = In poverty (SI = 1, NO = 0)

Variable	Coefficient	z
Socio-demographic characteristics		
Education of head	-0.207	-14.90*
Gender of head	0.110	1.13
Age of head	0.001	0.10
Age squared of head	-6.12E-05	-0.47
Head migrated last 5 years	-0.289	-2.52*
Land and credit		
Credit**	-0.333	-1.79*
Title deed for land	-0.108	-6.96*
Context variables (province)		
Road system	-0.896	-1.16
Unemployment	0.772	0.33
Writing illiteracy	4.606	6.78*
Primary health coverage	0.126	0.27
School building	0.706	0.71
Alcoholism or drug addiction	1.953	1.14
Abuses	1.273	0.25
Membership in Social Security	-6.363	-7.03*
Constant	0.861	1.61
Number of observations	4,508	
Chi²	787.22	
Prob > Chi²	0.0000	
Pseudo R²	0.1371	
Log Likelihood	-0.549	

*Coefficient significant at 95%.

**Credit from Caja Agraria, Banco Ganadero and/or Banco Cafetero.

Source: Authors' calculations based on CASEN and Quality of Life Surveys.

Table 5.11. Farmer Logit Models
Dependent variable = In poverty (SI = 1, NO = 0)

Variable	Model 1 Coefficient	z	Model 2 Coefficient	z
Socio-demographic characteristics				
Education of head	-0.205	-14.785*	-0.211	-7.643*
Gender of head	0.116	1.191	-0.063	-0.335
Age of head	-0.004	-0.277	-0.007	-0.26
Age squared of head	0.000	-0.191	0.000	0.058
Head migrated last 5 years	-0.289	-2.499*	0.458	1.781
Land and credit				
Farmcre****	-	-	-0.298	-2.992*
Credit***	-0.479	-2.518*	-	-
Log (household land)	-0.119	-7.766*	-0.130	-7.63 *
Title deed for land	0.309	3.341*	-0.148	-1.062
Context variables (province)				
Road system	-1.524	-1.929*	-3.475	-2.39 *
Unemployment	0.618	0.257	2.467	0.514
Writing illiteracy	6.108	7.103*	8.090	4.463*
Primary health coverage	-0.204	-0.437	-1.220	-1.638
School building	0.985	0.990	2.521	1.173
Alcoholism or drug addiction	0.588	0.333	-1.058	-0.313
Abuses	-4.338	-0.825	-17.521	-1.438
Membership in Social Security	-5.280	-5.540*	-4.560	-2.230*
Constant	1.240	2.417*	2.426	2.519*
Number of observations	4,508		1,694	
Chi²	808.70		343.56	
Prob > Chi²	0.0000		0.0000	
Pseudo R²	0.1409		0.1698	
Log likelihood	2465.9815		839.85213	

*Coefficient significant at 95%.
**D1farmi = (quintile i = 1, quintile i = 0) *log (land per capita).
***Credits from Caja Agraria, Banco Ganadero and/or Banco Cafetero.
****Farmcre = (credit = 1, no credit = 0) *log (land per capita).
*****Difc = D1farmi *(credit = 1, no credit = 0).
Source: Authors' calculations based on CASEN and Quality of Life Surveys.

The logit models for peasant farmers confirm the probability that poverty declines with years of education of the head of household and immigrant status. More land per capita helps to reduce poverty, as does access to credit for production. The contextual variables that influence the probability of poverty are the road system (-), illiteracy (+), and social security membership (-).

Access of the Poor to Labor Markets

The average rate of participation in the labor force for poor men and women is lower than that for the non-poor. This may influence poverty, but as participation is an endogenous variable, it is important to define its determinants for both men and women in urban and rural areas.

Following Ribero (1997), logit models were specified for labor participation for the urban and rural sectors, differentiating between men and women. The explanatory variables of labor participation are position in the household (whether or not the person is the head of the household), age and age squared, educational level, number of children under 5, ages 6-11 and ages 12- 17, spouse's total income, attendance at school and the person's non-labor income.

The participation rate for household heads is expected to increase with age and educational level. The number of children under 5 years old should have an impact on the participation of women, but its effect on men is not clear. The presence of older children in the household can stimulate the participation of other members because of the need for additional income to pay for their education. Clearly, the monetary income of the spouse and incomes of non-labor origin reduce participation, as does school attendance.

Tables 5.12 and 5.13 present the results of the logit models estimated for the urban and rural sectors, separating men and women. In the urban case, men's labor participation responds positively to being the head of household, decreasingly to age, educational level and the number of children under 5. In contrast, participation responds negatively to the number of children ages 12-17, spouse's income (if any), school attendance, and non-labor income.

The labor participation of urban women responds positively to being the head of household, increasingly to age, educational level, and the number of children ages 6-11. In contrast, participation is affected negatively by

Table 5.12. Determinants of Urban Labor Participation

Variable	Men		Women	
	Coefficient	z	Coefficient	z
Cte	-2.51	-22.12*	-3.77	-38.45*
Head	1.28	21.04*	0.91	20.01*
Age	0.22	36.14*	0.18	35.34*
Ed2	-0.00	-41.03*	-0.00	-37.14*
Educ	0.05	8.875*	0.10	30.09*
Children < 5	0.15	3.27*	-0.14	-5.22*
Children (6-11)	0.03	1.18	0.05	2.57*
Children (12-17)	-0.07	-3.7*	-0.02	-1.99*
Totinc.cony	0.02	-3.99*	-0.06	-26.70*
School att.	-2.51	-50.98*	-1.38	-30.30*
Non-labor income	-0.15	-31.00*	-0.08	-21.04*
No. of obs.	30,529		35,114	
Pseudo R²	0.45		0.16	

*Significant at 95%.
Source: Authors' calculations based on CASEN and Quality of Life Surveys.

Table 5.13. Determinants of Rural Labor Participation

Variable	Men		Women	
	Coefficient	z	Coefficient	z
Cte	-0.70	-3.06*	-3.29	-15.88*
Head	1.03	7.57*	0.93	8.55*
Age	0.18	14.87*	0.11	10.69*
Ed2	-0.00	-18.11*	-0.00	-11.09*
Educ	-0.02	-1.9	0.12	10.77*
Children < 5	-0.02	-0.31	-0.12	-1.87
Children (6-11)	0.08	1.42	0.03	0.71
Children (12-17)	-0.04	1.0	0.02	0.69
Totinc.cony	-0.08	-6.72*	-7.00E-02	-10.84*
School att.	-3.57	-27.87*	-1.81	-10.76*
Non-labor income	-0.11	-8.56*	-0.05	-4.86*
No. of obs.	7,912		7,038	
Pseudo R²	0.42		0.10	

*Significant at 95%.
Source: Authors' calculations based on CASEN and Quality of Life Surveys.

Table 5.14. Simulations of Labor Participation of the Poor

		Years of education		No. of children (<5, 6-12, >12)		Participation rate 1%		
		P	NP	P	NP	Observed	Simul 1*	Simul 2**
Urban	Men	5.10	7.50	(0.5,1.1,0.9)	(0.37,0.7,0.6)	65.41	66.92	65.65
	Women	5.00	7.25	(0.52,1.04,0.87)	(0.37,0.7,0.56)	31.84	37.26	32.09
Rural	Men	3.13	4.66	(0.6,1.28,0.99)	(0.35,0.65,0.49)	78.35	77.9	78.3
	Women	3.12	4.86	(0.62,1.3,0.92)	(0.38,0.68,0.48)	20	23.88	19.9

* Poor with average education of non-poor.
** Poor with age distribution of children of non-poor.
Source: Authors' calculations.

the number of children under 5 and from 12-17, spouse's income (if any), school attendance, and non-labor income.

For the rural sector, men's labor participation is affected positively by being the head of household and decreasingly by age. Surprisingly, educational level negatively affects participation, although its effect is small. Again, spouse's income discourages participation, as does school attendance and non-labor income. Children of any age have no significant effect on participation.

Finally, women's labor participation in the rural sector depends positively on being the head of household, decreasingly on age and on level of schooling. By contrast, children under five had a negative influence on participation, as did spouse's income, school attendance and non-labor income.

Table 5.14 presents the results of the labor participation of the urban and rural poor for men and women, assuming that the educational level of the poor were equal to that of the non-poor. For urban men, the participation rate increases from 65.4 percent to 66.9 percent, while the effect on women is more appreciable, rising from 31.8 percent to 37.3 percent, with similar changes in the number of years of magnitude for both men and women. The same simulation in the rural sector generates more modest and even contrary results. For men, participation falls from 78.3 percent to 77.9 percent; whereas for women, the rate increases from 20 percent to 23.9 percent. The conclusion is that raising the educational level of the urban and rural poor to the level of the non-poor would increase their participation rate. This does not guarantee they would leave poverty, but at least it becomes more probable, given that a significant proportion of these new participants would find jobs and thus improve household income.

The second simulation, presented in the same table, relates to the impact of applying the age distribution of children in non-poor households to the poor. Although these distributions differ significantly in magnitude, with a larger number of children in poor households, the impact on the participation of men and women would be very small in both urban and rural sectors.

Policies to Combat Poverty

Policy Simulations

Using the results of the logit models estimated above, simulation exercises show the possible effects of poverty reduction due to changes in certain exogenous or predetermined variables. The methodology quantifies the effect of improvements in points of incidence of poverty, which generates a value for the exogenous or predetermined variable for the poor that is the average value observed for the non-poor. This type of simulation gives a realistic notion of the different areas where efforts need to be focused to reduce poverty.

Table 5.15 presents the results in terms of the reduction of points of incidence of poverty at the national, urban, and rural levels, and for people who work in agriculture. At the national level, an increase in the average years of education of the heads of poor households from 3.4 years to 6.7 years (non-poor average) would reduce the incidence of poverty by 3.7 points. Obviously, achieving this depends on policies to expand coverage, which only have an effect in the medium term. Thus, it would be expected that a more aggressive policy of expanding primary education coverage to nine years, along with an improvement in educational quality, would decrease poverty over the years that followed.[9]

Targeting the poor with credit programs that support productive activities such as microenterprises or agricultural production would have a moderate effect on poverty reduction (.05 points), applying the existing cov-

---

[9] A specification where dummy variables are used for the different educational levels instead of years of education might generate weaker effects because the average years of education of non-poor households is in a segment in which the return on education is lower than that derived from a linear specification.

Table 5.15. Policy Simulations for Reducing Poverty (Reduction in Points of Incidence of Poverty)
(In percent)

	Sim1*	Sim2*	Sim3***	Sim4****	Sim5*****	Sim6******
National total	-3.72	-0.05	-12.82	-0.92	-	-
Urban	-3.92	-0.05	-13.23	-0.83	-	-
Rural	-3.99	-0.22	-4.65	-2.32	-1.99	-2.18
Farmers	-3.96	-0.22	-4.66	-2.08	-1.99	-2.37

* If poor heads of household had the same education as the non-poor.
** If the poor had the same access to credit as the non-poor.
*** If all the poor had access to credit.
**** If the poor had the same access to social security as the non-poor.
***** If the poor had the same amount of land as the non-poor.
****** If the poor had the same illiteracy rate as the non-poor.
Source: Authors' calculations.

erage of the non-poor, which is very low (1.5 percent). However, if credit were available to all the poor who do not now have access to it, the effect on poverty reduction would be -12.8 points. The impact of an expansion of coverage of social security for the poor from 17.5 percent to the rate of 24.1 percent enjoyed by the non-poor could reduce poverty by 0.92 points.

The same table gives the results of the simulations for the urban sector. In this case, an increase in the average education of heads of poor households to that of heads of non-poor households (3.98 to 7) would reduce the incidence of poverty by 3.92 points. Guaranteed access to credit for the poor at the level of the non-poor has no significant effect, but again if credit were available to all the poor who do not have access to it, urban poverty could be reduced by 13.2 points. The effect of greater coverage of social security at the level of the non-poor would reduce poverty by 0.83 points.

The effects of the different simulations on rural poverty can be seen in the same table. The increase in the average years of education of the heads of poor households to the level of the non-poor (from 2.28 to 3.98 years) would reduce the incidence of poverty by 4 points. Access to credit at the same level as the non-poor (from 2.5 percent to 5 percent) would have an effect of -0.2 points on poverty. If all the poor had access to credit the reduction would be 4.7 points. The simulation of giving land to the poor at levels that the non-poor have it (a ratio of 1 to 3) would reduce the incidence of poverty by 2 points. A fall in the illiteracy rate at the regional level to the levels of the non-poor (from 18 percent to 14 percent) would reduce poverty by 2.4 points. Finally, enhanced access to social security (from 5.3 percent to 8.7 percent) would reduce poverty by 2.1 points.

Lastly, Table 5.15 shows the possible reductions in poverty among people who work in agriculture. The results are very similar to those obtained for the poor rural population. The increase in the average education of heads of poor households to that of non-poor heads of households would reduce poverty by about 4 points, increase access to credit by 0.2 points, increase access to land by 4.74 points, reduce illiteracy by 2.4 points, and provide greater access to social security by 2.1 points.

Conclusions

Although in the past few decades the incidence of poverty in Colombia has decreased, it remains a major problem that must be addressed by public policies. Using a poverty line of US$2 (1985) per capita, 20.4 percent of Colombians (5.2 million people) in the urban sector and 60.4 percent (7.1 million) in the rural sector were found to be living in poverty. Decomposition exercises (per Datt and Ravallion, 1992) show that in the last decade the minor improvement in poverty in the urban sector was explained mostly by growth, which neutralized regressive redistribution. In the rural sector, it was progressive redistribution that helped to slightly reduce poverty. Econometric exercises confirm that economic growth was an important factor in reducing urban poverty and was reinforced by public spending and economic liberalization. Factors that exacerbated poverty were inflation, unemployment and the real depreciation of the exchange rate.

There is evidence of a link between poverty and the possession of assets, particularly human capital as measured by the number of years of education. An increase in human capital helps reduce poverty in two ways. First, it has a positive influence on labor participation, with more income earners in the household. Second, the income of the employed rises because of higher productivity.

In terms of policy, access to credit is an important resource for reducing poverty because it enhances economic activity. The Colombian credit market is an imperfect market to which the poor have limited access. Policies that reverse this situation by creating opportunities to generate jobs could prove important in reducing poverty in both urban and rural areas. Social security coverage is another resource to which the poor have had little access. The significant increase in coverage under way should help to reduce poverty. Improved access to land by peasant farmers is another way to reduce rural poverty, but it can be costly. To be effective, it has to be accompanied by other resources such as technical assistance and credit.

References

Bernal, R., N. Cárdenas, J. Núñez, and F. Sánchez. 1997. *Macroeconomic Performance and Inequality*. Working Paper #1. Bogota: Fedesarrollo.

Birdsall, N., and J.L. Londoño. 1997. *Asset Inequality Does Matter: Lessons from Latin America*. Inter-American Development Bank Research Department Working Paper 344, Washington, DC.

Bourguignon, F. 1996. Equity and Economic Growth: Permanent Questions and Changing Answers. World Bank, Washington, DC. Mimeo.

Coleman, J.S. 1990. *Foundations of Social Theory*. Cambridge, MA: Harvard University Press.

Datt, G., and M. Ravallion. 1992. Growth and Redistribution Components of Changes in Poverty Measures. *Journal of Development Economics* 38(3): 275-95.

Fukuyama, F. 1995. *Trust: The Social Virtues and the Creation of Prosperity*. New York: Free Press.

Knaul, F. 1997. The Importance of Family and Community Social Capital in the Creation of Human Capital in Urban Colombia. Paper presented at the Congress of the Latin American and Caribbean Economic Association, Bogota.

Leibovich, J. 1996. La migración interna en Colombia: un modelo explicativo del proceso de asimilación. *Planeación y Desarrollo* 27(4): 47-66.

Leibovich, J., and Núñez. 1999. *Los activos y recursos de la población pobre en Colombia*. Inter-American Development Bank Research Network Working Paper R-359, Washington, DC.

Leibovich, J., and L.A. Rodríguez. 1997. Análisis de la evolución de la distribución del ingreso rural en Colombia (1988-1995). Universidad de los Andes, Centro de Estudios Sobre Desarrollo Económico, Bogota.

Lipton, M., and M. Ravallion. 1995. Poverty and Policy. In J. Behrman and T.N. Srinivasan (eds.), *Handbook of Development Economics*. Volume 3B. Amsterdam: Elsevier.

Londoño, J.L. 1996a. Brechas sociales en Colombia. Inter-American Development Bank, Washington, DC. Mimeo.

———. 1996b. Cambios en la distribución del ingreso, la pobreza y el desarrollo humano en las últimas décadas. Inter-American Development Bank, Washington, DC. Mimeo.

López, R., and A. Valdés. 1996. Determinants of Rural Poverty in Colombia.World Bank, Washington, DC. Mimeo.

May, E. 1996. *La pobreza en Colombia: un estudio del Banco Mundial*. Bogota: Tercer Mundo/World Bank.

Nina, E. 1997. Análisis de la evolución del perfil de pobreza y desigualdad, 1978, 1988, 1991-95. Misión Social, Bogota. Mimeo.

Ocampo, J.A., M.J. Pérez, and C. Tovar. 1998. Macroeconomía, ajuste estructural y equidad en Colombia (1978-1996). Macroeconomic Archives Document 79, National Planning Department, Bogota.

Pérez, M.J. 1995. La situación social en Colombia. *Planeación y Desarrollo*. July-September.

Putnam, R. 1993. *Making Democracy Work*. Princeton, NJ: Princeton University Press.

Ribero, R. 1997. Análisis temporal de funciones de ingreso y participación laboral femenina y masculina en Colombia. National Planning Department, Bogota.

Székely, M. 1996. *El ahorro de los hogares en México*. Series of Economic and Sectoral Studies No. 001, Inter-American Development Bank Regional Operations Department 2, Washington, DC.

Tenjo, J. 1997. Determinantes de la calidad educativa a nivel de estudiantes y de planteles. Centro de Estudios Sobre Desarrollo Económico, Bogota. Mimeo.

World Bank. 1996. *La pobreza en Colombia*. Bogota: Tercer Mundo Editores.

CHAPTER SIX

The Capital of the Poor in Costa Rica: Access, Utilization and Return

Juan Diego Trejos
Nancy Montiel[1]

Over the past decade, between one-quarter and one-fifth of Costa Rican families were estimated to be living in poverty, when defined as insufficient income.[2] This relatively high incidence of poverty persists despite moderate economic growth and Costa Rica's long tradition of social policies and programs to assist the poor.[3]

The income of families depends principally on the quantity and use of their assets and the returns on them. These assets include human and social capital. Poverty is associated with the insufficient accumulation or unprofitable use of the different types of assets. The objective of this chapter is to study the assets of the poor in Costa Rica, their degree of utilization, the returns achieved on them, and their impact on the capacity of families to escape poverty.

Household surveys contain the best approximation of poverty trends, providing precise estimates of its absolute and relative extent. To obtain the most consistent and complete measurements, two comparable surveys covering the last decade were used. The earliest available survey, which dates to 1986 and is an ad hoc survey taken by the Institute of Economic Research (Instituto de Investigaciones en Ciencias Económicas, IICE) on poverty

---

[1] The authors are economists at the Instituto de Investigaciones en Ciencias Económicas of the University of Costa Rica.

[2] For this concept of poverty, the official estimates (DGEC, 1997) and ECLAC (1996) are in this range, but those of the IDB (Morley and Alvarez, 1992) and the World Bank (Psacharopoulos et al., 1993) are systematically lower. The treatment of the income and poverty lines used explains these discrepancies.

[3] See Trejos et al. (1994) and Trejos (1995a).

caused by the economic crisis of the first half of the 1980s. The second is the 1995 Multi-Purpose Survey of Households (Encuesta de Hogares de Propósitos Múltiples, EHPM) which has been taken every year since 1987 by the Statistics and Census Service (Dirección General de Estadísticas y Censos, DGEC, 1995).[4] Both of these national surveys were adjusted to be consistent with population projections and distribution, and to be coherent with the estimates of family income from the National Accounts.[5] In 1995, imputations were also included for non-replies and omission of income items (e.g., rent was imputed for home ownership).

Table 6.1 summarizes the estimates based on two alternative poverty lines: the official line and an international line.[6] When applying the official poverty line, which is very close to the one used by ECLAC, the incidence of poverty is between 20 percent and 25 percent. When a homogeneous international line is used, the poverty indicators are almost half that amount, close to the level that the official lines consider extreme poverty. Although the changes are modest, both the incidence and intensity decrease, a tendency that is not clearly demonstrated by the depth indicator. This could mean that there have been no changes in the most deprived groups. In both estimates, the absolute number of poor families and individuals increases, with the exception of the number of people below the international line.

Following Datt and Ravallion (1992), Table 6.2 gives a breakdown of these base estimates into a growth effect and a redistribution effect. This

---

[4] A previous IICE survey (1983) was rejected because it did not contain information on assets and because the characteristics of poverty were influenced by the severe economic crisis that was just coming under control that year. Similarly, DGEC household surveys of the same period were not used because the concept of income was very limited (primary cash income) and the additional information was inadequate. As the surveys require an income adjustment due to under-declaration, the most recent survey (1996) could not be used because the information from the National Accounts for that year was not available. For data on assets that were missing or of lower quality, the 1986 IICE survey was supplemented by the 1988 Survey of Income and Spending.

[5] As the base surveys are not surveys of income and spending, measurement of income is less precise. This is particularly true for the 1995 EHPM. The income adjustments were by source.

[6] The official line, calculated by the DGEC, establishes differences by urban and rural areas with respect to nutritional requirements (calories), structure of food consumption and the Engel coefficient. The international line corresponds to the equivalent of US$60 monthly at 1985 purchasing power parity and makes no distinction by area, which tends to overestimate rural poverty. The estimates of poverty are calculated by comparing magnitudes per capita with no adjustment for equivalent scales or presence of economies of scale. Third, these indicators apply to data grouped with the World Bank's POVCAL program.

Table 6.1. Costa Rica: Alternative Estimates of Poverty, 1986 and 1995

Indicator	Official poverty line[1]		International line[3]	
	1986	1995	1986	1995
Poor families (thousands)	141.4	166.2	77.9	85.5
Percentage of total families	23.7	20.5	13.0	10.5
Poor individuals (thousands)	773.3	790.7	438.6	388.3
Percentage of total population	28.5	23.4	16.2	11.5
Global indicators (%)[2]				
Incidence (P0)	23.7	20.5	13.0	10.5
Intensity (P1)	9.5	8.6	5.3	4.8
Depth (P2)	5.5	5.4	3.2	3.3
Poor families in rural areas (% of poor)	65.8	64.9	75.4	76.7

[1] Poverty lines obtained from the structure of consumption in 1988 with area differences for nutritional requirements, and patterns of food and non-food consumption.
[2] Traditional measures of the Foster-Greer-Thorbecke series (FGT) and applied to families.
[3] Equivalent value to US$60 monthly in 1985 purchasing power.
Source: Authors' calculations based on IICE (1986) and DGEC (1995).

Table 6.2. Costa Rica: Disaggregation of the Change in Poverty by Growth Effect and Redistribution Effect, 1986 and 1995

Indicator[1]	Official poverty line[2]			International line[3]		
	P0	P1	P2	P0	P1	P2
Value of indicator (%)						
1986	29.4	12.0	6.6	16.5	6.1	3.0
1995	25.6	10.2	5.4	12.7	4.2	1.9
Total change	-3.8	-1.9	-1.2	-3.8	-1.9	-1.1
Relative structure						
Total change	100.0	100.0	100.0	100.0	100.0	100.0
Growth effect	117.4	110.9	103.3	109.0	99.0	93.2
Redistribution effect	-17.2	-13.6	-6.6	-13.0	-3.2	4.0
Residual	-0.2	2.7	3.3	4.0	4.2	2.8

[1] Traditional measures of the Foster-Greer-Thorbecke (FGT) series and applied to individuals.
[2] Used by the DGEC according to structure of consumption of 1988 and with area differences.
[3] Equivalent value to US$60 monthly in 1985 purchasing parity.
Source: Authors' calculations based on IICE (1986) and DGEC (1995).

decomposition is presented for the three indicators and for the two alternative poverty lines.[7] In all cases, there is a reduction in poverty that is largely explained by an increase in real income thanks to economic growth. While no global changes are perceived in income distribution,[8] the redistribution effect, although small, neutralizes in part the reduction in poverty attributed to economic growth in all cases except one. The combined effect shows an even smaller change and, in all cases except one, contributes to the reduction of poverty.

Characteristics of the Poor

Studies on poverty in Costa Rica confirm a sociodemographic profile of poor households that has remained virtually unchanged since 1980 (Céspedes and Jiménez, 1995) and is reproduced even when alternative methodological approximations are used, such as the method of unsatisfied basic needs (De los Ríos, 1988) or the integrated method of poverty (World Bank, 1997).[9] There is a predominance of poverty in rural areas, in large households because of the higher number of children, and in the growing number of households with female heads. Among the poor, entry into the labor market is early and less successful—particularly among men—because of low educational levels. Women also have low educational levels, but they participate less in the labor market (Trejos, 1995b). Poor urban and rural children have broad access to primary education and generally stay in school. However, their participation in secondary education varies widely by region and income stratum (Rama, 1994). This is not the case with access to health services, where a national system provides broad coverage that even reaches poor rural families (Taylor-Dormond, 1991; Sauma, 1993; World Bank, 1990).

The sociodemographic profile of poverty in Costa Rica shown in Table 6.3 suggests several trends regarding the assets of the poor. First, the similar numbers of household members of working age in both poor and non-poor

---

[7] These indicators differ from those presented in Table 6.1 in three respects. First, they relate to individuals and not families. Second, a national average is used for the official poverty lines.

[8] The Gini coefficient moves from 0.498 in 1986 to 0.496 in 1995.

[9] In these cases, some characteristics become tautological. For example, individuals who do not attend school or do not have adequate housing are poor by definition.

Table 6.3. Costa Rica: Sociodemographic Characteristics of Families by Condition of Poverty, 1986 and 1995

	1986		1995	
Indicator	Poor	Non-poor	Poor	Non-poor
Percentage of families	23.7	76.3	20.5	79.5
Composition of household				
Persons per household	5.5	4.3	4.8	4.0
Persons under 12 (%)	37.9	25.6	30.4	19.1
Persons aged 12 or over	3.4	3.2	3.3	3.2
Dependents per worker	3.7	1.7	3.4	1.4
Female heads of household (%)	20.2	17.0	27.0	19.1
Average education of head (years)				
Male head	4.4	7.0	4.9	7.8
Female head	3.8	7.0	4.6	7.4
Labor participation (%)				
Net rate of participation	38.4	51.8	37.0	54.4
Rate of participation of head	74.7	84.2	66.9	82.8
Rate of open employment	9.8	3.6	12.3	3.9
Access to basic services				
% of 7-12 year-olds who attend school	91.1	95.3	96.2	98.5
% of 13-17 year-olds who attend school	40.9	53.7	62.4	69.7
% of families with health insurance	71.8	83.2	80 4	86.4

Note: Uses the DGEC poverty line.
Source: Authors' calculations based on IICE (1986) and DGEC (1995).

families suggest that the differences in the endowment of human capital, as shown by the lower educational levels of the heads, are due to different individual possibilities of accumulation. Second, the possibilities to accumulate human capital seem to be improving among the poor, judging from the attendance rates of those under 18 at educational facilities, and by access to health services. Third, lower and decreasing participation in the labor market and higher and growing unemployment among poor people who enter the market reveal a problem in the use of the human capital that households accumulate. Combined with the larger number of children in poor households, this implies heavier pressure on the household's human, productive and social capital. Thus, even an average return can be insufficient to overcome poverty thresholds.

A classification of families into socio-occupational groups offers additional evidence of changes in the assets of the poor over the last decade. These groups were defined bearing in mind seven variables: condition of activity, occupational category, size and location of establishment, branch of activity, institutional sector and occupational group. Initially, 14 categories were specified, which were later grouped into six for greater statistical representativeness. "Farm worker" covers all workers in that sector. "Formal skilled wage earners" include technical-professional wage earners in the non-farm public and private sector. "Formal unskilled wage earners" include non-technical or professional public and private wage earners in establishments of five or more workers. "Urban producers" comprise entrepreneurs, including owners of microenterprises and self-employed technical-professionals. "Informal workers" include other self-employed non-farm workers plus wage earners in microenterprises. The "floating population" covers the unemployed, workers in domestic service, non-remunerated workers and non-pensioner inactive persons. The final group comprises inactive people with pensions or in retirement.

These groups differentiate relationships through the means of production (holding of productive assets), sectors of activity (technology and linkage with external markets that affect the return on assets), and endowments of human capital and their utilization. All these elements are expected to differentiate the risks of poverty.[10] Table 6.4 confirms that poverty is associated with lower endowments and less utilization of assets as well as lower returns on them. The families with working heads that record the highest poverty levels have heads who work in agriculture, particularly linked to traditional agriculture (principally basic grains). In 1986, these families accounted for about one-third of total poverty. For them, the asset of land is the determining factor, although the concentration of poverty in traditional agriculture suggests that return and quality can be important explanatory elements of the probability of poverty.

The other two groups with a high incidence of poverty are those linked to informal urban activities, and the floating population. The former has little

---

[10] This means accepting that the occupational characteristics of the head are a good indicator of household income levels. Although surveys in Costa Rica follow the criterion of self-declaration by the head, the results indicate that in about 90 percent of families, the head is the principal breadwinner.

Table 6.4. Costa Rica: Profile of Poverty by Socio-occupational Groups, 1986 and 1995

Indicator	Total heads	Farm worker	Formal wage earner Skilled	Unskilled	Urban producer	Informal worker	Floating popultn	Inactive pensioner
Population weight (%)								
1986	100.0	24.0	8.5	26.4	9.0	9.8	16.3	6.0
1995	100.0	17.3	10.2	24.6	10.5	14.1	14.9	8.4
Change	0.0	-6.7	1.7	-1.8	1.5	4.3	-1.4	2.4
Incidence of poverty (Po)								
1986	23.7	36.5	1.4	12.4	11.7	24.6	41.5	22.0
1995	20.5	34.0	2.1	10.5	7.9	19.8	45.8	16.2
Change	-3.2	-2.5	0.7	-1.9	-3.8	-4.8	4.3	-5.8
Contribution to total poverty (%)								
1986	100.0	37.0	0.5	13.8	4.4	10.1	28.6	5.6
1995	100.0	28.7	1.0	12.6	4.1	13.7	33.3	6.6
Change	0.0	-8.3	0.5	-1.2	-0.3	3.6	4.7	1.0
Decomposition of total change (%)								
Total	100.0	89.9	-2.9	21.5	6.9	-12.2	-1.8	-1.3
Within	46.4	18.6	-1.9	15.6	10.7	14.7	-22.2	10.8
Among	45.6	76.5	-0.7	7.0	-5.8	-33.4	18.5	-16.5
Cross	8.1	-5.2	-0.4	-1.1	1.9	6.5	1.9	4.3

Source: Authors' calculations based on IICE (1986) and DGEC (1995).

human and productive capital and the latter under-utilizes the scarce human capital it has. The contribution of these two groups to total poverty is substantial and still growing, accounting for almost half of total poverty in 1995.

Conversely, urban producers (including microentrepreneurs and self-employed workers with assets) with higher endowments of productive and human assets show a low and decreasing incidence of poverty. Non-farm wage earners in formal employment, particularly those with the most human capital, also record a lower incidence of poverty. Only wage earners in the formal economy who are unskilled or have low human capital make a higher contribution to total poverty because of their greater relative weight among the total heads of household. This group, however, obtains a higher return on its human capital because it works with a higher productive capital; thus the rates of incidence of poverty are about half those of informal workers and one-third that of farm workers.

Although the results are as expected, the disaggregation of the changes in the incidence of poverty (Po) by socioeconomic group provides additional evidence of possible changes in the assets of the poor. Table 6.4 shows that the reduction in poverty is explained principally and in similar parts by changes among and between groups, indicating that the result is due to reductions in poverty within each group and to movements into less poor groups. Combining all the effects, households linked to agricultural activities account for 90 percent of the total reduction in the incidence of poverty. A similar conclusion by Morley and Alvarez (1992) cited the fact that the Costa Rican farm sector produces tradable goods that are favored by open trade policies and price liberalization. This suggests that the lower incidence of poverty within this socio-occupational group could be due to improvements in the return on their productive assets, although much of their contribution to total poverty reduction is owing to the movement of workers into groups with a lower risk of poverty.

Rodríguez and Smith (1994) estimated probability models of poverty using the 1986 survey for the base estimates. Their results confirm those described earlier—that the probability of poverty is increased by lower human capital (education of household head), lower utilization (unemployment of the head), heavy pressure on household assets (dependence of children), and reduced access to public social capital (residence outside the Central Valley[11] or in rural areas). In households with a working head, these variables combine with others for a lower return on human and productive capital (temporary employment, informal employment, traditional agricultural activities and small-scale activities). The variable that is not significant is the education of the head of household's parents, which suggests a certain capacity to accumulate human capital among poor households.

Table 6.5 includes the estimates made in this study for 1995, which are similar to those by Rodríguez and Smith (1994) for 1986. Still, some differ-

---

[11] The Central Valley of Costa Rica, despite its small area, is where two-thirds of the national population and the principal non-agricultural activities are concentrated. It is home to the capital and the next three largest cities.

Table 6.5. Costa Rica: Logistics Models of Probability of Poverty, 1995

Variables associated with head's characteristics[1]	Total households			Households with employed head		
	Total	Urban	Rural	Total	Urban	Rural
Gender (1: female 0: male)	0.5102 (0.0760)	0.6724 (0.1283)	0.4478 (0.0952)	1.0714 (0.1158)	0.9510 (0.1848)	1.1939 (0.1499)
Central Valley (1: Central Valley 0: other)	-0.7114 (0.0667)	-0.4735 (0.1093)	-0.8576[2] (0.0939)	0.3547 (0.0897)	n.s.	-0.5123 (0.1230)
Education (years of education)	-0.1880 (0.0087)	-0.1854 (0.0148)	-0.1870 (0.0114)	-0.1572 (0.0114)	-0.2113 (0.0204)	-0.1441[2] (0.0143)
Level of economic dependency (dependents per person employed)	0.7007 (0.0204)	0.7653 (0.0396)	0.6768 (0.0239)	0.7980 (0.0258)	0.8360 (0.0505)	0.8061 (0.0307)
Employment status (1: employed 0: other)	-0.4737 (0.0702)	-0.5080 (0.1248)	-0.4641 (0.0859)			
Stability of employment (1: permanent 0: temporary)				-0.6078 (0.1097)	-0.8362 (0.2300)	-0.5437 (0.1251)
Formality of employment (1: informal 0: formal)				1.1730 (0.0776)	0.7803 (0.1476)	1.2347[2] (0.0928)
Agriculture (1: works in agriculture 0: other)				0.9605 (0.0820)	0.5913 (0.2347)	
Modern agriculture (1: works in modern agriculture 0: other)						0.9695 (0.1051)
Traditional agriculture (1: works in traditional agriculture 0: other)						1.3543 (0.1135)
Constant	-1.2863 (0.0832)	-1.6461 (0.1666)	-1.1913 (0.0975)	-2.8464 (0.1574)	-2.1208 (0.2916)	-3.2082 (0.1871)
Number of cases	9,529	3,522	6,007	7,447	2,713	4,734
Poor = 1	2289	553	1,736	1,443	306	1,137
Poor = 0	7240	2,969	4,271	6,004	2,407	3,597
Correct predictions (%)	80.8	86.6	77.3	84.9	90.1	82.2
Likelihood ratio test	2652	809	1636	2210	530	1527
Significance	0.0000	0.0000	0.0000	0.0000	0.0000	0.0000

[1] Standard deviations in parentheses. All variables are significant at 99.99%. Zone, age and age^2 are not significant.

[2] The null hypothesis of equality of coefficients between zones was rejected, as $Z = (\beta_1 - \beta_2)/((se_{\beta_1})^2 + (se_{\beta_2})^2)^{1/2}$

n.s. = not significant.

Source: Authors' calculations based on DGEC (1995).

ences are apparent. First, the gender of the household head acquires statistical significance and the presence of female heads increases the probability of poverty.[12] Second, the rate of economic dependence (dependents per worker), as an indicator of the pressure on human and productive assets, contributes more to explaining the probability of poverty than the simultaneous consideration of the rate of demographic dependence and the number of workers in the household. Third, the link to agricultural activities, modern as well as traditional, continues to increase the probability of poor households.[13] This suggests that agricultural activity provides a lower return on productive and human assets in comparison with other productive activities. Finally, residence in a rural area ceases to be statistically significant in the determination of the probability of poverty because of the greater explanatory power acquired by other variables in the model or their high correlation with other variables.[14]

Based on the most recent profile, it can be concluded that poverty is more prevalent among households with female heads, heads who have little schooling, heads with temporary jobs in the informal sector (usually in traditional agricultural activities), and heads with a relatively high number of dependents, as well as in families that reside outside the Central Valley. This suggests that the poverty of families is explained by the endowment of assets, human or otherwise, the pressure exerted on them, and their utilization and return.

Assets of the Poor

The resources or assets to which the poor have access can have a variety of different effects. They can improve the quality of life, expand productive possibilities and increase the accumulation of human capital. Such is the

---

[12] Households with female heads accounted for 20 percent of total poverty in 1986 and 27 percent in 1995, rising to 32 percent when indicators other than Po and P2 are considered.
[13] Modern agriculture includes export products (coffee, bananas, meat, sugar plus nontraditional products). Traditional agriculture covers the remaining activities, particularly basic grains.
[14] Although the incidence of poverty is falling in rural areas, it still encompasses two-thirds of poor households, and there is no sign of a convergence of incidence or intensity of poverty toward the values of urban areas.

case of housing and basic services, for example. Productive and human capital can enhance people's income generating potential and thus help overcome deprivation. Private social capital can also alleviate privation, while public social capital in basic social services can help break the intergenerational transmission of poverty.

The 1988 Income and Spending Survey (DGEC, 1988) allows for a comparison of a series of variables relating to resources or assets with the probability of poverty in the household.[15] Based on the presence of capital income, households with productive and financial assets are identified and the Székely (1996) methodology is used to estimate their monetary value according to average returns in the market at the time. A similar approximation is performed for homeowners based on potential rent. For both productive assets and housing, an additional qualitative indicator was constructed that reflects the differences in the relative quantities of productive capital held by the different independent workers by branch of activity, number of workers and location of establishment, and access to quality housing according to materials and relative size. For rural areas, land (access and area cultivated) and the value of livestock are considered as additional productive assets. Human capital is estimated as the sum of equivalent years of education of family members of working age. The relative wages of 1990 were used to establish the equivalent years of education. Private social capital is approximated by participation in social organizations and productive cooperatives and by income transfers among family members. Public social capital, such as access to physical and social infrastructure, is approximated by residence in the center of the country.

Table 6.6 summarizes the results of three models—one for the country as a whole and the others for the urban and rural areas—that associate the probability of poverty with access to resources and assets. The results are not surprising: holding assets and resources or having access to them reduces the probability of poverty. Some observations, however, are pertinent. Productive capital, as a booster of family income, is inversely associated with the probability of poverty. For the aggregate model, both access to the asset

---

[15] The results of this survey for incidence of poverty are similar to the base estimates (23.7 percent in 1986 against 22.8 percent in 1988), and the area differences are unchanged. Because it is a survey of income and spending, only minor adjustments are required.

Table 6.6. Costa Rica: Probabilistic Poverty Models Based on Assets, 1988

Variables[1]	Households		
	Total	Urban[2]	Rural
Value of productive capital	-0.000004	n.s.	-0.0000053
(colones)	(0.000)		(0.000)
Holding of physical capital	-0.6974	-1.8706	n.s.
(1: have 0: do not have)	(0.280)	(0.443)	
Holding of financial capital	-0.9635	-0.8956	-0.957
(1: have 0: do not have)	(0.291)	(0.492)	(0.360)
Value of livestock	-0.0000015	n.s.	-0.0000014
(colones)	(0.000)		(0.000)
Access to physical and social infrastructure	-0.317	n.s.	-0.434
(1: have 0: do not have)	(0.101)		(0.135)
Membership of associations	-1.1236	-1.0627	-1.3501
(1: member 0: not member)	(0.252)	(0.356)	(0.357)
Family assistance as transfers	0.255	n.s.	n.s.
(1: have 0: do not have)	(0.120)		
Access to quality housing	-0.1599	-0.1502	-0.1674
(0: no access 6: full access)	(0.042)	(0.079)	(0.052)
Own home =	1.2685	1.5523	1.3623
(1: have 0: do not have)	(0.135)	(0.249)	(0.168)
Value of own home	-0.000076	-0.000081	-0.000085
(colones)	(0.000)	(0.000)	(0.000)
Human capital per capita	-0.1778	-0.1734	-0.2001
(equivalent years of education			
per household member)	(0.013)	(0.021)	(0.018)
Constant	0.8718	0.8112	0.9545
	0.156)	(0.317)	0.181
Number of cases	3,909	1,568	2,341
Poor = 1	1,070	271	799
Poor = 0	2,839	1,297	1,542
Correct predictions (%)	77.9	85.1	73.9
Likelihood ratio test	1139	404	597
Significance	0.0000	0.0000	0.0000

n.s. = not significant. The following were not significant in any model: the qualitative variable of physical capital, value of financial capital, access and land use and participation in production cooperatives.

[1] Standard deviations are in brackets. All the variables are significant at the level of at least 97 percent, except holding of financial capital and access to quality housing in the urban area, at 93 percent and 94 percent, respectively.

[2] The tests for difference of coefficients between areas do not reject the null hypothesis that the coefficients are equal between areas for all the variables.

Source: Authors' calculations based on the DGEC (1988).

and the value of it reduce the probability of poverty, but in urban areas only access is significant and in rural areas only value. The indicator of relative access to productive capital was not statistically significant in either case.

The presence of financial capital, savings and time deposits can improve the generation of income by financing working capital for productive activities as well as new investments in productive capital. It is also an indicator of the saving capacity of the household, since it results from the generation of income in excess of satisfaction of basic needs. In the three models of Table 6.6, the holding of financial capital rather than its value is statistically significant in reducing the impact on the probability of poverty. For the country as a whole, as well as for rural areas, the value of livestock is associated with low probabilities of poverty. However, neither access to farmland nor cultivated areas appear to support a statistically significant reduction of poverty. This is because access to land is similar among poor and non-poor rural families, and the area cultivated is even larger among the poor. In part, this reflects the fact that non-poor families hold their agricultural land in the form of companies and not as family enterprises, and that the result has to be controlled for quality of land, type of crop and the technology used.

A larger stock of human capital, adjusted for the size of the household and particularly for the presence of children, is also associated with lower probabilities of poverty both at the national level and in rural and urban areas.[16] Using the capacity to generate primary or labor income for households as the estimated indicator of human capital improves the adjustment of the model, ceteris paribus, compared to the use of education of the head of household as proxy, although in most cases (90 percent) the head is the principal breadwinner of the household. This highlights the need to consider the capacity for income generation of the other members of the household in order to determine the probability of escaping poverty.

Housing is an asset that dramatically improves the quality of life of families, although its role in enhancing income-generating capacity is also important. First, it can be transformed into a productive asset for microproducers who use their home as a productive establishment. Second,

---

[16] Although the coefficient of the rural area is greater than that of the urban area, the difference is not significant, which could mean that the human capital per capita of households has an equal impact on poverty reduction in both areas.

it can help in the accumulation of physical capital when used as mortgage security, and help the accumulation of human capital because adequate physical/sanitary conditions support the growth of healthy children who can take advantage of a basic formal education. The indicators included offer similar results in all three models but in opposite directions. In particular, access to one's own home shows a direct relationship with the probability of poverty, a result that is perhaps a dominant characteristic among poor and non-poor families. In fact, 67 percent of poor families have their own home versus 69 percent of non-poor households. This result is also partly due to the fact that the quality of housing is not controlled. When the value of the home is included as a reflection of its quality, the result is as expected. As the value of the home also reflects a consumption decision, an indicator was constructed for access (ownership, rent or transfer) to quality housing (by type, materials and size relative to the number of members of the household). In this case, access to better quality housing reduces the probability of poverty, showing that access to assets can be more important than ownership as a means of escaping poverty.

The last variables included in the models approximate the impact of access to social capital. Greater access to social and physical infrastructure, known as public social capital, reduces the probability of poverty by increasing opportunities for income generation and making greater degrees of accumulation possible, particularly of human capital. As expected, the impact is significant for the country as a whole and for rural areas. For private social capital, social participation measured as membership in social organizations reveals an inverse relationship with the probability of poverty, which is statistically significant for the country as a whole and for each area. However, participation in productive cooperatives, with some presence in the farm sector, was not statistically significant. Lastly, the presence of inter-family assistance, as an indicator of social assistance networks, was directly related to the probability of poverty and only significant for the whole country. Since only families that received assistance are captured, and not those that provided it, the finding could suffer from a causality problem. That is, the presence of assistance does not increase the probability of poverty, but the presence of situations of privation increases the probability of receiving assistance from other households.

The results further show that, with small justifiable exceptions, the increased presence of assets and funds in households reduces the probability of poverty. Access to assets, although important, can be insufficient. Further study is needed on the use and quality of assets, restrictions on accumulating them, and returns on them.

Human Capital

In countries such as Costa Rica, where most people have some educational background, human capital is the asset to which the poor have greatest access.[17] Even the poor generally attend and stay in primary school because public social capital facilitates the accumulation of human capital by providing free education and health care, among other services. However, attendance is concentrated in primary education, while at other levels (secondary and tertiary) the possibilities of the poor decrease.[18]

What impact does this broad access to primary education have on the distribution of human assets among the different income strata? To answer this question, it is first necessary to define how and for which group human capital is measured. Since human capital is important in escaping poverty because it contributes to the generation of income, its measurement is confined to household members of working age, which in Costa Rica is over 12 years old. The simplest way to measure this asset is in terms of years of education completed, although when the household is the unit of analysis this measure loses relevance because it grants the same value to the marginal year of education, whether first grade of primary or the last year of university education. As each year of additional education has a different return in the labor market, which can be approximated by the average wage of individuals with the same number of years of education, the procedure is to use these wages, relative to the wage of workers with no education, as weightings to create a measurement of the household's endowment or stock of human capital. The result is defined as the sum of the equivalent years of education

[17] If only the education of the head is considered, 87 percent of poor households had some level of human capital in 1995 (at least one completed year of education). If the education of all working members is used, access to some degree of human capital among the poor rises to 96 percent.

[18] Although secondary education is provided free of charge by the state, supply is concentrated in urban areas and opportunity costs are greater for poor families.

Table 6.7. Costa Rica: Distribution of Educational and Human Capital, 1986 and 1995

Unit of analysis[1]	Years of education		Human capital[2]	
	1986	1995	1986	1995
Population aged 12 or over				
Average value	6.5	7.4	12.4	14.0
Gini coefficient	0.14	0.15	0.26	0.25
Coefficient change	0.25	0.28	0.50	0.48
Theil index	0.03	0.04	0.11	0.10
Households				
Average value per household[3]	20.8	22.0	39.6	44.4
Average value per person	4.9	5.6	9.7	11.7
Gini coefficient	0.10	0.13	0.22	0.25
Coefficient change	0.19	0.22	0.43	0.47
Theil index	0.02	0.03	0.08	0.10

[1] Arranged by family income per capita.

[2] Equivalent years of education according to 1990 relative prices.

[3] Of its population of working age (aged 12 or over).

Source: Authors' calculations based on IICE (1986) and DGEC (1995).

of the population of working age.[19] This indicator measures the physical endowment of the stock of human capital in terms of years of education rather than measuring its monetary value, and also avoids the problem of price changes in intertemporal comparisons.[20]

Table 6.7 presents indicators of the distribution of human capital according to both approximations. Three comments seem pertinent. First, there is a generalized, though small, increase in the average levels of human capital. Second, with relatively low inequality, this asset doubles when consider-

---

[19] The relative wages are for 1990, the intermediate year of the period under analysis, in order to use fixed weightings. For a better approximation of these relative prices, eliminating different impacts on education, the calculation is limited to full-time wage earners (47 or more hours per week) with five to 15 years of labor experience.

[20] The weighting used is equivalent to the wage premium for each additional year of education. A measurement of the monetary value of the stock of human capital, namely the discounted value of wage premiums due to education, can be found in Pritchett (1996).

ing equivalent years of education (human capital), revealing that the less poor strata have the highest probabilities of continuing secondary and higher studies. Third, although inequality seems to increase slightly in relation to years of education, this does not happen with human capital and distribution among individuals. This suggests that people from households with low per capita income are increasing their opportunities to form human capital. This does not, however, counteract the trend towards greater inequality when the analysis focuses on households.

If the distribution of human capital among families is not so unequal, no large differences should be expected between poor and non-poor households. If this is the case, the question of utilization is added to that of endowments. Table 6.8 presents data on average human capital among the poor and non-poor and their utilization. In terms of the average values of human capital, inequality is in fact important because the human capital of potentially active individuals in non-poor households is nearly double that of potential workers in poor households, although this relationship has been unchanged in the last decade. Since poor households have more children, the gap in terms of per capita human capital is greater: in 1995 the capital available in non-poor households was almost three times that of poor households. Changes in the composition of the households also produced a widening of differences between 1986 and 1995 in relation to total human capital per household or member.

Along with these differences in the endowment of human assets, there are also wide gaps in utilization of those assets. Although the degree of utilization of human capital tended to increase in the period, in poor households only about one-third of capital is used, whereas in non-poor ones this figure almost doubles.[21] This lower utilization of human capital in poorer households affects both genders, but particularly women. In poor households, the human capital utilized does not even reach 20 percent among women, although their average human capital is similar to that of men. Not only do non-poor households use human capital more, but an important part of the explanation of unutilized capital also stems from the fact that it

---

[21] Note that these concepts do not incorporate underemployment as another source of underutilization of human capital. If it is accepted that underemployment affects poor workers more, the gaps in the utilization of human capital are even greater.

Table 6.8. Costa Rica: Utilization of Human Capital by Income Strata, 1986 and 1995

Indicator	1986		1995	
	Poor	Non-poor	Poor	Non-poor
Average value of human capital[1]				
Per household	24.1	44.4	23.5	49.8
Per member	4.5	11.2	5.1	14.4
Per person of working age	7.3	14.3	7.9	15.6
Utilization of human capital (%)[2]	34.7	58.8	36.9	63.3
Men	57.7	76.9	58.4	79.1
Women	12.7	40.9	19.1	47.3
Human capital not utilized (%)	65.3	41.2	63.1	36.7
Unemployment	4.2	1.5	6.3	2.3
Accumulation[3]	18.4	15.8	19.2	13.1
Retirement[4]	0.8	2.8	2.8	4.8
Other causes	41.9	21.1	34.8	16.5
Men	7.5	1.5	4.7	1.4
Women	34.4	19.6	30.1	15.1

[1] Equivalent years of education according to 1990 relative prices.
[2] Human capital of the employed/human capital of the population of working age.
[3] Members of the household who are studying.
[4] Pensioners and the retired.

Source: Authors' calculations based on IICE (1986) and DGEC (1995).

is still in the process of being accumulated (about one-third). In poor households, where efforts to accumulate are important and more human capital is committed to it, most of the non-utilization of human capital is related to unemployment and other causes. Thus, half the unutilized human capital in poor households is concentrated among women who are not studying or seeking work, or have withdrawn from work. These women are generally engaged in work in the home.

Potential Impact of Human Capital

Such marked differences in the endowment of human capital and its utilization between poor and non-poor households are most likely also accompanied by differences in the returns obtained by effectively utilized human capital. The question that then arises is what probabilities would poor households have of leaving poverty if they used their human capital more, with a higher return? For the answer, the potential labor income of household members of working age was estimated from their educational characteristics and work experience.[22] This potential income is produced by an equation of labor or primary income for each working member of the household. The equation incorporates the following explanatory variables: level of education, potential experience, degree of formality of employment (1 is informal), type of access to the labor market (1 is not a wage earner) and the "lambda" variable which corrects for selection bias, as proposed by Heckman (1979). This last variable comes from a model of the probability of participation in the labor market and incorporates as explanatory variables the age of the individual, relationship with the head of household, level of education and area of residence. Both models make separate estimates for men and women, and their results are shown in Table 6.9.

From these models and the coefficients of the variables relative to education, labor experience and the constant of the labor income equations, an estimate was calculated of the potential labor income of each working-age household member attributable to his or her human capital for 1995. The imputation of potential labor income excluded only inactive people over 65 years of age—who may have high potential experience but no real options in the labor market—and inactive people with severe disabilities. To reconstruct potential household labor or primary income, this potential income can be added to other sources such as current transfers and property rents. The result is an estimate of total potential family income.

To separate the impact of higher return from the impact attributed to greater utilization of human capital, several potential sources of family income were estimated. First, only the potential labor income of the employed person was considered. Since this potential income reflects the average return from human capital, variations in the incidence of poverty will cause a

---

[22] Labor experience is a proxy for age and educational level (age - education - 6). When the individual has less than six years' education, the estimate is age minus 12, which avoids overestimation. Similarly, if the individual is over 65, this limit is maintained as the upper limit in the age variable.

Table 6.9. Costa Rica: Models Utilized to Estimate Potential Labor Income, 1995

Variables	Males	Females
Participation model[1]		
Education	0.0552	0.0393
(years completed)	(0.0008)	(0.0007)
Age	0.0065	-0.0002
	(0.0002)	(0.0001)
Relationship with head	0.2570	0.2405
(1: Head 0: Other)	(0.0094)	(0.0114)
Zone	-0.0908	-0.0244
(1: Urban 0: Rural)	(0.0084)	(0.0079)
Cases (N)	14.527	14.633
With participation=1	11.100	4.490
With participation=0	3.427	10.143
Correct predictions (%)	74.63	69.82
Likelihood ratio test	1.795,37	809.78
Significance	0.0000	0.0000
Income model[2]		
Education	0.0687	0.1735
(years completed)	(0.0093)	(0.0143)
Experience	-0.0165	0.0232
(age-schooling-6)	(0.0019)	(0.0040)
Experience[2]	0.0003	0.0004
(experience squared)	(0.0000)	(0.0001)
Formality	-1.4997	-1.6700
(1: informal 0: formal)	(0.0657)	(0.1189)
Category	1.4766	2.0287
(1: unsalaried 0: salaried)	(0.0774)	(0.1475)
Lambda[3]	-2.5662	-1.2641
	(0.1331)	(0.2186)
Number of cases	14,527	14,633
R^2	0.1684	0.1385
Adjusted R^2	0.1680	0.1374
Standard deviation	3.2280	3.4253
F-statistic	374.3900	120.1500

[1] The dependent variable is participation (1: participates 0: does not participate).

[2] The dependent variable is the natural logarithm of hourly labor income. The variables are significant at the level of at least 95 percent, with the exception of women's age.

[3] Correction for selection bias using a two-stage Heckman procedure, which estimates probit models.

Source: Authors' calculations based on DGEC (1995).

"return" effect of the currently employed. Second, the actual or original income of the employed person was maintained and added to the potential income of the unemployed ones. This isolates the "utilization" effect. To avoid overestimating the impact of greater utilization, the potential income of all unemployed and inactive persons was not considered because it would imply accepting zero unemployment and 100 percent net activity and employment. Instead, an approximation was estimated of the levels of unemployment and labor participation shown by the non-poor households in each area. This was done by including 69 percent of the unemployed and 27 percent of inactive people in poor households as receivers of potential labor income, and accepting that their employment rate (workers over the population of working age) rises from 37 percent initially to 57 percent. Greater participation among the members of poor households was simulated by considering as part of family income 69 percent of the potential income of the unemployed (75 percent in urban and 65 percent in rural areas) and 27 percent of the potential income of the inactive (26 percent in urban and 28 percent in rural areas), excluding individuals over 65 years old or the disabled.[23] Finally, consideration was given to the combined effect of a higher return among the employed and greater utilization of the human capital of the household.

Table 6.10 presents the results for 1995, disaggregating by area of residence. The upper section of the table summarizes the global impact of each effect on the estimates of the incidence of poverty. Starting from the base estimates of an incidence of 20.5 percent, a higher return on the human capital presently utilized would reduce poverty to less than half (to 8.3 percent), while greater utilization of human capital, through the absorption of unemployed or inactive members, reduces incidence by about one-third (to 13.2 percent). The combined impact of both effects provokes a potential reduction in poverty of 72 percent, bringing the incidence to levels close to 6 percent. The return effect has the greatest impact on poor families in rural areas, while the utilization effect leads to a relatively larger reduction of poverty in urban areas. Both differential effects tend to be neutralized because the combined result produces similar reductions of poverty in both areas.

---

[23] This procedure reproduces the average increase in income arising from greater participation for poor households taken from a random selection, although there may be differences by household. This also avoids the need to incorporate additional assumptions on hours worked.

Table 6.10. Costa Rica: Impact of Human Capital on Poverty, 1995

Indicator	Country	Urban	Rural
Incidence of poverty (Po)			
Initial	20.5	14.1	27.1
With higher return	8.3	6.4	10.2
With more utilization	13.2	7.8	18.7
With more return and utilization	5.8	3.7	7.9
Decomposition of poverty (% of total)			
Poor families	20.5	14.1	27.1
By endowment	5.8	3.7	7.9
Only by return	2.5	2.6	2.3
Only by utilization	7.4	4.1	10.8
By return or utilization	4.8	3.7	6.0
Distribution of poor families (%)			
Poor families	100.0	100.0	100.0
Endowment	28.2	26.4	29.1
Only by return	12.1	18.6	8.7
Only by utilization	36.1	29.0	39.9
By return or utilization	23.6	26.0	22.4

Source: Authors' calculations based on DGEC (1995).

The second section of Table 6.10 presents a breakdown of the poor that interprets the preceding figures in the opposite direction, that is, by identifying families who remain in poverty despite higher returns or greater utilization. Of the families who are initially poor, 5.8 percent remain in that situation despite improving their return on and utilization of human capital.[24] These families, which account for a little over one-quarter of total families in poverty, suffer from an insufficient endowment of human capital. The rest of the poor families could potentially escape from the poverty thresh-

---

[24] This percentage is 3 percent when all the potential income of unemployed and inactive persons is considered.

olds by achieving a higher return on their utilized human capital, through greater utilization of their capital, or through a combination of both strategies. Not all families in this group, however, have the same options: 24 percent (equivalent to 4.8 percent of all families in the country) could escape from poverty by either of the two strategies. A much lower percentage—12 percent of poor families or 2.5 percent of the total—could only escape poverty by greater utilization of their human capital (they are poor because of return, not utilization). The largest group (36.1 percent of poor families) could only escape by obtaining a higher return on their presently utilized human capital. (They cannot leave the poverty threshold by utilizing more capital.) These results suggest that poverty is not solely associated with a problem of insufficient endowment of assets, particularly human capital. Therefore, more detailed study is needed of the determinants of the returns, as well as the utilization of and restrictions on the accumulation of human capital.

The low utilization of the human capital of poor households described above is explained by the scant participation of women in the labor market. Although this low level of participation is typical among all Costa Rican women, it is accentuated in poor households. The figures for the country indicate that the net rate of male participation is 76 percent, whereas the female rate is only 31 percent (based on averages for 1987-96). Furthermore, the female rate has increased only 0.6 percent annually in the last 10 years and is even lower among poor households. The data for 1995 indicate that the rate of female participation among poor households is about 43 percent lower than that of non-poor households. These differences remain even for women who are heads of household. Women participate less in remunerated activities and are the most affected by unemployment, especially if they are poor women. The open unemployment rate for women is around 6.6 percent, compared with 4.2 percent for men (1987-96 averages). The unemployment rate among active poor women is more than three times the rate for non-poor women.[25]

---

[25] Cultural factors, such as the role traditionally assigned to women, undoubtedly influence women's labor participation. But it is clear that other more economic variables affect these decisions. See the working paper version of this chapter (Trejos and Montiel, 1999).

Why Do Some People Accumulate less Human Capital than Others?

There are a variety of reasons why young people stop accumulating human capital while of school age. Table 6.11 summarizes rates of and reasons for non-attendance of the secondary-age population (13 to 17). The rates were about 50 percent in 1986, falling in 1996 to under 40 percent—still high for the country's level of social development. By 1996, the attendance of young people from poor households had reached levels that were similar to those of non-poor youth 10 years earlier. In 1986, the three most common reasons for nonattendance for both poor and non-poor were similar: "have to work" or "have to do household chores;" "cannot pay for studies" and "not interested in formal learning." Problems associated with the family, however, are more important for the non-poor than for the poor. This is contrary to expectations, but can be partially explained by the fact that the work of these young people in the home or in the labor market allows their households to leave poverty. In 1996, another reason was added: "it's hard to study"—associated with personal problems among both poor and non-poor youth. Among the poor, problems of supply prompted by their largely rural extraction take second place, whereas among the non-poor family problems predominate.

Differentiated by gender, the analysis for both years reveals that college-age women are prevented from continuing their education largely because of the need to help with domestic chores. This coincides with the previous analysis of female labor force participation, and is less related with having to work outside the home, which is a more important reason for men. The problems of access or supply also seem to affect women more, including the burden of travelling long distances to study. Poor girls in particular express a lack of interest in formal study.

This evidence shows that this problem needs to be addressed from a comprehensive perspective. The situation would be helped by the availability of more opportunities for well-paid jobs related to the general macroeconomic situation and the endowment of human capital, the existence of educational infrastructure that makes access possible, and the design of a relevant curriculum and its correct implementation to convince people of the economic value of education. This latter point touches on the subject of the quality of education and thus of the human capital accumulated, an aspect that cannot be developed further from the information available.

Table 6.11. Costa Rica: Reasons for Formal Education Nonattendance of Ages 13-17 by Condition of Poverty and Gender, 1986 and 1996
(In percent)

	1986				1996			
	Poor		Non-poor		Poor		Non-poor	
Reasons	M	W	M	W	M	W	M	W
Rates of nonattendance	59.9	58.1	45.8	46.1	42.8	42.0	33.4	26.8
Reasons for nonattendance	100.0	100.0	100.0	100.0	100.0	100.0	100.0	100.0
Associated with the family:	34.3	28.0	45.9	36.2	27.0	12.7	27.1	25.2
Have to work	32.4	1.2	4.4	12.8	26.6	2.9	26.8	10.1
Help with domestic chores	1.9	26.8	1.5	23.4	0.4	9.8	0.3	15.1
Associated with education supply:	32.1	39.4	21.5	26.9	34.9	36.2	19.5	24.1
Cannot pay for studies	29.2	31.3	17.4	20.4	29.3	25.7	15.0	14.8
Problems of access	2.9	8.1	4.1	6.5	5.6	10.5	4.5	9.3
Associated with student:	33.6	32.6	32.6	36.9	38.1	51.1	53.4	50.7
Pregnancy or marriage	n.a.	n.a.	n.a.	n.a.	0.0	4.5	0.0	5.8
Illness or disability	n.a.	n.a.	n.a.	n.a.	1.6	5.4	3.0	3.8
Difficulties in studying	n.a.	n.a.	n.a.	n.a.	15.0	14.3	14.2	14.1
Not interested	25.9	29.6	29.3	34.0	18.1	22.4	34.6	23.2
Not of age	0.6	0.0	0.0	0.0	0.0	0.0	0.1	0.9
Other	7.1	3.0	3.3	2.9	3.4	4.5	1.5	2.9

n.a.: not available. In 1986 the survey did not ask explicitly for reasons.
Source: Authors' calculations based on IICE (1986) and DGEC (1996).

Productive Capital

Farm Families and Land

The number of hectares of land to which a farm family has access—that is, land in use with or without title, rented or on loan—was found to be a determinant of poverty. This confirms that access to land is more important than ownership of it as a mechanism for escaping from poverty. The same result was also found for housing. The significance of the education of the head of household shows that human assets are also a factor associated with lower poverty and point toward the complementarity of assets. The type of farming that the head of household does is also important. Those working in traditional farming have a greater probability of falling into poverty than those working in modern farming (associated with products for the external sector such as bananas, coffee, livestock, sugar cane) or the non-farm sectors (industry and services). This stems from the low productivity of traditional agriculture, which confirms that the endowment of and the returns on assets are important to leaving poverty. It also suggests that the difference in the quality of the asset is another variable that explains the return differentials and the direction of poverty.

Households with members who work off the farm have a lower probability of poverty, and the same occurs as the household employment rate rises. And farm families that reside in the Central Valley have less probability of being poor because of the better supply of social capital in terms of infrastructure, job opportunities, access to markets and education and welfare services. But in the case of agriculture, an association is also found between export products, such as coffee, and a lower probability of being poor.

These results are evidence that the socioeconomic situation of farm families in Costa Rica is influenced by the type of farming (traditional versus modern), which reflects differences in the returns from the land asset associated with technology, the quality of the land, and geographic location. This, in turn, reflects social capital and the area of accessible land, which reflects endowment irrespective of legal possession. The results suggest that even in families that depend on specific assets to generate income to leave poverty, human capital and its utilization are basic determinants because they complement this specific asset or offer means of diversifying the sources of income for the household.

Since access to land is an explanatory factor of non-poverty, its impact can be analyzed in relation to adequate utilization in terms of returns. Table 6.12 measures the impact of land use on poverty. The income of farm families was re-estimated with their poverty levels, taking into account in all cases the average return from the land. The results indicate that only a small percentage of farm families have insufficient land (3 percent of total, 11 percent of poor farm families) and that a similarly low percentage (5 percent) escapes from poverty thanks to a better return from the available land. About 90 percent of poor farmers could remedy their situation if the quantity of

Table 6.12. Costa Rica: Estimate of the Impact of Land on Poverty of Farm Families, 1986

Stratum	Families	%	%
Total	76,302	100.0	
Poor by income	21,501	28.2	100.0
Insufficient land	2,276	3.0	10.6
Land with low return	19,225	25.2	89.4
Non-poor by income	54,801	71.8	100.0
Better land use	3,829	5.0	7.0
Sufficient land and return	50,972	66.8	93.0

Source: Authors' calculations based on IICE (1986).

the asset available were utilized with a higher return. This suggests that for agricultural producers, overcoming poverty is not just a matter of increased access to land assets, but also access to a series of collateral services that increase return, such as improved seed, infrastructure, marketing facilities and technical assistance.[26]

Urban Microproducers

In Costa Rica, there is a modest but longstanding tradition of assisting microenterprises through credit and technical assistance from public and private institutions that offer internal and external financing. A survey examined the possible impact of these policies on combating poverty by facilitating processes of accumulation among urban microproducers. The survey covered a sample of microproducers in the San José metropolitan area. Following Trejos (1991), the objective was to determine the factors that explain the relative success or failure of microenterprises in terms of generating income, and the impact of public credit and technical assistance policies. The

---

[26] These results must be seen only as an approximation since there are no indicators that measure differences in quality of land and thus the real possibilities of substitution between specific crops. Additionally, constant unit returns were used, which implicitly assumes that they are independent of the stock.

sampling framework was the set of people in the metropolitan area who stated they were independent non-professional workers (self-employed and owners of microenterprises) in the DGEC Household Survey of July 1997. This refined sampling framework consisted of 509 cases, from which DGEC experts prepared a subsample of 217 complete and usable surveys.[27]

Equivalent to 45 percent of the sampling framework, the sample is representative of the scope of activities of microproducers: 71 percent are self-employed workers, 22 percent are in manufacturing, 12 percent in construction, 29 percent in commerce, and the rest in other services, particularly personal services. On average, the microenterprises have 1.8 employees, and 72 percent of microproducers are heads of household. Their average education is approximately eight years, and one-third are women. Of these households, 20 percent are under the poverty line and have an average of 4.3 members. In order to determine the role of asset markets in the capacity to generate income for the poor and non-poor, the survey researched aspects such as the experience of the producer, degree of linkage to the formal market, degree of formality of the activity, operating rationale, accumulated assets, and access to credit. This information was supplemented by data on the nuclear family.

The starting point was to explain the income of microenterprises in terms of the assets available for the productive process. The assets considered include human, physical, financial and social capital. For human capital, consideration was given to the workers of the establishment (KEH) and the specific human capital of the microproducer (KHME). Both variables represent weighted years of education where the weightings also consider years of experience. The physical capital (KFIS) represents the replacement value of the different assets used—although not necessarily owned—by the enterprise, including buildings, vehicles, machinery and equipment, furniture and other property. Financial capital (KFIN) includes cash plus deposits. Social capital (DKS) is constructed as a dichotomous variable. Its existence is shown (value 1) in cases where interest-free financial assistance from rela-

---

[27] The framework was refined to exclude workers linked to agriculture and members of the same family in the same business. The sample consisted of 239 interviews of which 22 were excluded because of unemployment (8) or change to wage earning (14). No replies accounted for 2 percent.

tives or friends was used to start the enterprise, to purchase machinery and equipment, or for working capital. There is also social capital in cases of nonremunerated work by family members in the enterprise.

Three additional fictitious binary variables were included to help explain the return on different assets. These variables approximate the degree of formality, the link to the market and the operating rationale. The degree of formality considers the characteristics of the establishment: that is, legal constitution, organization and business license, social contributions and taxes. The link to the market considers the type of customers and suppliers and the use of credit in transactions. Finally, the operating rationale identifies conduct that tends either toward accumulation of assets or toward subsistence or survival. Other factors taken into account are the reasons for starting the enterprise, the interest in or possibility of expanding production, the presence of future expansion plans, and recent investments.

Table 6.12 summarizes the results of the three models. Based on the model that explains the income of the microenterprise (intermediate column), all the variables associated with stocks of assets were significant, but not those incorporated to specify returns. Stocks of financial and physical capital provide the best explanation of the income of microenterprises. However, both social and human capital are also significant in explaining the income of establishments. In relation to human capital, the contribution made by microproducers themselves and their employees is important. Although these are the expected results, as larger stocks of assets imply higher income, two questions seem relevant. Are these stocks sufficient to enable families to leave poverty, or is there an additional problem of returns? And, if the quantity is determinant, why do some accumulate and leave poverty while others do not?

As the unit of analysis for poverty is the household and not the establishment, in reply to the first question, the household has to be the unit used to determine the weight of income generated by the microenterprise in family income. The results of the survey show that only one-third of families depend exclusively on the income generated by the microenterprise, although for 41 percent of households this income accounts for at least 75 percent of total family income. For an appreciable percentage of families (39 percent), this income contributes less than 50 percent of income. In this situation, income from microenterprises cannot explain the totality of family income or the family's situation of poverty or non-poverty.

Since the additional income of the household comes from the diversified labor of its members, human capital of the household is a key variable. This household human capital was estimated by the method described earlier, that is, considering members aged 12 or over and using years of education weighted by their relative prices. The difference here is that in order to consider labor diversification, the relative prices discriminate by type of access to the labor market (occupational category), and have been qualified using trend estimates with 1997 data. The idea here is that work outside the establishment is not only associated with higher returns per unit of human capital but can also reduce the vulnerability of family income to the cycle of the microenterprise. Table 6.12 (first column) confirms that the human capital of the household contributes to the explanation of family income. This means that the deprivation of the household can be reversed by acting on the accumulation of the household's human capital and other types of assets.

Bearing in mind the explanatory weight of household human capital in the determination of family income and its condition of poverty, it is possible to simulate the effect that a higher return on the establishment's assets would have on the household's condition of poverty. To do this, the expected income of the microenterprise was estimated on the basis of the endowment of assets of each establishment and their average return (as appears in Table 6.13) in order to estimate a new expected family income. The comparison of both family incomes against the poverty line reveals the changes in the condition of poverty associated with changes in the returns on the assets.[28] These results are summarized in Table 6.14. About 20 percent of microproducers were below the poverty line in 1997, and almost half remain there, even considering the average return on their assets. They are poor because of the insufficient stock of assets in the microenterprise. This means that the other half of microproducers could be above the poverty thresholds if they made better use of their available assets, as about 6 percent of microproducers are in fact doing. This small group has succeeded in leaving poverty thanks to returns on their assets that are above the average

---

[28] In order to isolate only the impact of the microenterprise, no modifications were introduced in the return on household human capital or in its utilization. Note the maintenance of the limitation that considers the average return as independent of the stock of assets. Thus, the results must be seen as a first approximation.

Table 6.13. Costa Rica: Models Using Assets of Microproducers in Metropolitan San José, 1997

| Variables | Dependent variable | | |
	Family income[1]	Income of microenterprise[2]	Physical capital[3]
Constant	10.262.0	36.976.1	n.s.
	(8.642.67)	(8.645.48)	
Human capital of family (KHA)	1.206.23		
(Years of education weighted)	(125.34)		
Income of microenterprise (YMICRO)	0.802		
(colones)	(0.050)		
Human capital of enterprise (KHE)		16.776	
(Years of education weighted)		(5.819)	
Human capital of producer (KHME)		1.221.59	n.s.
(Years of education weighted)		(592.914)	
Physical capital (KFIS)		0.006	
(colones)		(0.002)	
Financial capital (KFIN)		0.038	
(colones)		(0.008)	
Social capital (DKS)		21.967.99	
(1 = have, 0 = do not have)		(10.675.97)	
Branch of activity (DRAMA)			2.176.075.20
(1 = high KFIS, 0 = low KFIS)			(488.796.47)
Access and use of credit (DCRE)			955.290.95
(1 = use credit, 0 = do not use)			(452.358.29)
Operating rationale (DLF)		n.s.	1.065.935.76
(1 = accumulation, 0 = subsistence)			(517.334.49)
Degree of formality (DGF)		n.s.	2.466.310.54
(1 = more formal, 0 = less formal)			(505.289.02)
R^2	0.69	0.39	0.30
R^2 adjusted	0.69	0.38	0.29
Standard deviation	64980.04	73077.09	3279347.84
F-statistic	239.56	27.39	23.04
Number of cases	217	217	217

n.s. = not significant. The following were not significant: linkage to markets, return on physical capital and years of operation of enterprise.

[1] All variables are significant at 99.99 percent confidence, except the constant.

[2] All variables are significant at 99.99 percent confidence, except KHME and DSK, which are significant at 95 percent.

[3] All variables are significant at 99.99 percent confidence, except DCRE and DLF, which are significant at 95 percent.

Source: Authors' estimates based on the Survey of Small Establishments in Metropolitan San José, IICE-DGEC, 1997.

Table 6.14. Costa Rica: Estimate of the Impact of Productive Capital on Poverty of a Sample of Microproducers in Metropolitan San José, 1997

Stratum	Microproducer	%	%
Total	217	100.0	
Poor by income	44	20.3	100.0
By insufficient productive capital	21	9.7	47.7
By productive capital with low return	23	10.6	52.3
Non-poor by income	173	79.7	100.0
By better use of productive capital	12	5.5	6.9
By productive capital and sufficient return	161	74.2	93.1

Source: Authors' calculations based on the Survey of Small Establishments in Metropolitan San José, IICE-DGEC, 1997.

of the sample under study. The estimates also confirm that three out of every four microproducers fall outside poverty thresholds because they have sufficient assets and achieve adequate returns.

Given that the quantity of assets is as important as their return, it is possible to reply to the second question on the variables that contribute to accumulation. For this purpose, it is useful to concentrate on physical capital, because it is the best measure of the establishment's accumulated stock. In this case, it is possible to construct a model in which the amount of physical capital accumulated by the establishment is associated with a set of variables. These variables include the human capital of the microproducer and the binary variables mentioned earlier: the link to the market, degree of formality and operating rationale. A fictitious variable on the branch of activity can be added to separate branches that require more physical capital than others (transport or industry against retail trade or personal services), a binary variable on access and use of credit, and two additional variables, namely, return (earnings on physical capital) and years of operation of the establishment.

The results of the estimate of the model appear in Table 6.13 (last column). Several comments seem pertinent. Although the formal human capital of microproducers does not appear significant, the operating rationale does show an important incidence. This means that microproducers who follow a rationale of accumulation and who are interested in the expansion of the enterprise—in other words, who have a more entrepreneurial attitude—are successful in accumulating assets. This brings to light a special element of microproducers, not necessarily acquired from formal education, which is the entrepreneurial spirit and intuition required for successful productive activity, which is in itself one more productive asset.

Aside from the branch variable, which indicates that people who enter certain activities require more capital, the two other significant variables have important policy implications. One of them relates to access and use of credit, which is significant even in a context of very limited access to this type of enterprise since it highlights an area that requires additional assistance.[29] The last significant variable to be considered is the degree of formality, which has two elements. First, the greater the informality the greater the restrictions on access to the financial system; and second, greater informality means that the microproducers need more support such as technical assistance and reforms to the regulatory framework of the enterprises. In fact, one-third of the microproducers surveyed who had outstanding loans cited guarantees and paperwork as the principal limitations on access to credit. A further 31 percent said they needed credit but did not apply because they had no capacity to repay (50 percent of those in need of credit), considered it costly (31 percent), or saw the process as involving guarantees or onerous paperwork (19 percent).

Conclusions

Estimates of poverty in this study reveal that about one-fifth of Costa Rican families are under the thresholds based on the official poverty lines, a proportion that falls by one-tenth when a uniform international line is used. These measurements of the extent, intensity and depth of poverty indicate a moderate, although not widespread, reduction in poverty during the last decade of economic reforms. This reduction is based on growth of real fam-

---

[29] Only 11 percent of interviewees had an outstanding loan, while an additional 5 percent stated they had applied for a loan. In about half the cases, the application was made through a formal source (banks), mainly for physical capital. Estimates indicate that in 1997 only about 0.3 percent of the portfolio of the state banks and 0.1 percent of the banking system were credits for micro and small enterprises.

ily incomes and on improvements in the conditions of families whose heads worked, at least initially, in the farm sector.

The results suggest that the persistence of poverty reflects difficulties for the poor in gaining access to sufficient quantities of human, physical and social capital assets. Three additional factors related to the endowment of assets need to be mentioned. First, access to or control of assets rather than ownership helps explain the lower probability of poverty. For housing, farmland and the productive assets of urban microproducers, the relevant variables were access rather than ownership. This points the way to policies that promote broader and more generalized forms of renting or leasing of assets, perhaps with the option to buy—which are beginning to appear in the region—but with some system of subsidiary state guarantee.

A more detailed review of the role of assets shows that access is very broad, at least for basic quantities of them. The simulations of potential family income obtained average returns on the assets, and greater utilization in the case of human capital. This indicates that a percentage of families—at least half of those currently poor—could obtain sufficient income to escape poverty. This suggests that differences in utilization of and returns on assets are as important as access and are elements that help explain the high probabilities of poverty. These results highlight the need for complementary policies to guarantee a basic endowment of assets, coupled with others to improve the utilization and returns on these assets at basic levels.

In the cases of farm families and urban microproducers, the presence of greater human capital is clearly associated with higher returns from productive capital. This suggests that the important factor is not access to each independent asset but the possibility of supplementing the assets available to the household. It further suggests that minimum endowments of human capital are required if access to productive assets is to have an economic impact.

Human capital is the asset that the poor can access most easily, thanks to the state's contribution of public social capital in the form of health and education services that provide the entire population with a minimum quantity of this capital. These services have permitted the poor to accumulate a certain amount of human capital, even growing over time. However, gaps open after primary education. Educational opportunities do exist, but there are other factors that prevent the poor from keeping their children in the education system. Expanding the opportunities for accumulation among young people requires action on the supply side to facilitate access to quality education, and the inclusion of incentives to promote demand. These incentives should compensate these families for the opportunity costs of maintaining children outside the labor market.

For the productive capital of microproducers, lack of access to credit and the absence of real entrepreneurial human capital seem to be the main factors that curb the possibilities of accumulation. The survey of urban microproducers shows that the financial market plays no significant role in the creation of physical capital for these enterprises. What little access to credit that exists is associated with increased possibilities of capital accumulation. This suggests that public credit policies and the policies of nongovernmental organizations that target this population are not achieving their objectives. The very modest flow of funds into this sector—less than 0.3 percent of banks' portfolios—is evidence of the small scale of credit assistance for microproducers. As with housing, the strategy of poor families is to gradually construct assets with assistance from more informal sources. However, unlike housing, public social capital has a lower profile and complementarity in this sector, and state action may even hinder rather than help these processes.

To conclude, it is important to call attention to an inherent limitation of this type of analysis of the possibilities of accumulation. The selection of microproducers necessarily leaves out the most successful cases; that is, poor entrepreneurs who have succeeded in accumulating sufficient assets to become medium-sized or large enterprises. On the other hand, it also leaves out the unsuccessful ventures that have already disappeared. Therefore, the approach loses sight of how successful entrepreneurs overcome the restrictions to accumulate assets, as well as the costs of those for whom economic activity did not prosper precisely due to the absence of assets.

References

Céspedes, V.H., and R. Jiménez. 1995. *La pobreza en Costa Rica: concepto, método y medición.* San José: Academia de Centroamérica.

Datt, G., and M. Ravallion. 1992. Growth and Redistribution Components of Changes in Poverty Measures: A Decomposition with Applications to Brazil and India in the 1980s. *Journal of Development Economics* 38(3): 275-95.

De los Ríos, R. 1988. Pobreza, necesidades básicas y estrategias de sobrevivencia familiar: el caso de la región central de Costa Rica. Centro Latinoamericano de Demografía, San José. Master's thesis.

Dirección General de Estadísticas y Censos (DGEC). 1997. *Principales resultados de la Encuesta de Hogares de Propósitos Múltiples.* San José, Costa Rica: Dirección General de Estadísticas y Censos.

_____. 1988. *Encuesta Nacional de Ingresos y Gastos de las Familias Costarricenses.* San José: Dirección General de Estadísticas y Censos.

_____. Various years. *Encuesta de Hogares de Propósitos Múltiples.* Data records for 1987, 1990, 1995, 1996.

Economic Commission for Latin America and the Caribbean (ECLAC). 1996. *Panorama social de 1996.* Santiago: Economic Commission for Latin America and the Caribbean.

_____. 1994. *Panorama social de 1994.* Santiago: Economic Commission for Latin America and the Caribbean.

_____. 1991. *Magnitud de la pobreza en América Latina en los años ochenta.* Serie Estudios e Informes de la CEPAL No. 81. Santiago: Economic Commission for Latin America and the Caribbean.

Fields, G. 1980. *Poverty, Inequality and Development.* New York: Cambridge University Press.

Funkhouser, E. 1994. *Changes in the Returns to Education in Costa Rica.* Working Paper 21/94. Santa Barbara, CA: University of California at Santa Barbara, Department of Economics.

Gindling, T.H. 1992. Why Women Earn Less than Men in Costa Rica. In G. Psacharopoulos and Z. Tzannatos (eds.), *Case Studies in Women's Employment and Pay in Latin America.* Washington, DC: World Bank.

_____. 1991. Labor Market Segmentation and the Determination of Wages in the Public, Private-Formal, and Informal Sectors in San José, Costa Rica. *Economic Development and Cultural Change* 39(3): 585-605.

Gindling, T.H., and A. Berry. 1992. The Performance of the Labor Market during Recession and Structural Adjustment: Costa Rica in the 1980s. *World Development* 20(11): 1599-1616.

Gindling, T.H., and D. Robbins. 1997. *Liberalización comercial, expansión de la educación y desigualdad en Costa Rica.* Serie Divulgación Económica No. 27. San José: Instituto de Investigaciones en Ciencias Económicas, University of Costa Rica.

Heckman, J.J. 1979. Sample Selection Bias as a Specification Error. *Econometrica* 47(1): 153-161.

Instituto de Investigaciones en Ciencias Económicas (IICE). 1986. *Encuesta sobre las características socioeconómicas de las familias costarricenses.* San José: Instituto de Investigaciones en Ciencias Económicas, University of Costa Rica.

Marenco, L., A.M. Trejos, J.D. Trejos, et al. 1998. *Del silencio a la palabra: un modelo de trabajo con las mujeres jefas de hogar.* San José: Mundo Gráfico S.A./Government of Costa Rica.

Ministry of Public Education (MEP). 1994. *Pertinencia de la educación secundaria en Costa Rica.* Informe preliminar. San José: Ministry of Public Education.

Montiel, N. 1995. Estudio Econométrico de la ficha SISBEN del Instituto Mixto de Ayuda Social. Instituto de Investigaciones en Ciencias Económicas, University of Costa Rica, San José. Mimeo.

Montiel, N., and H. Rojas-Romagosa. 1997. *Algunos determinantes de la conclusión de la educación secundaria en Costa Rica.* Working Paper No. 191, Instituto de Investigaciones en Ciencias Económicas, University of Costa Rica, San José.

Morley, S., and C. Alvarez. 1992. *Poverty and Adjustment in Costa Rica.* Inter-American Development Bank Working Paper No. 123, Washington, DC.

Piñera, S. 1979. *¿Se benefician los pobres del crecimiento económico?* Santiago: Economic Commission for Latin America and the Caribbean.

Pritchett, L. 1996. *Where Has All the Education Gone?* World Bank Policy Research Working Paper No. 1581, Washington, DC.

Psacharopoulos, G., and Y.C. Ng. 1992. *Earnings and Education in Latin America: Assessing Priorities for Schooling Investment.* Washington, DC: World Bank, Latin American Caribbean Region Technical Department.

Psacharopoulos, G., S. Morley, A. Fiszbein, et al. 1993. *Poverty and Income Distribution in Latin America: The Story of the 1980s*. Washington, DC: World Bank.

Rama, G. 1994. A la búsqueda del siglo XXI: nuevos caminos de desarrollo en Costa Rica. Report of the Pilot Mission of the Social Reform Program of the Inter-American Development Bank, San José. Mimeo.

Ravallion, M. 1992. *Poverty Comparisons: A Guide to Concepts and Methods: Living Standard Measurement Study*. World Bank Working Paper No. 88, Washington, DC.

Rodríguez, A., and S. Smith. 1994. A Comparison of Determinants of Urban, Rural and Farm Poverty in Costa Rica. *World Development* 22(3): 381-97.

Sáenz, M.I., and J.D. Trejos. 1993. *Las formas de inserción de la mujer al mercado de trabajo en Costa Rica*. Working Paper Series No. 165, Instituto de Investigaciones en Ciencias Económicas, University of Costa Rica, San José.

Sauma, P. 1993. *Acceso a los programas sociales*. Working Paper Series No. 143, Instituto de Investigaciones en Ciencias Económicas, University of Costa Rica, San José.

Sauma, P., and A. Hoffmaister. 1989. Una aproximación a los determinantes y características principales de la pobreza en Costa Rica. *Revista Ciencias Económicas* 9(1/2): 95-110.

Sauma, P., and J.D. Trejos. 1990. *Evolución reciente de la distribución del ingreso en Costa Rica: 1977-1986*. Working Paper Series No. 132, Instituto de Investigaciones en Ciencias Económicas, University of Costa Rica, San José.

Sauma, P., and L. Garnier. 1997. Efecto de las políticas económicas y sociales sobre la pobreza en Costa Rica. San José. Mimeo.

Seligson, M.A., J. Martínez, and J.D. Trejos. 1996. *Reducción de la pobreza en Costa Rica: el impacto de las políticas públicas*. Serie de Divulgación Económica No. 51, Instituto de Investigaciones en Ciencias Económicas, University of Costa Rica/United Nations Development Programme, San José.

Székely, M. 1996. *El ahorro de los hogares en México*. Serie de Estudios Económicos y Sectoriales No. 001, Regional Operations Department 2, Inter-American Development Bank, Washington, DC.

Taylor-Dormond, M. 1991. The State and Poverty in Costa Rica. *ECLAC Review* 43: 131-48.

Trejos, J.D. 1995a. Costa Rica: la respuesta estatal frente a la pobreza: instituciones, programas y recursos. In D. Raczynski (ed.), *Estrategias para combatir la pobreza en América Latina: programas, instituciones y recursos.* Santiago: Corporación de Investigaciones Económicas para Latinoamérica/Inter-American Development Bank.

———. 1995b. *Síntesis cuantitativa de la pobreza.* Working Paper Series No. 163, Instituto de Investigaciones en Ciencias Económicas, University of Costa Rica, San José.

———. 1992. *Mercado de trabajo y pobreza urbana en Costa Rica.* Working Paper Series No. 162, Instituto de Investigaciones en Ciencias Económicas, University of Costa Rica, San José.

———. 1991. Informalidad y acumulación en el área metropolitana de San José, Costa Rica. In J. P. Pérez-Sáinz and R. Menjívar (eds.), *Informalidad urbana en Centroamérica: entre la acumulación y la subsistencia.* Caracas: Editorial Nueva Sociedad/Facultad Latinoamericana de Ciencias Sociales.

Trejos, J.D., L. Garnier, G. Monge, and R. Hidalgo. 1994. Sistema de entrega de los servicios sociales: una agenda para la reforma en Costa Rica. In C. Aedo and O. Larrañaga (eds.), *Sistema de entrega de los servicios sociales: una agenda para la reforma.* Santiago: Instituto Latinoamericano de Doctrina y Estudios Sociales/Inter-American Development Bank.

Trejos, J.D., and N. Montiel. 1999. *El capital de los pobres en Costa Rica: acceso, utilización y rendimiento.* Latin American Research Network Working Paper R-360. Inter-American Development Bank, Washington, DC.

World Bank. 1997. *Costa Rica: Identifying the Social Needs of the Poor. An Update.* Report No. 15449-CR. Inter-American Development Bank, Washington, DC.

———. 1990. *Costa Rica: el gasto público social en los sectores sociales.* Report No. 8519-CR. World Bank, Washington, DC.

Yang, H. 1992. Female Labor Force Participation and Earnings Differentials in Costa Rica. In G. Psacharopoulos and Z. Tzannatos (eds.), *Case Studies in Women's Employment and Pay in Latin America.* Washington, DC: World Bank.

CHAPTER SEVEN

Distribution, Access and Complementarity: Capital of the Poor in Peru

Javier Escobal
Jaime Saavedra
Máximo Torero[1]

Both income distribution and poverty levels have shifted significantly in Peru over the last four decades. Setting aside problems of compatibility between surveys and methodological differences associated with calculating these indicators, the evidence suggests a decrease in the dispersion of income distribution and a significant reduction in poverty, especially in the 1970s. In the 1980s and 1990s the dispersion in income distribution continued to fall, although at lower rates. At the same time, however, there were important fluctuations in poverty levels, associated with abrupt macroeconomic changes. Although the most significant changes in poverty, income distribution and spending occurred between 1960 and 1980, important modifications in patterns of poverty have taken place since the mid-1980s. The availability of a database using four household surveys (1985-1986, 1991, 1994 and 1996) as well as a panel of households from 1991 to 1994 opens the way to explore changes in the holding of assets by the poor, and the impact of those assets on poverty and income distribution.

This chapter analyzes the possession of and access to assets by the poor. Private, public and organizational assets are the principal determinants of household spending. Income flows are therefore crucial in determining whether a family is successful in leaving poverty. In this respect, public poli-

---

[1] The authors are research economists with the Grupo de Análisis para el Desarrollo (GRADE) in Lima, Peru.

cies need to be carefully designed to resolve unequal access to certain assets that are suitable for state intervention. These policies must facilitate access to household assets, accumulation of them, and higher returns on them. The chapter first examines the nature and characteristics of poverty in Peru, as well as trends in income distribution, spending and assets. This is followed by an analysis of how these assets are dispersed and possessed by the poor, as well as the extent to which the poor have access to them. Relationships between the different types of assets and the status of poverty are then evaluated along with the mobility of households on the scale of income and spending. The effect of ownership of or access to some public or organizational assets on the return from private assets is also determined.

Historical Background

In the 1960s and 1970s, the empirical literature that analyzed income and spending focused on income distribution, neglecting estimates of the magnitude of poverty. In general, trends in income distribution, changes in welfare, and poverty were implicitly treated as biunivocally interrelated concepts (i.e., an increase in income concentration would necessarily result in an increase in poverty). To assert that poverty was increasing, it was sufficient to establish that a high percentage of low-income families would receive a decreasing proportion of total income or spending. At the same time, the existence of a national poverty line was presumed without taking into account the disparity of regional baskets and relative regional price structures. This meant that the same level of spending could be associated in one region with a poor family, and in another with a non-poor one. Moreover, there was no discussion of more complex relationships such as the possibilities of distributive improvements as poverty increased, or of more unequal distributions as poverty declined.

The study uses the 1970-71 National Food Consumption Survey (ENCA) to estimate the long-term change in the poverty rate. To compare the poverty rates from this survey with those calculated more recently from the National Surveys of Standard of Living (ENNIV), the lines were adjusted to make them methodologically comparable with the lines associated with

Table 7.1. Poverty Indicators by Region for 1971, 1985, 1991, 1994 and 1996
(Family spending in percentages)

Region	1971-72	1985	1991	1994	1996
Peru	64.0	43.1	59.0	53.6	50.5
Urban	39.6	36.0	53.3	46.3	45.5
Rural	84.5	55.2	80.7	70.6	68.0
50% Poorest	10.7	18.8	21.0	22.9	24.5
20% Richest	60.9	51.4	46.6	45.4	42.9
Gini	0.55	0.48	0.43	0.41	0.38

Source: Authors' calculations based on ENCA (1971-72) and ENNIV 1985-86, 1991, 1994 and 1996.

the ENNIV.[2] Note that both surveys use family spending and the coverage of spending.

Table 7.1 shows that poverty levels declined substantially in Peru between the early 1970s and 1985, particularly in the rural sector.[3] Since then, most information reveals a clear pro-cyclical pattern in the poverty rate, which increases dramatically in 1991, followed by three years of declining production during the implementation of a drastic macroeconomic stabilization program. In 1994, after the economic recovery, poverty fell by five points, a trend that continued until 1996. Thus, although in 1996 poverty rates were still above their 1985 level, poverty was 15 points below the rates of 25 years earlier.

The results also show that the composition of poverty in Peru has changed dramatically. While in the early 1970s poverty was largely rural—two-thirds of the poor were rural dwellers—the picture was reversed in the

---

[2] Two adjustments were made to the data from Amat y León (1981): homogenization of calorific consumption of both surveys to construct a basic food spending index, and use of the same method to extrapolate the global spending required (i.e., the line) from basic food spending.

[3] The methodology on which the ENNIV calculations of poverty are based is shown in Escobal, Saavedra and Torero (1999). It is possible to introduce some additional modifications to the lines estimated by Amat y León to strengthen their comparability with the results derived from the ENNIV, since the Amat y León data are based on a normative basket that contains not only a minimum calorific consumption such as the ENNIV, but also protein and other lesser nutrients.

mid-1990s, when two-thirds of the poor were urban dwellers. Urban poverty rates over that period increased by six points, while rural poverty fell 16 points. Thus, the entire long-term reduction in poverty could be viewed as a rural phenomenon, in the context of a major migratory process.[4]

Table 7.1 also shows a clear decline in dispersion since 1971. The Gini coefficient of family income fell from 0.55 to 0.40 between the early 1970s and the 1990s. The percentage of total income received by the poorer half of the population rose from 10.7 percent to 24.5 percent in 1996, while the share of the richest half fell from 61 percent to 43 percent.

The trend in income distribution from the 1970s can also be corroborated by the indicators of concentration based on family spending. The reduction in the dispersion of family or personal income or spending could have taken place both during periods when average income was falling (e.g., 1985-86 to 1991) and when it was rising (1991 to 1994 or 1996). Bruno, Ravallion and Squire (1998) demonstrate that the empirical support for Kuznets' suggested systematic relationship between growth and inequality is very weak. The Peruvian case also shows that there is no evident association between the economic cycle and inequality.[5]

Birdsall and Londoño (1998) suggest that one of the fundamental causes of income inequality is unequal access to and possession of assets. In this respect, it should be possible to find changes in the distribution of key assets that underlie these long-term shifts in income distribution. Although no detailed information at the household level is available on possession of assets before the 1980s, the evidence presented below suggests that improvement in the distribution of two key assets—land and human capital—played an important role in reducing the concentration of income/spending and in reducing poverty.

In fact, declining levels of income dispersion and poverty from the 1960s to the 1980s coincided with an increase in the average endowment of land and education, as well as with a decline in the dispersion of these assets.

---

[4] The 1991 survey does not include the tropical forest areas and rural coast, while the other surveys are representative at the national level. Estimates were made limiting the sample of the 1985, 1994 and 1996 surveys to the domains of the 1991 survey, and the results did not vary significantly.

[5] More evidence on the time trend of inequality of income and spending using different databases is found in Saavedra and Díaz (1998).

For example, the Gini coefficient of land distribution fell from 0.94 to 0.81 between 1961 and 1971, and then to 0.61 in 1994.[6] The average endowment per farmer went over 1971-94 from one to two hectares (standardized in equivalent units of irrigated coastal land). This occurred because of a substantial expansion of the agricultural frontier through irrigation in the desert coastal strip, expansion of the agricultural frontier in forest areas, and an increase in farming hectares under irrigation.

Improvements in the distribution of land, however, did not occur smoothly. At the end of the 1960s, Peru's military government began an agrarian reform process. However, before redistributing the land expropriated from large landowners, the government collectivized agriculture, creating large cooperatives on the coast and in the sierra. The failure of this reform by the late 1970s led to splitting up the cooperatives, a process formalized in 1980 by the Belaúnde administration and carried out during the decade that followed. By 1994, according to the agricultural census, most Peruvian farmers again owned isolated and small holdings, with the exception of peasant communities in the Sierra, which retained large areas of relatively infertile land. Approximately 50 percent of agricultural holdings on the coast and 62 percent in the Sierra were less than three hectares. Furthermore, each producer had an average of three non-contiguous plots of land; this is particularly characteristic of the sierra, where almost one-third of producers have five or more plots averaging less than one hectare.

The other important change in average ownership and asset distribution was in education, as school enrollment has increased massively since the 1950s. While in 1940 30 percent of children aged six to 14 attended school, by 1993 this figure had risen to 86 percent. Beginning in the early 1970s, this expansion extended to post-secondary education. The changes in enrollment had an impact on the level of education of the population and labor force. While almost 60 percent of the population over 50 had no education in 1948, that rate had dropped to 15 percent by 1996. In 1940, less than 5 percent of the population had completed the secondary level; by 1996, this figure had jumped to one-third. Average years of schooling have risen consistently from two in 1940 to six in 1981 and eight in 1996.

---

[6] The 1961 figure comes from Webb and Figueroa (1975). Those for 1970 to 1994 are the authors' own calculations based on information from the agricultural census.

It is clear that educational expansion and redistribution of land resulted in a change in the pattern of asset ownership among the poor. As the return on these assets has not fallen over time, it can be expected that these structural transformations raise, at least partially, the average income of the poorest sectors and improve income distribution. The most notable caveat to this assessment is that, in the case of land, there is evidence of a reduction in the return on the asset associated with the restrictions that the agrarian reform imposed on trading in this asset. This could have affected farmers' opportunities for using land as a means of raising their income and reducing poverty. In contrast, for education the evidence provided by Psacharopoulos and Woodhall (1984) for rates of return in the 1970s and early 1980s, and by Saavedra (1997) for the mid-1980s and early 1990s, shows little probability of a fall in the private return on education in the last three decades. The notable increase in urban and rural educational levels and the reduction in the dispersion of these assets indicate that the educational transformation over the last few decades is one of the variables that explain the changes identified in poverty and income distribution.

The Growth-Inequality Decomposition

Using the methodology proposed by Datt and Ravallion (1992), a decomposition was made of the changes in the poverty rates. Table 7.2 shows that the changes in both average spending and distribution are important for understanding changes in the poverty indicators. At the national level, between 1971 and 1985, 52 percent of the 21 point reduction in poverty was attributable to an increase in average family spending, while 26 percent was attributable to a reduction in the dispersion in the structure of family spending.

When the period of analysis is extended to 1996, the relative importance of the distribution effect increases dramatically, explaining 64 percent of the 14 point reduction in poverty between 1971 and 1996.[7] Thus, in a period of 25 years, the decline in poverty was largely attributable to a reduction in the dispersion of purchasing power.

---

[7] The decomposition of the indicators of the gap and the severity of poverty over 1971-96—not reported—make the role of the reduction in the dispersion of family spending even more evident.

Table 7.2. Decomposition of Changes in the Poverty Rate by Region
(In percent)

Region/Period	Total	Growth effect	Distribution effect	Interaction effect
Peru				
1971-85	-20.9	-11.0	-5.5	-4.4
1971-96	-13.6	-2.7	-8.7	-2.2
Rural				
1971-85	-29.2	-23.6	-0.9	-4.8
1971-96	-16.5	-13.0	3.8	-7.3
Urban				
1971-85	-3.6	1.0	-4.8	0.1
1971-96	5.9	14.1	-12.7	4.5

Source: Authors' calculations based on ENCA (1971-72) and ENNIV (1985-86 and 1996).

When a separate decomposition is performed for the urban and rural sectors, the results are qualitatively different. In the rural sector, the increase in family purchasing power resulted in a reduction in poverty. In the urban sector, until 1985 poverty fell basically because of a redistribution effect. Extending the analysis period to 1996, poverty worsened because the redistribution effect reduced the impact of the growth effect on poverty. The difference between the results for rural and urban areas, and the fact that the redistribution effect predominates in the national analysis, reveals a convergence of income and spending between urban and rural sectors.

It can be concluded that income dispersion has clearly fallen during the last 25 years. In the periods when spending grew, it contributed to a further reduction in poverty, and in the periods when spending fell, poverty intensified. In terms of well-being, although the reduction in the dispersion of spending had a positive effect, producing less poverty in the long run, this took place in a context in which average spending and income per capita were stagnant—although with fluctuations—for 25 years. So, the average Peruvian is in the same condition as 25 years ago, but all incomes are nearer the average. It is clear then that the Peruvian problem is more one of low average incomes than of distribution. While in the 1960s inequality was sufficient to prevent growth from having a positive impact on poverty reduction, in the future initial inequality could have a less negative impact on the interaction between poverty and growth (Ravallion, 1998).

Distribution of Assets

The dispersion of spending or income, as well as probabilities of people or families being poor or non-poor, depends on their stock of assets and its return or market price. Assuming that aside from possible interactions between different assets, the return on possession of an asset of physical, human, financial, public or organizational capital does not depend on its level, the distribution of assets plays an important role in the determination of the distribution of income and spending.

Table 7.3 shows the average level of possession of or access to different assets in the urban sector by spending quintile for 1985 and 1994. For example, in 1985, when the average years of education of heads of household was 6.9, the same value was only 4.9 years for heads of household in the poorest quintile but 10.5 years in the richest quintile. Access to a private educational institution, which on average reaches 10 percent of heads of household, clearly increases with the level of spending and triples in the richest quintile compared with the poorest. Potential experience, which approximates a person's time in the labor market, together with specific experience, which measures time in a firm or a job, does not show a clear pattern of variation by income quintile.[8] On the other hand, the youngest heads of household tend to be in the poorest income quintiles. Family size, which in large measure can approximate levels of human capital of the family not observed with other variables, changes dramatically by quintile, dropping from 7.2 members in the poorest quintile to 5.3 in the richest. Migration, an asset that represents the investment made to find a place where other assets are more productive, has a growing relationship with income. Thus, while among the poorest, 30 percent of household members have migrated, the figure is 51 percent for the rich. Other assets show much greater polarization. Only 21 percent of families in the poorest quintile have access to credit, rising to 50 percent in the richest quintile. For durable goods, average ownership for the richest decile was 15 times the figure for the poorest. Access to

---

[8] These data are based on the characteristics of the head of the family. When the same analysis is done for income distribution including all active members—heads and other family members who work—a very clear relationship is observed between experience and position in the income scale.

Table 7.3. Average Value of Assets by Per Capita Income Quintile: Urban Peru

Assets	Quintiles					
1985	Average	I	II	III	IV	V
Years of education of head of household	7.74	5.51	7.01	7.28	8.43	10.45
Average years of education of family	6.92	4.92	5.98	6.82	7.68	9.22
Heads of household who attended private schools (%)	0.10	0.07	0.07	0.09	0.11	0.19
Age of head of household	46.02	44.28	44.13	46.70	46.78	48.19
Labor experience	10.06	9.48	10.40	9.61	10.94	9.89
Potential experience	32.28	32.77	31.12	33.42	32.35	31.74
Family size	6.40	7.20	7.01	6.74	5.85	5.22
Migrants in the household (%)	0.41	0.31	0.36	0.41	0.43	0.51
Access to credit	0.37	0.22	0.28	0.42	0.44	0.50
Value of financial savings[2]	465.52	45.50	103.69	201.04	577.11	1,400.26
Value of durable goods[2]	6,438.49	1,430.70	3,081.01	4,532.87	6,353.57	16,794.32
Have water in home	0.71	0.54	0.65	0.70	0.79	0.89
Have sewerage in home	0.69	0.44	0.60	0.70	0.80	0.89
Electric power	0.86	0.72	0.81	0.86	0.92	0.97
Have telephone	0.14	0.03	0.05	0.08	0.17	0.37

Assets	Quintiles					
1994	Average	I	II	III	IV	V
Years of education of head of household	8.57	6.19	7.54	8.28	9.26	11.59
Average years of education of family	8.09	5.68	7.24	7.95	8.93	10.66
Educational institution of head of household[1]	0.07	0.05	0.04	0.05	0.06	0.17
Age of head of household	49.37	46.11	48.01	49.57	51.19	51.95
Labor experience	9.14	9.14	8.85	9.05	9.78	8.90
Potential experience	34.80	33.92	34.47	35.30	35.94	34.36
Family size	6.08	7.35	6.52	6.01	5.70	4.84
Migrants in household (%)	0.26	0.18	0.25	0.26	0.29	0.32
Access to credit	0.16	0.15	0.16	0.12	0.17	0.21
Value of financial savings[2]	203.23	16.50	90.96	40.41	132.20	736.06
Value of durable goods[2]	1,532.11	390.50	614.28	897.34	1,589.47	4,168.94
Have water supply in home	0.83	0.66	0.81	0.82	0.90	0.96
Have sewerage in home	0.70	0.43	0.63	0.69	0.85	0.92
Electric power	0.94	0.81	0.94	0.97	0.98	0.99
Have telephone	0.18	0.02	0.06	0.11	0.21	0.51

[1] Percentage of people who attend a private educational institution.

[2] Monetary values are expressed in 1996 dollars.

electricity, telephone, water and sewerage has a clear positive relationship with the position in spending distribution.

Obviously, the stock of assets is not a totally endogenous variable. The possession of assets depends on the possession of other assets, on changes in acquisition prices, and on the expected return on assets. However, patterns of possession of and access to assets by position on the scale of spending were relatively similar in 1994, although the average in some cases had changed. For example, access to water increased, while access to electric power had become almost universal, with the exception of the poorest quintile. Access to telephones, average level of education, average years of experience, and the age of the head of household also rose, although the distribution did not vary substantially.[9]

Table 7.4 shows the distribution of different assets by quintile for the rural sector. The changes in the averages and the pattern of ownership and assets between 1985 and 1994 are evident. In 1985, the level of schooling of heads of household was very low and unequal in the rural sector. A decade later, average years of education had increased from 2.9 to 5, and inequality had declined. Among the poorest sectors the schooling of the head almost doubled, while among the richest the increase was 50 percent. The average family size in the poorest quintile was 50 percent higher than the average in the richest quintile. On the other hand, access to credit was relatively segmented, being very low in the poorest quintile. The 1994 survey revealed that although global access to credit had fallen from 23 percent of farmers to 16 percent, it had increased for the poorest quintile and fallen for the other quintiles, particularly the richest. This is explained by the disappearance of the development banks, which concentrated on larger scale agriculture. In the case of access to basic services (electricity, water and sewerage), levels of access were low and not very equitable in 1985. In contrast, by 1994, access to water and electricity had doubled, reaching 27 percent and 24 percent of households, respectively. However, dispersion in access by spending decile is now much more pronounced.

With respect to the variables for agricultural activity, the sample is limited to agricultural producers. Dispersion of the ownership of livestock—

---

[9] Access to public services was expected to increase significantly by 1997 under commitments made by the companies that acquired privatized public enterprises.

Table 7.4. Average Value of Assets by Per Capita Spending Quintiles: Rural Peru

Assets	Quintiles					
1985	Average	I	II	III	IV	V
Years of education of head of household	2.92	2.28	2.45	2.88	3.28	3.72
Average years of education of family	2.78	2.15	2.38	2.87	2.96	3.54
Age of head of household	46.96	47.70	45.90	47.23	45.54	48.43
Labor experience of head of household	21.29	22.90	21.86	21.20	19.19	21.30
Potential experience of head of household	38.04	39.43	37.45	38.35	36.26	38.71
Family size	6.49	7.30	7.18	6.60	6.31	5.08
Migrants in household (%)	0.26	0.23	0.22	0.26	0.26	0.33
Access to credit	0.23	0.09	0.25	0.23	0.31	0.28
Value of financial savings[1]	74.74	4.63	22.36	48.23	78.63	219.85
Value of durable goods[1]	924.87	285.32	708.78	786.95	984.34	1,858.97
Have water in home	0.12	0.10	0.12	0.13	0.12	0.14
Have sewerage in home	0.03	0.01	0.01	0.03	0.04	0.05
Have electricity	0.12	0.04	0.07	0.13	0.17	0.18
Stock of livestock[2]	25.54	17.27	19.21	31.78	23.14	36.31
Stock of land[2]	8.20	4.24	5.10	9.64	10.87	11.14
Use of fertilizers[2]	18.87	16.48	19.10	20.08	18.77	19.92
Value of agricultural equipment[2]	633.13	27.37	53.58	467.60	184.15	2,432.94
Value of livestock[2]	3,977.11	1,932.70	2,650.81	5,000.43	3,856.92	6,444.69
Value of land[2]	8,020.46	3,338.84	5,396.56	6,682.89	6,930.81	17,753.18

Assets	Quintiles					
1994	Average	I	II	III	IV	V
Years of education of head of household	4.53	3.28	4.02	4.32	4.93	6.11
Average years of education of family	4.96	4.21	4.50	4.63	5.15	6.32
Age of head of household	45.71	45.16	44.05	44.44	46.08	48.79
Labor experience of head of household	18.25	19.83	17.83	17.01	18.46	18.11
Potential experience of head of household	34.74	34.96	33.55	33.81	34.92	36.47
Family size	6.32	7.67	6.98	6.06	6.02	4.88
Migrants in household (%)	0.11	0.08	0.08	0.11	0.12	0.16
Access to credit	0.16	0.10	0.15	0.20	0.17	0.19
Value of financial savings[1]	54.53	17.42	2.28	4.80	33.32	214.85
Value of durable goods[1]	391.83	71.28	179.72	146.01	490.20	1,071.92
Have water in home	0.27	0.26	0.26	0.21	0.26	0.34
Have sewerage in home	0.02	0.00	0.00	0.00	0.02	0.09
Have electricity	0.24	0.09	0.21	0.19	0.28	0.41
Stock of livestock[2]	18.99	20.47	15.32	19.14	16.30	23.74
Stock of land[2]	5.59	2.70	3.19	3.18	12.00	6.90
Use of fertilizers[2]	48.30	42.33	47.07	47.39	50.37	54.37
Value of agricultural equipment[2]	231.03	79.77	79.55	120.33	468.28	407.22

[1] Monetary values are expressed in 1996 dollars.

[2] The sample is restricted exclusively to agricultural producers.

measured in sheep equivalents—is relatively low, since the richest decile owns only double the poorest decile, although the disparity is greater when the value of livestock is used. A reduction of 35 percent was found in the average size of livestock units, although not observed among producers in the poorest quintile. However, this was very pronounced in the upper 60 percent of the distribution because the producers closest to the market were obliged to reduce their capital to cushion fluctuations in consumption in a context of falling real agricultural prices. The ENNIV also reveals that income from livestock forms a higher proportion of total income for the poorest producers, so it is more difficult for them to cushion consumption.

In the case of land, the differences in ownership between rich and poor are more marked than for livestock, while the disparity is even more evident for the value of agricultural equipment. For land, drastic changes took place in average levels of ownership between 1985 and 1994; however, the distribution of land ownership did not change significantly.

Assets of the Poor

Ownership of assets is analyzed as a determinant of the status of poverty. In other words, is possession of certain private assets or access to certain public or organizational assets a good predictor of poverty? Table 7.5 shows the proportion of poor urban households that possess certain assets. It is important to normalize these figures with respect to the poverty rates in each region, which are reported in the last line of the table. For example, in 1985, of urban households with water in the home, 28 percent were poor, a lower figure than the poverty rate of 33 percent for that year, which indicates that access to water is proportionately less among poor households. The figure for access to water rises to 36 percent in 1994; the poverty rate in that year, however, was 41.3 percent, so the relative access of the poor to this public service increased only slightly. In several public services such as electricity, water and sewerage, there was an increase in the proportion of poor with access to these services and in relative access to the service by the poor.[10]

---

[10] That is, the percentage of poor who have access to the service grew more rapidly than the poverty rate.

Table 7.5. Percentage of Urban Poor Who Have Specific Assets

Variables	1985	1994
Water in home	27.5	36.4
Sewerage in home	24.0	31.0
Make donations	21.2	13.7
Use electric power	28.3	38.7
Use kerosene	60.8	82.6
Have telephone	9.5	7.5
Have savings	17.3	13.9
Have over 770 soles in durable goods[1]	24.4	14.5
Have access to credit	22.3	32.2
Head has primary education	43.1	57.1
Head has secondary education	28.8	37.4
Head has higher education	10.0	11.9
Head has over 6 years of education	22.8	35.4
Family size of 7 or more	48.3	60.8
Poverty rate	33.0	41.3

[1] Monetary values are expressed in soles of June 1994.

Source: Authors' calculations based on ENNIV (1985-86 and 1994).

On the other hand, as the gap between the proportion of poor with access to an asset and the poverty rate widens, the asset is increasingly dispersed between the poor and the non-poor. For example, kerosene—a fuel inferior to electricity or gas—is used by a majority of the poor: in 1994, 82.4 percent of users were poor, with poverty rates of 41.3 percent. In this case, kerosene use increases the probability that a family can be classified as poor. Consistent with the results obtained by Saavedra and Díaz (1998), higher education reduces the probability of being poor, while primary education alone increases it. Finally, a very low percentage of families that have telephones, or over 770 soles (US$350) in durable goods or savings, can be defined as poor.

Table 7.6 shows the results of a similar analysis for the rural sector. Many assets in the rural sector do not necessarily "discriminate," in the sense that a high percentage of the poor own livestock, possess over two hectares

Table 7.6. Percentage of Rural Poor Who Have Specific Assets

Variables	Survey	
	1985	1994
Obtain water from river or ditch	56.5	70.5
Use electric power	31.4	49.9
Use kerosene	55.2	73.6
Have over 750 soles in durable goods[1]	34.8	29.0
Have over 300 soles in agricultural equipment[1]	35.9	56.5
Have livestock	50.6	69.3
Have over two hectares	53.2	58.2
Have access to credit	39.3	63.6
Have savings	34.1	33.4
Head has over 6 years of education	29.7	63.0
Head has primary education	52.3	70.2
Head has secondary education	32.7	56.6
Head has higher education	7.1	38.5
Family size of 7 or more members	66.1	81.4
Poverty rate	51.5	66.8

[1] Monetary values are expressed in soles of June 1994.

Source: Authors' calculations based on ENNIV (1985-86 and 1994).

of land, and use seeds and fertilizers.[11] There was, moreover, a clear increase in electric power by the poor from 1985 to 1994. As observed, the percentage of poor among those who own land or livestock is similar to the poverty rate. Assets that do seem to clearly differentiate the poor from the non-poor are education, savings and possession of durable goods.

Poverty and Demography

The incidence of poverty is not uniform between people with different characteristics. Table 7.7 shows that poverty is, as expected, greater among the

---

[11] This problem can be resolved by a joint analysis of the impact of access to or possession of several assets on levels of poverty, as will be seen later.

Table 7.7. Urban Poverty Indicators by Access to Assets

Variables	1985				1991				1994			
	%	FGT0	FGT1	FGT2	%	FGT0	FGT1	FGT2	%	FGT0	FGT1	FGT2
Educational level of head												
No education	5.2	48.8	19.7	11.7	4.7	70.3	30.6	16.8	5.7	69.5	26.7	14.0
Primary-initial	43.7	43.1	14.8	7.3	34.2	63.3	23.3	11.2	36.9	57.1	20.3	9.6
Incomplete secondary	14.1	33.2	9.5	4.1	14.6	59.1	20.9	10.2	13.5	48.2	14.3	5.8
Complete secondary	20.4	25.8	6.1	2.7	26.4	45.7	14.1	6.1	23.4	31.1	8.7	3.4
Incomplete higher	4.2	17.4	7.4	5.0	5.8	35.1	10.1	4.1	6.0	15.6	3.1	0.9
Complete higher	12.3	7.5	3.1	2.1	14.4	21.3	4.3	1.3	14.4	10.3	2.0	0.9
Gender												
Women	14.5	33.1	11.4	5.9	16.3	47.6	16.7	8.2	17.6	37.2	12.3	5.6
Men	85.5	33.0	10.7	5.3	83.7	51.3	17.5	8.1	82.4	42.2	13.8	6.2

less educated. For example, in 1994 the urban poverty rate, which averaged 41.5 percent, exceeded 57 percent among individuals with primary or lower education, and 40 percent of the poor had this educational level. In contrast, the incidence of poverty among people with higher education was only 10 percent, and this group constituted only 14 percent of all poor. In 1991, when the poverty rate rose, participation of the more educated (i.e., those with completed secondary or higher education) in the total poor also increased. This could be counterintuitive, if it is assumed that the more educated are better prepared for macroeconomic crises. There is evidence, however, that during the period immediately after hyperinflation, the return on educational assets declined. What determines the probability of being poor is not only possession of certain assets, but also their market price at any given time. On the other hand, the poverty gap is much greater among the less educated.

Unlike in other countries in Latin America, the incidence of poverty in Peru is lower in households headed by women. This has been the case since 1991 and is consistent with the increase in the rate of activity of women and the increase in their income relative to men.[12]

Table 7.8 shows similar indicators for the rural sector, where poverty is much more concentrated among people with a lower educational level. Only 10 percent of the poor have completed secondary or further education. However, given the high incidence of poverty in general in the rural sector, the incidence of poverty only falls below 20 percent in the case of people with a completed higher education. The poverty gap between the more and less educated is much larger in the urban areas. In the case of gender in rural areas, the incidence of poverty is, as in urban areas, lower among families headed by women.

Relationship between Assets, Returns and Poverty: A Static Analysis

Depending on the conceptual framework, the relationship between possession of or access to certain assets and poverty can be seen either as a profile of poverty or an attempt to understand its determinants. Based on the static

---

[12] This does not necessarily mean that gender differences, ceteris paribus, are important in explaining differences in the state of poverty or in the transition between non-poor and poor. This requires "control" through possession of the other assets.

Table 7.8. Rural Poverty Indicators by Access to Assets

Variables	1985-86				1991				1994			
	%	FGT0	FGT1	FGT2	%	FGT0	FGT1	FGT2	%	FGT0	FGT1	FGT2
Education of head												
No education	27.3	59.1	26.8	16.4	13.3	79.6	33.5	17.2	15.3	79.2	31.3	16.5
Primary-initial	63.2	52.3	22.1	12.4	60.9	74.0	35.1	20.3	59.9	70.2	28.7	15.0
Incomplete secondary	5.0	30.9	12.6	7.3	11.3	78.9	40.7	24.7	13.2	61.2	20.7	9.7
Complete secondary	3.2	35.5	12.4	5.8	11.0	63.6	29.5	16.5	8.9	49.9	16.4	7.6
Incomplete higher	0.7	12.9	1.4	0.2	1.5	43.8	17.6	10.9	1.2	62.8	23.0	11.7
Complete higher[1]	0.6	-	-	-	2.0	30.4	10.0	3.5	1.5	19.8	5.5	1.6
Gender												
Women	11.3	44.1	21.3	13.1	9.5	65.8	26.2	13.7	8.0	52.7	19.1	9.5
Men	88.7	53.0	22.4	12.8	90.5	73.5	34.9	20.1	92.0	69.0	27.2	14.0
Land												
Yes	19.0	50.9	22.8	14.2	6.2	75.2	34.2	18.6	8.2	69.5	28.7	14.9
No	81.0	52.2	22.2	12.5	93.8	72.7	34.1	19.5	91.8	67.6	26.3	13.5
Total	100.0	52.0	22.3	12.9	100.0	72.8	34.1	19.5	100.0	67.7	26.5	13.6

[1] This variable is only defined for 1991 and 1994.

model of optimization of household decisions on production and consumption, it is possible to derive a relationship between household spending and possession of assets, which is susceptible to empirical evaluation.

In fact, assuming that households as producers maximize benefits subject to the usual technological restrictions (i.e., production function), and as consumers maximize their welfare by optimizing their consumption and work decisions given the level of gains obtained, it is possible to establish a direct connection between the household's possession of and access to assets, and its levels of spending. The reduced form of this problem of optimization can be represented in terms of the following spending equation:

$$G = G(p;A) = G(p;A_{hum}, A_{fis}, A_{fin}, A_{pub\&org})$$

(1)

where p is the price vector and A is the vector that includes all the assets to which the household has access. These assets can in turn be classified as assets associated with human capital (A_{hum}), physical capital (A_{fis}), financial capital (A_{fin}) and public and organizational capital ($A_{pub\&org}$).

This equation establishes a direct connection, given an economic context, between possession of or access to assets by a household and its spending capacity. If our definition of poverty is based on the indicator of household spending, it is possible to rewrite equation (1) as follows:[13]

$$P = P(A_{hum}, A_{fis}, A_{fin}, A_{pub\&org})$$

(2)

where P indicates the probability of a household being poor or non-poor.

Tables 7.9 and 7.10 show the estimates of equation (6), which has been performed as an estimate of a probit model at urban and rural levels for each year for which information from ENNIV is available. In general, the results for 1985-86 are consistent. Variables of human capital such as years of education of the head and members over age 14, family size, financial

---

[13] Assuming separability between the price vector and the assets, equation (5) can be expressed as $G^* = G^*(A_{hum}, A_{fis}, A_{fin}, A_{pub\&org})$ where the regional price vector is included in the spending calculation; that is, the spending is expressed in this case at constant values of the city of Lima.

Table 7.9. Estimates of the Determinants of Urban Poverty
(Marginal effects)

Variables	1985-86	1991	1994	1996
Intercept	0.1409	0.7232	0.3995	0.0214
	(2.789)	(4.750)	(4.399)	(0.105)
Years of education of head	-0.0109	-0.0156	-0.0204	-0.0195
	-(2.142)	-(1.346)	-(2.452)	-(1.570)
Years of education of head squared	0.0002	-0.0001	-0.0001	0.0000
	(0.683)	-(0.103)	-(0.120)	(0.005)
Years of education of rest of household	-0.0090	-0.0361	-0.0245	-0.0135
(over age 14)	-(4.773)	-(8.081)	-(7.597)	-(2.829)
Potential experience (head)	0.0000	-0.0015	-0.0003	-0.0026
	-(0.084)	-(1.219)	-(0.386)	-(2.075)
Marital status (married)	-0.0002	0.0959	0.0695	0.1132
	-(0.008)	(1.861)	(1.766)	(2.040)
Gender of head of household	-0.0120	-0.0542	0.0160	-0.0925
	-(0.502)	-(1.006)	(0.386)	-(1.596)
% of migrants in household	-0.0559	-0.1353	-0.1221	0.0004
	-(2.426)	-(2.719)	-(3.043)	(0.005)
Days of illness (head)	-0.0070	0.0076	-0.0029	-0.0314
	-(1.606)	(0.717)	-(0.339)	-(0.999)
Family size	0.0328	0.0802	0.0675	0.0864
	(10.000)	(11.650)	(12.692)	(10.604)
Proportion of people				
with 6 years or more	-0.0724	-0.3040	-0.1848	-0.0505
	-(1.756)	-(3.028)	-(2.635)	-(0.394)
Financial savings	-0.1190	-0.1023	-0.1417	-204.8
	-(6.922)	-(2.781)	-(3.246)	-(2.357)
Durable goods	-0.0124	0.0001	-0.0084	-0.0940
	-(8.647)	(1.230)	-(2.536)	-(5.440)
Own home	-0.0018	0.0707	-0.0370	-0.0661
	-(0.143)	(2.341)	-(1.680)	-(1.986)
Potable water in home	-0.0480	-0.0787	-0.1187	-0.0343
	-(2.611)	-(1.367)	-(3.045)	-(0.578)
Sewerage in home	-0.0394	-0.0631	-0.0850	-0.0630
	-(2.595)	-(1.302)	-(3.340)	-(1.463)
Have electric power	-0.0600	-0.2642	-0.1121	0.1215
	-(2.140)	-(2.624)	-(2.047)	(0.791)
Have telephone	-0.0411	-0.3091	-0.2424	-0.1959
	-(1.816)	-(7.275)	-(6.205)	-(4.779)
Membership of associations	-0.0700	-0.1211	-0.1132	-0.0540
	-(3.897)	-(2.281)	-(2.269)	-(0.794)
Pseudo R²	0.265	0.246	0.318	0.347
Prediction rate	0.821	0.746	0.802	0.810

Note: The z-statistics are in brackets.
Source: Authors' calculations based on ENNIV (1985-86, 1991, 1994 and 1996).

Table 7.10. Estimates of Determinants of Rural Poverty
(Marginal effects)

Variables	1985-86	1991	1994	1996
Intercept	-0.2318	0.2578	0.4114	0.4851
	-(2.456)	(1.470)	(3.625)	(1.951)
Years of education of head	-0.0116	-0.0308	-0.0315	-0.0692
	-(1.153)	-(1.643)	-(2.471)	-(2.686)
Years of education of head squared	-0.0004	0.0000	0.0002	0.0030
	-(0.409)	-(0.030)	(0.242)	(1.490)
Years of education of rest of household	-0.0177	-0.0318	-0.0264	-0.0301
(over age 14)	-(3.668)	-(4.352)	-(5.331)	-(2.991)
Potential experience (of head)	0.0005	-0.0061	-0.0019	-0.0009
	(0.560)	-(3.534)	-(1.554)	-(0.362)
Marital status	0.0238	-0.1262	0.0143	0.0674
	(0.599)	-(1.584)	(0.228)	(0.537)
Gender of head of household	-0.0076	0.1182	0.0754	-0.0693
	-(0.168)	(1.236)	(1.077)	-(0.482)
% of migrants in household	-0.0273	-0.0685	-0.1895	-0.1425
	-(0.666)	-(0.594)	-(2.791)	-(0.804)
Days of illness (head)	0.0106	-0.0341	-0.0045	-0.0608
	(1.306)	-(1.790)	-(0.385)	-(1.025)
Family size	0.0709	0.1186	0.0875	0.1434
	(12.665)	(8.464)	(11.241)	(8.258)
Proportion of people with				
6 or more years	-0.0343	-0.2220	-0.5144	-0.7783
	-(0.429)	-(1.353)	-(5.105)	-(3.418)
Financial savings	0.0055	-1.2029	-C.2038	-421.6
	(0.374)	-(1.229)	-(3.154)	-(2.278)
Durable goods	-0.0492	-0.0001	-0.0002	-0.2784
	-(8.305)	-(0.832)	-(0.145)	-(4.321)
Size of land	-0.0001	-0.0029	-0.0001	0.0020
	-(0.844)	-(1.037)	-(0.171)	(0.359)
Own home	-0.0311	0.0656	-0.0079	0.0342
	-(0.989)	(0.888)	-(0.213)	(0.443)
Potable water in home	-0.0133	0.1025	-0.0324	0.0870
	-(0.546)	(1.981)	(1.070)	(1.382)
Sewerage in home	-0.0586	0.0217	-0.1461	-0.1301
	-(1.409)	(0.448)	-(3.461)	-(1.614)
Have electric power	-0.0113	0.0224	0.0310	0.0414
	-(0.242)	(0.318)	(0.667)	(0.410)
Membership of associations	-0.2248	-0.2000	-0.0871	-0.2339
	-(6.580)	-(1.840)	-(1.361)	-(2.932)
Pseudo R²	0.155	0.249	0.219	0.316
Prediction rate	0.696	0.757	0.731	0.796

Note: z-statistics are in brackets.

Source: Authors' calculations based on ENNIV (1985-86, 1991, 1994 and 1996).

capital (savings, durable goods or home ownership), access to public services and organizational capital (water, sewerage and electricity, along with membership in organizations) are consistently significant with the correct sign. Migratory experience in times of crisis also appears as significant (e.g., in 1991).

In the urban sector, the variables of access with guarantees to the capital market are significant (durable goods and home ownership), as are the human capital variables mentioned above. In the rural sector, the variables associated with public and organizational capital are important (access to water and sewerage and membership in associations), followed by variables associated with financial capital (financial savings and durable goods). It is interesting to note that, confirming what was mentioned above, access to land does not discriminate between the poor and non-poor in the rural sector. Nor were differences found by gender of head of household. The gender difference identified in the preceding section was diluted when controlled by possession of and access to the other assets.

The negative sign of the variable of family size is very strong.[14] A possible interpretation is that smaller families are better able to increase their assets to leave poverty. However, this variable could also be appearing as a proxy for other variables of human capital that are not observed.

Another interesting indicator that can be derived from the per capita spending equations is the "cross elasticity" between asset i and asset j:

$$\varepsilon_{A_i A_j} = \frac{\partial(\frac{\partial G}{\partial A_i})}{\partial A_j} \; x \; A_{jover} \; \frac{\partial G}{\partial A_i} \tag{3}$$

---

[14] The negative relationship appears in both the spending equations and the probit equations. This relationship between larger families and lower spending or greater probability of being poor maintains its sign and significance even when economies of scale in consumption are incorporated, although it can obviously change in magnitude. Simulations with a parameter of economies of scale in consumption from 0.5 to 1 confirmed this statement, since economies of scale would require an implausible magnitude to reverse the signs of the relationships. See Annex 2 of Escobal, Saavedra and Torero (1999).

As $\dfrac{\partial G}{\partial A_i}$ is a proxy for the return on asset A_i; $\varepsilon_{A_i A_j}$ it simulates the percentage rise in return on one asset in relation to a percentage increase in the possession of the other assets.[15] The estimated spending equation is semi-logarithmic and includes the interactions between assets. Given the functional form chosen, the elasticities vary throughout the range of interest of the assets which, although complicating the calculation, gives much more flexibility, permitting the estimate of different values for the elasticities at the average values of each quintile.[16]

Table 7.11 shows these estimates for the return on the assets of education and land in relation to changes in the possession of other assets of human capital (family size) and access to public assets (sewerage, electricity, roads). In all cases, except in relation to changes in family size, the cross elasticities are positive, and the changes in the return on education and land in relation to a change in the access to public goods are greater in the richest strata. Family size is again negative and "progressive" in the sense that the reductions in the return on education are higher in the richest quintile. Finally, the simulations show that one more year of education increases the return on land by 3 percent to 4 percent, evidence of the complementarity of both assets.

Assets and Transition between States of Poverty

Access to assets of human, physical and financial capital and public or organizational capital would not only raise the return on private assets but also have an effect on the process of asset accumulation. Thus, the original possession of assets, their process of accumulation and the existence of external shocks would be the determinants of the transition of households along the scale of income or spending. Under this criterion, it is possible to derive an

---

[15] This "return" is approximated by the effect generated by an additional unit of an asset on the value of its marginal product, measured in terms of household spending.

[16] If a double-logarithmic functional form of the parameters of the cross products had been used, the elasticities would be constant, but this would obviously be less interesting because the effect of a change of assets would be the same between rich and poor.

Table 7.11. Change in the Return on Education and Land in Relation to an Increase in Selected Assets

(Simulation)

Variable	Quintile				
	1	2	3	4	5
Urban 1985-86	Return on education				
One additional member in family	-12.0	-12.3	-13.1	-14.0	-16.2
Access to sewerage in home	8.1	8.7	10.3	10.5	10.9
Access to electric power	14.1	14.2	14.8	14.2	15.6
Urban 1994	Return on education				
One additional member in family	-12.1	-12.7	-12.1	-12.7	-12.9
Access to sewerage in home	8.0	11.3	13.4	14.5	14.4
Access to electric power	13.8	14.0	15.6	15.1	15.1
Rural 1985-86	Return on education				
One additional member in family	-15.6	-16.6	-17.5	-18.1	-22.6
Access to sewerage in home	0.5	1.0	1.4	2.3	2.5
One additional hectare of land	2.4	0.9	1.1	1.2	1.0
	Return on land				
One additional year of education	4.1	3.8	3.6	3.5	3.2
Rural 1994	Return on education				
One additional member in family	-29.6	-30.2	-29.6	-30.0	-29.0
Access to sewerage in home	1.3	1.5	1.8	2.1	4.3
Access to electric power	11.3	9.4	6.4	4.6	-0.6

Note: The values show the percentage change in the profitability of education and land in relation to a discrete change in their selected variables. The results are evaluated on the average values of each quintile. The quintiles are ordered from lower to higher.

Source: Authors' calculations based on estimates of semi-logarithmic spending equations.

equation that represents the transition of a household from one level of spending to another, or alternatively from states of poverty or non-poverty:

$$\Delta P = P(A_{i\,0},\, A_{j\,0},\, A_{k\,0},\, A_{l\,0};\; \Delta A_i,\, \Delta A_j,\, \Delta A_k,\, \Delta A_l, \eta\,) \; ; \; i \in A_{hum},\; j \in A_{fis},\; k \in A_{fin},\; k \in A_{pub\&org}$$

(4)

where all the variables have been defined, except η, which represents a vector of short-term shocks that affect current income/spending. This chapter introduces two variables to capture short-term shocks: the spending of the Compensation and Social Development Fund (FONCODES) between 1991 and 1994 and the change in labor status between both years (the difference between the household occupation rate measured as the number of household members who work compared with the number of members over age 14). Both variables attempt to capture short-term modifications in the macro-environment that have not yet resulted in changes in the possession of assets.

To evaluate the transition between states of poverty, a panel of 1,316 households surveyed in 1991 and 1994 was used. To see how representative the panel is with respect to the 1991 sample, the panel information for the principal variables under study was compared with data that do not form part of the panel because the households were not present in the 1994 survey. The coverage of the panel represents 71.5 percent of the 1991 sample. The results, based on the principal variables under study, show that the information at panel level does not contain significant differences in relation to the total 1991 sample. However, the panel assigns greater weight to the urban north coast and lesser weight to metropolitan Lima. In relation to the poverty rate, the panel captures the distribution of the total sample, although with a slight bias, since it captures 74 percent of the poor and only 71 percent of the non-poor.

The estimate of equation (4) requires the use of a discrete variable to indicate the changes between the different states, and the use of a multinomial logit to estimate the effect of the possession of different types of assets on the probability that, for example, a household might remain in poverty or make a successful transition out of it. The advantage of the multinomial logit approach used here, as opposed to direct maximum likelihood, is that it explicitly identifies the effects of the possession of different assets on the transition process.

Since certain changes in the possession of assets can be considered endogenous to the process of household decision-making, the changes have to be instrumentalized, especially for changes in key assets such as education, financial saving, land or livestock. Changes in public assets are considered exogenous to the process of household decision-making and are not therefore instrumentalized. For instrumentalization, the endowment of initial assets is used, both those that appear in the estimate and others not considered in the estimated model (e.g., education of the rest of the household). Since the set of explanatory variables shows an important degree of collinearity, certain restrictions were imposed. In particular, the estimated model assumes that the changes in possession of assets help explain the transitions but do not affect the households that remained in the same state between 1991 and 1994. It is also assumed that the asset levels help explain why certain households remain poor or non-poor but are less important in explaining the transition.[17] In addition, because of the small number of panel observations for the rural sector, the model was estimated for the entire sample.

Table 7.12 shows the results obtained from the proposed multinomial logit model. The model maintained 15 explanatory variables previously analyzed that are indicators of the assets of human capital (education of head of household, potential labor experience, gender differences, migratory ability, illnesses in the household and family size), assets of physical and financial capital (savings, durable goods, land, livestock), and of public and organizational capital (access to water, electricity, sewerage, telephone and membership in social organizations). The prediction rate of the model is reasonably high for households that remain in their initial state (poor or non-poor). In contrast, the prediction rate for households that make the transition from states of poverty is low, reflecting the inability to capture adequately all short-term shocks that affect the transitory income or spending of the households.

The multivariate logit-type models have the property of independence of irrelevant alternatives (IIA), that is, to add or reduce alternatives or states does not affect the relative probabilities of the state maintained in the model.

---

[17] These assumptions appear reasonable in light of the results of the unrestricted logit model, with the sole exception of the educational variable in the equations that explain the transitions (the variable that was introduced in the model). It should be noted that due to the high collinearity verified between the changes in the assets and their levels, these restrictions were imposed ex ante.

Table 7.12. Multinomial Analysis of Changes in States of Poverty
(Marginal effects)

I: In transition	Poor to non-poor		Non-poor to poor	
	Coefficients	z-statistic	Coefficients	z-statistic
Education of head of household	-0.002	-0.519	-0.006	-2.500
Gender	0.018	0.433	0.006	0.241
(Education of head of household)[1]	0.007	1.489	-0.012	-4.098
(Potential labor experience)	-0.002	-1.623	0.002	-2.127
(Migration)	0.146	2.486	-0.078	-2.053
(Land)[1]	0.021	1.552	-0.003	-1.384
(Access to potable water)	0.017	0.310	0.063	2.218
(Access to sewerage)	0.021	0.290	0.000	-0.007
(Access to electricity)	0.029	0.324	-0.063	-0.938
(Access to telephone)	0.051	0.670	-0.100	-1.174
(Family size)	-0.034	-5.124	0.028	6.842
(Financial savings)[1]	-0.014	-0.068	0.045	0.345
(Livestock)[1]	-0.001	-0.882	-0.001	-1.796
(Community capital)	-0.062	-0.799	-0.003	-0.075
(Labor status)	0.052	1.806	-0.057	-3.184
FONCODES	0.000	0.304	0.000	-0.864
Constant	-0.058	-0.922	-0.063	-1.870

II: Constant	Poor to non-poor		Non-poor to poor	
	Coefficients	z-statistic	Coefficients	z-statistic
Education of head of household	-0.032	-7.047	0.049	8.713
Potential labor experience	-0.005	-4.193	0.008	5.416
Gender	0.031	0.883	-0.086	-1.668
Migration	-0.202	-3.569	0.137	1.992
Illness	-0.002	-0.147	-0.003	-0.232
Family size	0.062	8.357	-0.092	-10.011
Financial savings	-0.466	-2.842	0.315	3.450
Durable goods	0.000	1.186	0.000	-0.682
Land	0.000	0.008	0.001	0.347
Access to potable water	-0.018	-0.520	-0.056	-0.988
Access to sewerage	-0.003	-0.104	0.077	1.607
Access to electricity	-0.049	-0.906	0.101	1.148
Access to telephone	-0.446	-4.417	0.418	6.016
Community capital	0.448	1.845	0.063	0.179
Livestock	0.002	2.234	-0.004	-2.333
Labor status	0.077	3.397	-0.102	-2.918
FONCODES	0.000	-0.003	0.000	-0.085
Constant	0.181	2.162	-0.156	-1.239
Pseudo R^2			0.195	

[1] These variables were instrumentalized to correct possible bias due to endogenous effects.

Table 7.13. Hausman Test for IIA

Excluding alternative poor-poor	13.7563
Excluding alternative poor/non-poor	10.9349
Excluding alternative non-poor/poor	11.1669
Excluding alternative non-poor/non-poor	62.6985

Test: Where s indicates the estimators based on the restricted subset of alternatives, and f indicates the estimators with all the set of alternatives. The critical value is 75.35 at the level of 1 percent.

Table 7.14. Probability of Transition
(In percent)

States	Effective	Estimate
Poor to poor	29.3	35.7
Poor to non-poor	21.0	10.5
Non-poor to poor	10.0	3.0
Non-poor to non-poor	39.7	50.8
Total	100.0	100.0

This property could be undesirable in a model such as that proposed here because the states are conditional on the initial position of each household. To verify that this property does not generate important biases in the results obtained, the statistical test developed by Hausman and McFadden (1984) was used. As shown in Table 7.13, in our case the tests show that the estimates of the proposed model were not affected by this assumption; the probabilities of transition are presented in Table 7.14.

The results reveal that human capital assets (years of education of head of household, potential experience of head, migratory experience and family size), financial capital (savings), physical capital (livestock) and public and organizational capital (access to telephone and membership in associations) are crucial in explaining why certain households remain in a state of poverty or non-poverty. Changes in some human capital assets (migratory experience and family size) as well as the positive shocks associated with change in the labor status are the variables that best explain the transition from poverty. Conversely, the variables that best explain why certain households that were not poor in 1991 had become poor by 1994 are the level and change in educational achievement of the head of household, changes in labor and migratory experience, lack of access to public goods, and the adverse shock associated with the change in labor status.

Gender differences are not important in any of the four states analyzed. In addition, of the short-term shocks identified (FONCODES spending and change in labor status), only the second has explanatory power for understanding the reasons why a household moves into or out of poverty. Lastly, as expected, family size reduces the probability of improving status and is a determinant in explaining why some households remain in poverty.

Conclusions

In spite of long-term reductions and improvements in the 1990s, there is still an extreme amount of poverty in Peru, and poverty continued to affect almost half the population in the mid-1990s. This study has empirically verified the key assets that characterize the country's poor. It has attempted to better understand the connection between assets and poverty, analyzing changes in the distribution of assets, the link between access to or holding of these assets and poverty, and the connection between their return and poverty. Given that many of these assets are reasonably exogenous, at least in the short term, an understanding of these relationships enriches the debate on which public policies could have the greatest effect on poverty reduction.

In the Peruvian case, the study shows the importance of variables such as education and family size for classifying the state of a person's poverty through the analysis of probit models and spending regressions. The analysis also confirms that access to credit and ownership of assets that can be used as collateral have a positive effect on spending and on the probability of not being poor. Finally, statistical evidence showed a similar impact from variables of public and organizational capital such as membership in organizations, and access to basic public services such as water, sewerage, electricity and telephone. In this respect, the empirical analysis is consistent with the view that the lack of access to certain key assets, which generate sufficient income for loans for a part of the population, underlies the problem of poverty.

The level of assets and the changes in returns on them are as important as the possession of assets in the determination of the status of poverty. These returns can also be modified by access to complementary key assets (for instance, the complementarity between public and private assets). This points to the role of public policy in terms of providing services and infrastructure as a mechanism to strengthen the return on private assets to help reduce poverty.

An analysis of the effect of ownership of assets on mobility between poverty and non-poverty found the initial levels of assets sufficient to explain the transition, although they are crucial in explaining permanence in one state or the other. This is to be expected, since the sample of households in panel form was for a relatively short period (1991-94). Education, labor experience and family size, as well as savings, access to telephone service and ownership of livestock, are the most important variables in explaining whether a household will remain in its original state of poverty. Thus, there is a close relationship between assets and chronic poverty. If the root causes of this problem are not tackled—that is, the lack of income-earning assets and the restrictions on acquiring them—it is highly likely that poverty will continue to be one of Peru's major challenges for many years to come.

References

Amat y León, C. 1981. *Distribución del ingreso familiar en el Perú*. Lima: Centro de Investigación de la Universidad del Pacífico.

Amat y León, C., and L.D. Curonisy. 1990. *La alimentación en el Perú*. Lima: Centro de Investigación de la Universidad del Pacífico.

Birdsall, N., and J.L. Londoño. 1998. Assets Inequality Matters. *American Economic Review* 87(2): 32-37.

Briceño, A., A. Pascó-Font, J. Escobal, et al. 1992. *Gestión pública y distribución del ingreso: tres estudios de caso para la economía peruana*. Working Paper 115. Inter-American Development Bank/Grupo de Análisis para el Desarrollo, Washington, DC.

Bruno, M., M. Ravallion, and L. Squire. 1998. Equity and Growth in the Developing World: Old and New Perspectives on the Policy Issues. In V. Tanzi and C. Key-Young (eds.), *Income Distribution and High Quality Growth*. Cambridge, MA: MIT Press.

Caballero, J.M., and E. Alvarez. 1980. *Aspectos cuantitativos de la reforma agraria (1969-1979)*. Lima: Instituto de Estudios Peruanos.

CEPAL. 1989. Antecedentes estadísticos de la distribución del ingreso Perú, 1961-1982. Serie Distribución del Ingreso. Santiago.

Datt, G. 1998. *Computational Tools for Poverty Measurement and Analysis*. Discussion Paper 50. International Food Policy Research Institute, Washington, DC.

Datt, G., and M. Ravallion. 1992. Growth and Redistribution Components of Changes in Poverty Measures: A Decomposition with Applications to Brazil and India in the 1980s. *Journal of Development Economics* 38(3): 275-95.

Escobal, J., J. Saavedra, and M. Torero. 1999. *Los activos de los pobres en el Perú*. Latin American Research Network Paper R-361. Inter-American Development Bank Research Department, Washington, DC.

Escobal, J., and M. Castillo. 1994. *Sesgo en la medición de la inflación en contextos inflacionarios: el caso peruano*. Working Paper 21, Grupo de Análisis para el Desarrollo, Lima.

Figueroa, A. 1982. *El problema distributivo en diferentes contextos socio-políticos y económicos: Perú 1950-1980*. Working Paper 51. Centro de Investigaciones Sociológicas, Económicas, Políticas y Antropológicas, Lima.

Glewwe, P. 1987. *The Distribution of Welfare in Peru: Living Standard Measurement Study.* Working Paper No. 42, World Bank, Washington, DC.

Hausman, J., and D. McFadden. 1984. A Specification Test for the Multinomial Logit Model. *Econometrica* 52: 1219-240.

Instituto Cuánto. 1994. *Retrato de la familia peruana: niveles de vida.* Volume I. Lima, Peru: Instituto Cuánto.

———. 1993. *Niveles de vida: Perú: subidas y caídas.* Lima: Instituto Cuánto/UNICEF.

Instituto Nacional de Estadística e Informática (INEI), and Ministry of Agriculture. 1995. *Tercer Censo Nacional Agropecuario, Perú Compendio Estadístico: Avance de resultados.* Volume II. Lima: INEI.

Maletta, H. 1996. Sustitución en el consumo, medición del costo de vida y tipo de cambio en Argentina, 1960-1885. Report presented to the World Bank, Buenos Aires. Mimeo.

Maletta, H., and K. Makhlouf. 1987. *Perú: las provincias en cifras 1876-1981. Volumen III: Estructura agraria.* Statistical Series No. 2, Universidad del Pacífico, Lima.

Medina, A. 1996. Pobreza, crecimiento y desigualdad: Perú 1991-1994. In G. Moncada and R. Webb (eds.), *¿Cómo estamos? Análisis de la Encuesta de Niveles de Vida.* Lima: Instituto Cuánto/UNICEF.

Moncada, G., and R. Webb (eds.). *¿Cómo estamos? Análisis de la Encuesta de Niveles de Vida.* Lima: Instituto Cuánto/UNICEF.

Psacharopoulos, G., and M. Woodhall. 1984. *Education for Development: An Analysis of Investment Choices.* New York: Oxford University Press.

Ravallion, M. 1998. *Reaching Poor Areas in a Federal System.* Policy Research Group Working Paper 1901, World Bank, Washington, DC.

Rodríguez, J. 1991a. Distribución salarial y educación en Lima Metropolitana: 1970-1984. Grupo de Análisis para el Desarrollo, Lima. Mimeo.

———. 1991b. Distribución del ingreso en el Perú: una relectura de las evidencias. Grupo de Análisis para el Desarrollo, Lima. Mimeo.

Saavedra, J. 1997. *¿Quiénes ganan y quiénes pierden con una reforma estructural? Cambios en la dispersión de ingresos según educación, experiencia y género en el Perú urbano.* Notas para el Debate No. 14. Grupo de Análisis para el Desarrollo, Lima.

Saavedra, J., and J.J. Díaz. 1998. Desigualdad del ingreso y del gasto en el Perú antes y después de las reformas estructurales. Report presented to ECLAC. GRADE, Lima. Mimeo.

Webb, R.C. 1977. *Government Policy and the Distribution of Income in Peru, 1963-1973*. Harvard Economic Studies 47. Cambridge and London: Harvard University Press.

Webb, R.C., and A. Figueroa. 1975. Distribución del ingreso en el Perú. Perú Problema 14. Instituto de Estudios Peruanos, Lima.

CHAPTER EIGHT

Where to from Here? Generating Capabilities and Creating Opportunities for the Poor

Miguel Székely

Poverty is present in all modern societies. Even in the richest countries in the world, few would disagree that some people have unacceptably low living standards.[1] How to address the problem of poverty, however, is still unclear. Recently, an old debate has been revived: is the solution to reduce poverty through economic growth, or should governments actively pursue poverty reduction policies? There are basically two opposing views. One is that incomes of the poor grow one-for-one with economic growth; therefore, policies that guarantee growth implicitly contribute to poverty reduction, and the justification for additional social policies is unclear.[2] The other view is that incomes of the poor grow less than one-for-one with average income.[3] The poor might in fact benefit from growth, but since the effect is rather small, growth alone will take too long to solve the problem—if it does so at all. According to this view, the state should foster growth-enhancing policies as well as those aimed at improving the well-being of those most in need.

---

[1] If one uses a definition of poverty of $2 per day, the proportion of poor in most developed countries turns out to be very small (around 2 percent of the total population). But this type of definition, which might be appropriate for developing countries, is meaningless in the context of rich countries. In the developed world, the poverty line is usually relative to the standard of living of each population. These definitions always yield poverty rates well over the absolute poverty levels.

[2] See Dollar and Kraay (2000), Gallup, Radelet and Warner (1999), and Roemer and Gugerty (1997).

[3] See Bourguignon (2001), Birdsall and de la Torre (2001) and Foster and Székely (2001).

This book has argued that growth alone does not guarantee a solution to the poverty problem, at least in Latin America. Consider the following two examples. Between 1996 and 1998, GDP per capita increased in Mexico by 9.7 percent in real terms, which is a spectacular gain as judged by the country's macroeconomic performance during the previous 16 years. However, poverty hardly declined. In fact, the incomes of the poorest 30 percent of the population contracted during this period. The huge increase in mean income was due entirely to income gains among the richest 30 percent— particularly the richest 10 percent—of the population.[4]

The second example is Chile, which has been characterized as one of the most successful economic growth stories in Latin America for the past decade. Between 1992 and 1996, Chilean GDP per capita expanded by more than 30 percent in real terms. During the same period, moderate poverty registered a substantial decline from 20 to 16 percent—a reduction of 20 percent in the head count ratio. But income inequality also increased during the period (the Gini index rose by 7 percent). In fact, had the income distribution remained the same as in 1992, the proportion of poor would have actually declined to 10 percent, rather than 16 percent—that is, the poverty rate would have been cut by one half, instead of by 20 percent.[5]

These two examples show that growth by itself does not necessarily guarantee a solution to the poverty problem, and that growth alone may result in much lower poverty reduction, especially if its benefits are concentrated among the wealthier sectors of the population. This suggests that while growth-enhancing policies should be given high priority, poverty reduction should be actively pursued through a wider set of policies.

The objective of this book has been to outline a framework to think about which policies can lead to substantial poverty reduction. The introductory chapter and the country studies have generated evidence supporting the idea that income is just the tip of the iceberg. Once one goes beyond income and looks into what is behind the process of income generation (the

---

[4] See Székely and Hilgert (2001).

[5] This result is obtained by using the CASEN household survey for 1992, and multiplying all incomes by 1.3 to simulate the growth rate registered between 1992 and 1996. The poverty rate computed after this adjustment can be interpreted as the poverty that would have been observed had the distribution remained unchanged between the two years. Obviously, this is only a simulation for illustration purposes, since there is no guarantee that growth would have been the same under a static distribution.

asset-based approach), a whole new range of possibilities arises. This chapter discusses the policy implications of the asset-based approach in more detail. Before delving into the policy discussion, a brief review of the recent history of social policy approaches in Latin America helps put the asset-based approach into perspective.

Evolution of Social Development Strategies in Latin America

Although the experience with social policy has varied widely from country to country, Latin America's social strategy can be broadly classified into four phases:[6] (i) import substitution, (ii) the debt crisis of the 1980s, (iii) the structural adjustment packages of the mid to late 1980s, and (iv) the incipient recovery of the 1990s.

The first phase covers the period between the Second World War and the late 1970s. These were the golden years of Latin America in terms of economic growth. The industrial sector in most countries was growing vigorously, fueled by the import substitution development strategy that prevailed in those decades. The urban middle classes were expanding,[7] and all kinds of subsidies were granted for industrial production under the belief that industrialization was the best engine for growth.

This first generation of social policies provided a range of subsidies for goods and services for the entire population. Its main beneficiaries were the expanding middle classes. Some of these subsidies—like those for food consumption—were justified as an indirect subsidy to industrial sector wages. Since high growth rates financed these widespread consumption subsidies, there was a virtuous circle. On the one hand, the middle classes contributed to economic growth by joining the industrial sector and migrating from rural areas. On the other, the policies introduced to facilitate the import substitution process raised the standard of living of vast sectors of the population by guaranteeing low prices for basic goods and by supplying subsidized services.

---

[6] Obviously, all countries did not follow the same strategy, nor were they exactly synchronized. This characterization is made for purposes of simplifying the discussion.

[7] See Székely (1998) for a description of Mexico.

In essence, the social strategy and the wider development strategy were one and the same. And the same was true for the rural sector. In the spirit of the import substitution strategy, rural areas played the key role of providing primary goods and natural resources for industrial production at low prices, as well as low-cost goods for consumption by the expanding middle class. This implied in many cases subsidizing rural production. But it also implied land redistribution, since high priority was given to minimizing idle resources and the underutilization of land. Again, social policy was seen as a fundamental part of the overall development strategy.

In spite of the large declines in poverty and inequality that accompanied this development strategy, at some point it proved unsustainable.[8] During the late 1970s and early 1980s, declining international oil prices triggered the debt crisis that pulled Latin America into a deep recession. Thus began the second phase of social development policies.

Under the new macroeconomic constraints of the early 1980s, widespread subsidies to goods and services were simply prohibitive. Governments had to cut all expenditures—especially in social areas, which were not a priority at the time—in order to reduce public deficits. With escalating inflation rates, devaluation, and GDP declines, the policy priority was to stabilize the economy at all costs. It was hoped that once the macroeconomic situation was under control, growth would resume, and with it the expansion of the middle classes and the social development of past decades. People would have to endure some sacrifices in order to return to the glory days, perhaps at the cost of substantial declines in living standards. The sacrifice, however, would only be temporary and would not discriminate by each person's position in the social ladder. Everybody would have to pay for the excesses of the good old days.

Consequently, the second phase began by dismantling the previous social development strategy. It coincided with an identity crisis for the state. It was unclear whether the government's role should go beyond setting the rules of the game, intervening only perhaps when markets failed. In this context, widespread subsidies and social policies in general became an obstacle to growth rather than an engine of it, as in the past.

---

[8] See Londoño and Székely (2000) for evidence on poverty and inequality trends for Latin America during the 1970s.

Growth did not resume immediately, however. Latin America went through a period of economic reform, intense volatility and stagnation that lasted for nearly the entire decade, and this prolonged the population's sacrifice well beyond initial expectations. The previous social strategy of providing widespread subsidies to the population at large proved to be financially unsustainable. However, signs were appearing that the shift to the opposite extreme of dismantling the previous system and minimizing the role of the state could also be unsustainable from the social point of view. Toward the end of the decade there was increasing evidence of growing inequality, and most worrying, of substantial increases in poverty.[9] This marked the end of the second generation of social policies, and the start of the third.

The third phase began with the acknowledgement that structural adjustment programs and economic reform could impose greater burdens on the poor. It was recognized that the poor generally have fewer means of protecting their incomes from unexpected shocks, or from the erosion of liquid assets entailed by high inflation. They are also the least likely to engage in sectors of activity with higher productivity and with a higher probability of surviving external competition.

The policy solution was to introduce compensatory policies through implementation of safety nets. In a set of influential papers, Ravi Kanbur (1985, 1987a, 1987b) initiated what became the feasible alternative to introducing a safety net: targeting resources to the poor.

The concept of targeting is quite simple. It suggests that when budgets are limited in times of economic hardship, the policy problem is how to allocate scarce means in order to obtain the largest possible poverty reduction per dollar spent. Since there are administrative costs of finding the people who are most in need, the population is generally classified into subgroups according to some characteristic (geographic location, gender, schooling, etc.). To target specific subgroups it is necessary to have the guidance of poverty maps or profiles that identify the populations with the highest poverty rates and which are most sensitive (in terms of poverty reduction) to funding allocations. If one finds the subgroups that will generate higher poverty declines per unit of the budget spent, then one should allocate the

---

[9] Cornia, Jolly and Stewart (1987) articulate the worries that adjustment programs were causing excessive social distress.

funds to these units until there are others where the marginal dollar would produce greater poverty reduction.

This third generation of policies has had two important features. First, they entail a totally different way of distributing resources. In fact, they entail new "costs," since to find the poor, one has to look for them. Thus, there has to be a balance between the administrative costs involved in finding the target population and the benefits of finding them. From this perspective, first-generation policies were inducing high "leakage," since many of the non-poor or the not-so-poor were benefiting from resources that should have perhaps been allocated only to the poorest of the poor. Most of the gains from targeting originate precisely in reducing leakage. However, this comes at a cost. Since finding all the poor would be too costly, almost inevitably some of the poor will be "missed." Thus, the main challenge is to find a balance between administrative costs, leakage, and under-coverage.

The second and perhaps most important feature of the third generation of policies is that there is a deep change in the spirit of social policy. Policies aimed at increasing the standard of living of the poor or at protecting them against the unfavorable macroeconomic environment are compensatory, and thus have to be small, specific and tightly focused. The development strategy of countries in terms of growth might well be totally disconnected from these social policies. More often than not, social and macroeconomic goals in the third generation of social policies were *not* part of an integrated strategy, and were in fact regarded as having opposite objectives. Perhaps due to the profound scars of the "lost decade" of the 1980s, the main objective of governments was to keep tight budgetary controls; thus, social programs, although perhaps necessary, were a potential threat to public deficits and to macroeconomic stability. Social policies and a country's growth strategy became two separate lines of action that are practically opponents challenging one another for public resources.

The early 1990s mark a shift in the macroeconomic environment in Latin America. The first years of the decade saw the recovery of positive economic growth in most countries in the region. Economic performance was far from spectacular—with the sole exception of Chile—but in general governments could afford to start looking beyond the objective of macroeconomic stability. The worldwide trend towards globalization became apparent during the middle of the decade. If the economic reforms implemented in the 1980s implied opening up Latin American economies and exposing them to world markets, during the 1990s this process was part of a similar global trend in other regions of the world. Globalization made it clear that to survive in the modern world, it would be necessary to be competitive.

This change in the economic environment had crucial consequences for social policy, mainly because it implied that if a country wanted to be competitive, having large sectors of the population living in poverty would be a serious constraint. Those at the end of the social ladder are not usually endowed with means for being "productive" in terms of the new economic order. For instance, if poor families have limited means to finance the education of their children, and if large sectors of the population live in poverty, then the country will have limited human capital endowments and may not be able to attract investment to finance development. To be competitive, countries must have natural resources, or human, physical, or other factor endowments that enable them to produce goods or services at relatively low cost. Having an army of unskilled workers with low wages is not necessarily sufficient. First, workers need to have at least some minimum skills (such as the ability to read or write) and must be physically able to engage in economic activity. Second, the awareness of human rights triggered by the access to information in the new economy imposes some restrictions on the use of labor, such as minimum standards in working hours and wages.

These developments have been accompanied by a fourth generation of social policies. Programs such as *Progresa* in Mexico, *Bolsa Escola* in Brazil, and *Chile Joven*[10]—all of which are a centerpiece in the social development strategy of their respective countries and are being replicated across the region—have shifted away from the concept of only having temporary

---

[10] *Progresa* is the Spanish acronym for the Programa de Educación, Salud y Alimentación (Education, Health and Nutrition Program). The program provides cash transfers and a nutritional supplement to families in extreme poverty in rural areas. Cash transfers are conditioned on children's school attendance rates of at least 85 percent, and regular attendance at health clinics for checkups and follow-ups. The cash transfer is given to the mother, who also has to attend a series of courses on health practices. *Bolsa Escola* is a similar program that provides scholarships for disadvantaged children. Part of the cash transfer is held in a special account, which the beneficiary can access after completing a schooling cycle. *Chile Joven* is also a program of cash transfers, but in this case they are provided to young adults as a training incentive. A detailed description and evaluation of the *Progresa* program can be found at www.ifpri.org/country/mexico.htm. A description of the *Bolsa Escola* program can be found at http://www.mec.gov.br/home/bolsaesc/default.shtm.

safety nets to compensate the poor. They provide assistance to the poor, but by including strong incentives to the accumulation of human capital. The idea is to help by equipping the poor with the tools to enable them to help themselves in the new economic environment.

The fourth generation of social policies continues to use targeting mechanisms to allocate resources, but it has two key features that distinguish it from the previous generation. The first is that in one way or another, these policies attack the causes of poverty and not only its consequences (low incomes). If one of the reasons for poverty is that the poor have scarce human capital, then improving their human capital endowments through investments in schooling or health (as in the case of *Progresa*) may help their situation well beyond the duration of the program. Even if these programs are eventually discontinued, they can permanently improve the standard of living of their beneficiaries over the long term if they improve income-earning capacities.

The second key feature of these fourth generation programs is that they are connected in some way to the overall development strategy, as is the case of traditional targeted safety nets. These new policies can even be viewed as contributing to some extent to economic growth in the long run. For instance, it is normally agreed that education is an important requirement for faster GDP growth. So by contributing to higher educational levels, these programs in some sense may be fueling the economic system with resources that are useful for expanding production and competitiveness.[11]

The fourth generation policies are nevertheless generally viewed as a separate set of programs aimed at specific subgroups of the population that need assistance from the state and that are a cost to the economic system. These programs still have to compete fiercely for public resources and have not been institutionalized in any country to date. In many ways, they are still viewed as a necessary cost that society has to pay for compensating the disadvantaged.

These types of programs also entail some risks. Perhaps the main danger is confusing the implementation of such a program with the full social policy strategy of a country. While these programs have the capacity to improve the well-being of the poor, they cannot be regarded as a solution to

---

[11] See Birdsall, Pinckney and Sabot (1998).

the poverty problem. For instance, they may improve schooling levels among poor children, but if there are no opportunities to put human capital to work, the expected impact on income-earning capacity might not be realized. For a country to rely on these programs as its entire social strategy is like throwing the poor a life preserver during a violent storm—it might help keep them temporarily afloat, but it does nothing to subdue the storm that is drowning them.

Where to from Here?

The main limitation of the fourth generation of social policies described above is that programs such as *Progresa* or *Bolsa Escola* do not change the economic environment or the underlying elements in the structure of the economy that are causing poverty. Having low human capital endowments is certainly one of the reasons why the poor have low incomes, but this is not the whole story. The factors generating poverty are in the system, since they are deeply rooted in the functioning of the economy. If the forces that are generating poverty are not dealt with, these policies will always be swimming against the tide, or will have a much smaller impact than expected.

In the case of Latin America, it seems that poverty is due not so much to the insufficiency of resources to satisfy each individual's basic needs as to inequalities in the distribution of such resources. Londoño and Székely (2000), for example, estimate that if Latin America were to have its current income levels but with the income distribution of any other region of the world, poverty would be cut by at least one half. If Latin America had its same income but with the distribution of Asian countries, for example, the poverty rate would be around 10 percent of what it actually is.[12]

---

[12] Of course, this does not apply to the same extent to all countries. There are cases where GDP per capita is low, and income redistribution would have a lesser impact. In any case, since the average income in all Latin American countries is well above international and country-specific poverty lines, it could be argued that poverty is to a large extent a problem of inequality, and not one of insufficient resources. This exercise is only performed for the sake of illustration, since there is no guarantee that if the distribution of resources were to be modified, the level of income would remain the same.

If poverty is to a large extent the consequence of high levels of inequality, the natural question to ask is why is there so much inequality. Part of the reason is people are different in many dimensions: schooling, age, gender, regional location, occupation, sector of activity, etc. But these characteristics typically explain only about one third of income differentials.[13]

Furthermore, in countries with high levels of inequality, those inequalities are seen at all levels. Table 8.1 shows the Gini inequality index for household per capita incomes for 19 countries—17 from Latin America, plus Thailand and Taiwan. The first column presents the index at the national level, while the second column shows the average Gini coefficient obtained from estimating inequality within each of the smallest geographic areas that can be identified in the corresponding household survey. In Argentina, for example, the overall Gini is .493, while the average Gini coefficient from all 28 states is .467. The third column presents the standard deviation of the Gini coefficient for each state. The fifth column indicates the smallest geographic area that can be identified in each country, while the last presents the number of geographic units identified.

There are two interesting features from the table. The first is that there is a very high correlation of .97 between the overall Gini index and the average Gini of the geographic areas within each country. The second is that, on average, the standard deviation of the Gini within each country is only 7.6 percent of the average Gini. The highest standard deviation is for Guatemala, with 15.4 percent, and it is lower than 10 percent in 16 out of 19 countries. This means that in countries with high inequality at the aggregate level, large inequalities are also found in each region, state, municipality or city. In countries such as Brazil, which is among the most unequal in the world, inequality is reproduced in each of the 27 areas into which the country can be disaggregated. The standard deviation of the Gini by state is not even 6 percent in Brazil. In contrast, in countries such as Taiwan, which have much lower inequality, low inequalities are also found in each city in the country.

To some extent, these inequalities reflect differences in personal characteristics, but typically, around two-thirds remain unexplained after accounting for them. The other two-thirds reflect aspects of the economic

---

[13] See Chapter One. It reports a set of Mincer regressions for several countries, which were used to estimate the returns to schooling. In none of the cases reported did the R^2 in the regression exceed 27 percent. See also IDB (1998) for comparisons across countries.

Table 8.1. Inequality in Latin America and East Asia by Geographic Area

Country	Year	Gini: total population	Average Gini of all geographic areas	Std. dev. Gini of all geographic areas	Std. dev. as a % of average for geographic areas	Geographic identifier	Number of geographic identifier
Argentina	1998	0.493	0.467	0.029	6.1	State	28
Bolivia	1999	0.601	0.586	0.049	8.3	State	9
Brazil	1997	0.585	0.569	0.032	5.7	State	27
Chile	1998	0.559	0.536	0.032	6.1	Region	13
Colombia	1999	0.555	0.530	0.032	6.0	State	25
Costa Rica	1998	0.461	0.437	0.022	5.1	Region	7
Ecuador	1998	0.557	0.564	0.015	2.6	Region	3
El Salvador	1998	0.559	0.543	0.045	8.3	Region	5
Guatemala	1998	0.562	0.494	0.076	15.4	Region	8
Honduras	1998	0.585	0.555	0.055	9.9	Region	18
Mexico	1998	0.538	0.488	0.045	9.3	State	33
Nicaragua	1998	0.602	0.546	0.061	11.2	State	17
Panama	1999	0.563	0.533	0.034	6.4	Province	9
Peru	2000	0.569	0.410	0.021	5.1	State	7
Paraguay	1998	0.493	0.508	0.071	14.0	State	16
Uruguay	1998	0.439	0.409	0.026	6.2	State	19
Venezuela	1999	0.467	0.444	0.030	6.7	State	23
Taiwan	1996	0.285	0.262	0.021	7.9	City	45
Thailand	1998	0.516	0.463	0.018	3.8	State	5
Average		**0.526**	**0.492**	**0.038**	**7.6**		

Source: Authors' calculations using household survey data.

environment where people live—aspects that are deeply entrenched in the system and reproduced at all levels. The reason why Brazil, Chile, Mexico and Colombia have such inequalities is not due to regional differences. In each region or state, very high inequalities are also found. Similarly, the main reason why Taiwan and Uruguay have the lowest inequalities among the countries in the table is *not* that there are few regional differences. Even in each city or state within the country, there are low inequalities.

If inequality, and therefore poverty, in Latin America is deeply entrenched in the economic system, as Table 8.1 suggests, it is highly unlikely that the poverty problem will be solved unless some fundamental elements of the system are modified. Again, specific programs such as *Progresa* or *Bolsa Escola* can certainly do much good, but the broader forces generating inequality will limit their impact.

The Asset-Based Approach: A Fifth Generation of Social Policies?

The main policy implication of the asset-based approach to poverty reduction is that the solution to the poverty problem must go well beyond income. It is necessary to examine the determinants of income in order to identify those that are prone to change through policy action.[14]

Chapter One of this book organized this discussion by stating that the income of each individual in society is the product of five elements. First, it depends on the income-earning assets owned by each household member. Broadly speaking, assets are classified into human, physical and social capital. Second, it depends on the rate of use of the assets, since assets only generate income when they are put to work in the market. Third, on the production side of the economy, income-earning assets are viewed as factors of production. The extent to which they generate income depends not only on the ownership and the rate of use of the asset, but also on the price paid for factors of production. Depending on the extent to which factors are demanded and supplied, prices can be high or low, and depending on the

---

[14] Poverty is a multi-dimensional concept that includes aspects of culture, freedom, democracy, empowerment and others. To make the concept tractable from a policy point of view, the analysis is restricted to income poverty. As will be seen later, this scheme can be easily adapted to more comprehensive definitions of poverty.

degree of trade openness of each country, the prices will be set by internal forces or by international markets. The fourth element is the income received independently of income-earning assets. It includes transfers (public or private), gifts, etc. that individuals receive not because they are putting an asset to work, but because of other factors. The safety nets of the third generation of policies would enter into this category. Finally, a person's income depends on the size of the household where he or she lives and on the way in which resources are shared within the household. For simplification purposes it is assumed that household resources are added up and that access of each member of the household to resources is the same.

From the policy point of view, there is scope for public action on all five fronts, and several suggestions were already proposed in Chapter One. The main implication of the asset-based approach is that it leads to a different policy strategy, and to a different way of thinking about social policy than do the second, third and fourth generation policies. It means that social policies are not separate from the overall development strategy; on the contrary, they are at the heart of it. Their main objective is to improve the standard of living of the poor, but to do so in a way that contributes to growth, increases the productivity of factors of production, and improves factor allocation in the economic system.

To simplify the discussion, the items listed above can be reframed into two broad policy categories: (a) the *capabilities* that people have to obtain resources (all income-earning assets), and (b) the *opportunities* available for putting income-earning assets to work (including the rate of use and prices). In this scheme, the role of social policy is to generate income-earning capabilities and to create opportunities for using them productively.[15]

There are four types of capabilities that are clearly prone to policy action: education (formal schooling as a proxy for human capital), health, investment capacity, and housing and basic services.[16] Education can be

---

[15] The concept of capabilities employed here is not exactly the same as that pioneered by Amartya Sen (1985, 1987, 1989). Sen defines capabilities as the ability to achieve. The concept of capabilities used here (income-earning assets) also includes the opportunities to put them to work. For present purposes, the concept of capabilities (income-earning assets) is separated from opportunities to simplify the policy discussion. In Sen's framework, capabilities are a means to attain functioning, or living conditions. In the present scheme, income plays the role of functioning because the definition of poverty is restricted to income poverty.

[16] Social capital is not included here because it is a more elusive concept.

thought of as a measure of the human capital or skills that a person can offer in the labor market, or which can be used to create his or her own employment. Health refers to the mental and physical capacity to perform economic activity. Investment capabilities are people's possibilities for creating economic activities through means other than their labor. Housing and basic services are measures of the availability of basic infrastructure to operate in society.

In terms of opportunity, the two clear areas of intervention are employment and investment opportunities. Employment opportunities refer to the conditions, costs and incentives in the labor market that influence the prices paid for different kinds of labor and the demand for skills. Investment opportunity comes from the existence of an efficient financial market that gives access to credit. Credit can be used to create economic activity and to take advantage of the economic environment to generate income.

Creating Capabilities

Policies for Human Capital Accumulation

There are at least two clear areas where public policy can support the accumulation of skills through education.

First, to be able to invest in the education of its members, a household has to be able to afford the private costs of schooling. Even when access to public schools is available, households must pay for books, clothing, nutrition, and perhaps most importantly for poor households, the opportunity cost of sending their children to school instead of sending them to work. If households lack the means to finance even these basic investments, it is most likely that they will under-invest in human capital. Programs such as *Progresa* or *Bolsa Escola*, which provide direct financial support to households conditioned on investing in the education of their members, are perhaps one of the best policy options available to enhance human capital accumulation by the poor. But even these could be complemented with school supplies, meals, and transportation services for students to make the effect stronger.[17]

---

[17] In the case of *Progresa*, a key issue is that by definition, some of the poorest of the poor do not have access to its benefits because they live in isolated and remote areas where no school or health clinic exists. If the program were accompanied by supply-side efforts, support for temporary reallocation during the school year, or subsidies to transport costs, it could perhaps reach these sectors of society.

Second, making investment in schooling an attractive option for a household requires that services of a certain quality be available. As discussed in IDB (1996 and 1998), resource allocation in the schooling systems of most Latin American countries is shaped by payment commitments to large bureaucracies, and not by the level and quality of educational results. Higher income families may have the chance to escape to private schools where there is competition and quality standards, but the poor are basically stuck with the public system. When it is of low quality, differences in human capital are intensified. The government can play a decisive role if it devotes at least part of its efforts to generating information, setting quality standards and assuring that schools receive funds from public resources based on the quality and quantity of the education they provide, instead of focusing only on bureaucratic and budgetary controls.[18] There is also scope for introducing new ways of teaching for the disadvantaged. Education by television is an innovative way to reach the poor in remote areas, and it has not yet been exploited to its full potential.[19]

An additional problem is that many of the poor are already beyond school age and will not benefit from improvements in the standard schooling system. They are the ones who dropped out early because their families could not finance the investment any longer, or those who never went through more than a couple of years of schooling due to the low quality of public schools or to pressing household financial needs. For these people, training policies may be one of the only ways to reverse the disadvantage they face in the labor market. But here, too, there are problems of investment capacity and in the supply of training services, since it is normally more costly to train people the lower their schooling level. From the investment side, one option could be to create *Progresa*-type programs for training. If pressure to make ends meet at home is one of the reasons why the poor who are beyond

---

[18] This will be even more of a challenge for Latin America in the future because of demographic factors. Chapter One shows that the main bottleneck for the poor appears to be their low chances of enrolling and going beyond secondary schooling. IDB (2000) estimates that to meet the demographic challenge of a changing age structure over the next 10 years, the number of teachers in secondary schools will have to increase from 1.8 million to 2.6 million just to keep pace with higher demand.

[19] As discussed by IDB (2000) there are examples of success in the region. *Telecurso* in Brazil and *Telesecundaria* in Mexico are among the most notable.

school age do not continue their schooling, direct incentives in the form of cash transfers conditioned on training might be a feasible option.

On the supply side, the problem is that in Latin America technical education and training programs—especially those targeted to the poor—became obsolete decades ago (IDB, 2000). Some countries are beginning to experiment with different organizational approaches to introduce incentives to improve the operation of these programs. There are some recent experiences where the private sector has created its own training centers financed by payroll taxes, but the quality of this option is not always good, and these facilities are difficult to monitor. Perhaps the scope for action is in redefining the role of the government as regulator of the system rather than focusing on providing the service. If this is combined with income-support programs, there might be better chances for the poor to acquire the training they would need to increase their income-earning power.

Policies for Improving Health

The health of the poor is usually more precarious than that of wealthier people[20] because the poor have fewer means for investing in health to at least maintain their income-earning capacity, and because they normally lack appropriate health insurance and therefore end up having access only to lower quality public services.

There are two ways of thinking about which public policy could improve this situation. First, governments can provide families with direct income support to finance health services. *Progresa* is a good example, but even these types of programs fall short of the needs of the poor because they do not normally include support for medication or preventive services for infants. Expanding income support to include these areas could have a strong impact on improving, or at least maintaining, the precarious income-earning potential of the poor.

On the supply side, governments have usually ignored private health insurance markets, seeking instead to support the poor by building hospitals to directly provide high-cost treatment. The problem is similar to that

---

[20] As reflected in higher infant mortality, lower life expectancy and being more prone to disease. For some examples, see IDB-RES (2000), which illustrates this clearly for the case of Mexico.

of public education in the sense that efficiency is low, and in the end it is not clear whether the objective is providing health services or supporting the huge bureaucracies that have grown up around them. As in the case of schooling, perhaps the main challenge is to find ways of creating effective regulatory frameworks that guarantee access of the poor to basic health services. Acknowledging that resources for spending in the health sector are limited, and that potential improvements could be achieved by enhancing efficiency, IDB (1996) proposes measures to change the organization of public health services. These include increasing the autonomy of local providers, building mechanisms of accountability through information, empowering consumers through choice, and allocating resources on the basis of outcomes instead of budgetary needs. These are deep changes, but they have the potential to benefit the poor, or at least to improve their access to health services.

Investment Capabilities

In the absence of formal credit markets, economic activity can be financed either by saving or by having access to informal credit markets. But if incomes are too low and there is no access to banks to deposit those savings, it is difficult, if not impossible, to create savings for investment. Savings must therefore be held in a non-monetary form (building materials, livestock, etc.) or in cash. But both of these strategies are risky. They tend to have a lower return and incur high transaction costs, such as converting illiquid assets into cash. The problem is worse in a context of economic uncertainty, where savings can only be used as a buffer-stock to face unexpected shocks, and where they cannot be used for long-term ventures with at least medium-term maturity periods. Moreover, if the poor are not able to save they are more exposed to fluctuations in the economic system and, worst of all, will be unable to accumulate the income-earning assets that could lift them out of poverty.

With respect to access to informal sources of credit, the family or other networks may be good sources of resources, but for the poor these resources are limited because the people in their networks are often impoverished as well. So people have to turn to informal credit markets that charge huge prices for credit, reducing the profitability of the proposed investment or making it prohibitive altogether.

There are at least two areas for policy action in terms of creating savings capabilities. The first and most obvious is to promote the existence of small-scale financial institutions that provide the poor with safe ways to save through liquid savings accounts, and which yield some return even when the investment is low. These can be fostered by setting the rules of the game in ways that introduce some regulation and supervision at the time when guarantees to investors are provided. The second is by creating insurance mechanisms such as unemployment insurance or self-insurance through social security accounts, which reduce the risk of abrupt income declines. Schemes of this type could enable the poor to invest with longer-term objectives—such as accumulating income-earning assets—and to gain access to investments with higher yields, which would make their savings and investment more profitable. A stable macroeconomic environment could also be considered as an important contribution to reducing risk for the poor.

Housing and Basic Services

Housing, basic infrastructure, and services such as electricity, potable water and drainage are necessary to function in a modern society. Without them, people's human capital and health are severely undermined. Moreover, the chances of creating economic activity are crippled. This is especially so in the case of women. Latin American women traditionally have been responsible for domestic chores, and with inadequate electricity, water, etc., they end up spending a huge amount of time and effort in these activities.

Although the urban poor in particular may have some access to housing and public services, most of the poor rarely have them in adequate quality and quantity. In part this is because the priority for governments has been to keep prices and tariffs low in the hope that this will result in broad access (IDB, 1998). The result is that the wealthy and middle classes, which consume the most, have received subsidized services while the poor in rural and marginal urban areas have very limited access, if any.

Since these services are usually publicly provided, there is a clear role for the state in covering the deficits accumulated in the past by the poor. But in the case of housing, there is also scope for helping to create both financial markets and a regulatory framework suitable for the poor. One example of the limitations of current regulatory frameworks is that in most countries, public or private mortgage options are only available for "finished" housing, defined as units that have been completely built and that have access to basic services. One of the reasons is that the house itself is normally the collateral, so it has to have some minimum value to make it worthwhile for banks or other creditors to engage in the deal. The problem is that the poorest of the poor either do not have access to these mechanisms, because they are employed in the informal sector, or they do not meet the minimum requirements to qualify for a loan for the full price of a house. Either a regulatory framework promoting the financing of unfinished units, or the creation of a market for unfinished housing could improve the chances of the poor to acquire housing of acceptable quality as well as access to services.

Generating Opportunities

Employment Opportunities

Opportunities, as defined here, are about prices and about the chances for using assets to generate income flows. From the point of view of the rate of use of assets such as human capital, Chapter One showed that the main difference between rich and poor is found in the labor force participation of women. Practically all males of prime age, regardless of their social position, work and are income-earners, while in the case of women, the participation rate among those who have better opportunities due to their education is much higher than among those who have less schooling.

One reason for this outcome is that traditional mechanisms for protecting labor in Latin America were designed by men, for men. Their objective was to generate formal employment with benefits, and with guarantees of stable jobs. But this implicitly induces discrimination against women, both because these mechanisms impose higher implicit costs for hiring women (due to maternity leave and allowances), and because restricting employment to full time and limiting flexibility in hours makes employment a prohibitive venture for some women. These efforts at protection result in reality in much lower participation rates among poor uneducated women.

There are at least four ways in which public policy can contribute to reducing restrictions to female participation in the labor force. The first is by providing access to basic infrastructure and services that lower the cost of household chores and free some time for women. The second is by enhancing child care services and preventive health services that create a support network for women who wish to engage in the labor market, but who do not do so because of the restrictions imposed by household tasks. These services could either be subsidized by the state or promoted through appropriate tax incentives, or other schemes, for private firms. A third way is by socializing maternity costs. If these costs were financed through fiscal revenue rather than charged to employers, the incentives to hire women would improve, and with that, their opportunities.

The fourth way is through labor legislation. As argued by IDB (1998), labor protection laws and regulations end up favoring people who are able to participate in the formal sector—normally those that are endowed with some schooling and health—while leaving the rest uncovered. Labor legislation could introduce greater flexibility into contracting conditions to help part-time or temporary workers who also have to deal with household tasks. But this must be accompanied by the corresponding (proportional) benefits enjoyed by full-time workers. A second measure would be unemployment protection to stabilize workers' income if they temporarily lose their jobs or are transiting between jobs. Many countries have already established individual savings accounts that can be used as personal unemployment insurance, but the main limitation is that this is restricted to the formal sector of the economy. For those in informal employment, it could be possible to establish collectively financed social safety nets that could play the role of social insurance. Individual savings accounts could possibly be expanded to cover these groups.

Apart from the differences in labor force participation between the rich and poor, the poor also have the strong disadvantage of receiving lower remuneration for the precarious human capital that they own. As shown in Chapter One, in Latin America the returns to primary and secondary schooling are relatively low, while the returns to higher education are huge. Perhaps the most straightforward option would be to influence the level of the minimum wage in the hope that by increasing it, the returns to the assets of the poor would increase. The problem is that high minimum wages often result in even more discrimination against women with low education, and unskilled workers in general, so in the end they do not serve their purpose of redistributing income.

In an era of globalization, it is difficult to think of policies that promote higher wages and employment for the poor without referring to trade policy. Since most Latin American countries are now open to international trade, their wages are set not only by the internal supply and demand for labor, but also by the scarcity or abundance of different types of labor in world markets. Therefore, minimum wages have an even more limited role than before. Perhaps the best example of this situation is the entry of China and India into world markets. These are the two most populated countries in the world, and when they started opening up to trade more than a decade ago, the availability of unskilled labor in the world increased substantially. Latin America is no longer a region abundant in unskilled labor, at least by world standards, and thus, it is not clear that it has the comparative advantages that attract investment and generate demand for local labor.

This means that to improve the wages of the poor it is necessary to have a trade policy that promotes the use of their human capital. According to IDB (1998), one way of dealing with this is to advocate flat and moderate tariff structures that protect all sectors alike and do not privilege imports of capital in industrial activities that are normally complementary to skilled labor. Tariff structures that favor intermediate inputs or factors of production complementary to relatively unskilled labor (by Latin American standards) would have better chances of increasing the demand for the labor of the poor.

Investment Opportunities

Efficient financial markets are one of the main vehicles for social mobility. Financial markets provide the institutional framework with which savings are mobilized to finance investment ventures. For people with low savings capacity, these markets often are the only way of accessing resources to create economic opportunities. Unfortunately, Latin American countries have inefficient and small financial systems that result in credit scarcity. This inhibits the opportunities of the poor considerably and reduces their capacity to put their meager income-assets to work. Therefore, reform to create or improve the functioning of financial markets in Latin America could enhance the income-earning capacity of the poor.

One way to do this is to promote lending institutions that make micro loans.[21] The role of the state in this case might be to create the regulatory

---

[21] Perhaps the most successful of many examples in Latin America are the Banco Sol and Caja los Andes in Bolivia and the Banco del Pacífico in Ecuador. Worldwide, the Grameen Bank in Bangladesh is perhaps the best-known success story of micro lending for the poor.

framework for these institutions to flourish. This requires setting clear rules of the game, imposing restrictions on the use of financial resources by banks for investing in certain instruments, monitoring the operation of banks, and creating guarantees that reduce the risk of their investment.

The problem is that micro lending institutions are to date only a minuscule part of the financial sector in Latin America. Altogether, they do not account for even 1 percent of the credit provided by commercial banks in the region. This points to the need for policies that generate widespread access to credit. The option of creating and managing state-owned banks that provide subsidized credit is not the solution, at least as judged by their low rate of success and high inefficiency in the region. To know where there is scope for intervention, it is first necessary to identify the obstacles that impede the credit relationship.

According to IDB (1998), "the fundamental problem lies in the first step in a credit relationship: the creditor must give the borrower money based on a promise of repayment." The credit relationship therefore depends on the ability to and willingness to repay loans. The question is, what can ensure that ability and willingness? Apart from introducing appropriate regulation and supervision of banking institutions, there are at least four mechanisms that governments can use to create or expand competitive and efficient financial systems that reach the poor: punishment, collateral, reputation and relationships.

Punishment is basically about the effectiveness of the legal system in enforcing the law. While enforcing the law does not necessarily benefit creditors on a case-by-case basis, it does provide incentives to debtors to repay if they possibly can. For financial systems that serve smaller borrowers, there need to be additional ways of ensuring willingness to pay. Areas for improvement include operational restrictions of banks (in terms of flexibility of times and forms of operation), simplification of documentation requirements, and lowering capital requirements on loans.

Collateral is one of the key mechanisms that make financial systems work because it implies some guarantee of repayment. The problem in the context of poverty reduction is that the poor normally lack collateral. One option is the introduction of new financial products such as leasing and factoring, or at least creating the regulatory framework so that they can exist. These types of instruments are closer in spirit to the concept of "renting" capital, rather than selling it. For instance, in leasing, the lending institution normally retains ownership of the equipment or other form of capital, while the debtor pays a monthly rent (which includes interest and amortization) for its use and eventually becomes an owner. One way in which public action can promote these types of arrangements is by facilitating rapid and low-cost repossession of the leased equipment in the event of default. Tax schemes tailored to the needs of these schemes, and the elimination of regulatory barriers, can also intervene to facilitate the creation and expansion of formal credit in the economy.

Reputation can be an effective mechanism for lowering the costs of monitoring the ability and willingness of borrowers to repay loans. Anybody can develop a good credit reputation, regardless of his or her socioeconomic condition. One feasible policy for introducing reputation mechanisms into the financial system is to create credit bureaus. These information-sharing mechanisms concentrate credit histories that are made available to lenders. This punishes default by limiting future access to credit to those with a bad history. Credit bureaus are a rare commodity in Latin America. Interestingly, small banks that provide micro loans are among the few places to use them. These types of institutions provide credit progressively in larger loans to an individual or group, with default resulting in loss to access. Rates of repayment of micro loans are usually very high, to a large extent due to such arrangements. Creating public credit bureaus on a larger scale could be one of the policy alternatives for providing incentives to create and expand credit markets in the region.

Promoting *relationships* is another important way to promote the creation of financial institutions. For instance, one common credit mechanism is group lending, where default by one member of the group results in loss of access to credit for the entire group. These schemes take advantage of the relationship that borrowers have with each other by introducing self-monitoring mechanisms that dramatically reduce the cost of monitoring lending. One way in which public policy can promote the use of group lending is through fiscal incentives to entities or groups that provide these types of loans. In addition, there is scope for policy intervention in setting the regulatory framework, or even creating insurance mechanisms that reduce the risk of default.

Social and Development Policy: One and the Same

It is time to start thinking about new ways of designing social policies in Latin America. Policies must support the poor in a way that also contributes to growth and development. This can only be done if social policy is at the heart of a country's development strategy, rather than being just one more sector constantly competing for public resources and seen as undermining macroeconomic stability. Therefore, the solution is not compensatory measures, but policies that promote efficiency in the economic system and improve the productivity of the poor.

If we go beyond income, and ask what determines the income of each individual, it is possible to outline some of the elements of such a strategy. This discussion has been framed in terms of policies that generate capabilities and create opportunities. The idea is that creating capabilities and opportunities for the poor will raise their incomes and give them access to a better standard of living.

But when we start thinking about what is needed to improve capabilities and opportunities, we end up talking about cash transfer programs such as *Progresa* or *Bolsa Escola*, health policy, incentives for saving, housing and basic services, labor market regulations, trade policy, the introduction of credit bureaus to expand access to credit, and even the promotion of alternative financial instruments such as leasing to help the poor overcome their lack of collateral. In other words, we end up talking about the economic environment as a whole. And what is most interesting is that many of these proposals are rarely conceived of as part of social policy, but rather as part of a country's overall development strategy.

This chapter has outlined a scheme within which the various public policies can be viewed as part of this integrated strategy. By framing it in this way, it is obvious that programs such as *Progresa* are an important part of the strategy. But they cannot be regarded as *the* strategy for poverty reduction. If other elements of the economic environment are not modified, these types of government intervention will always be swimming against the tide. But, on the contrary, if these efforts are complemented by a wide set of policies that generate capabilities and create opportunities for the poor, their chances of contributing to solving the poverty puzzle may be multiplied.

References

Birdsall, N., and A. de la Torre. 2001. *Washington Contentious: Economic Policies for Social Equity in Latin America*. Washington, DC: Carnegie Endowment for International Peace.

Birdsall, N., T. Pinckney, and R. Sabot. 1998. Why Low Inequality Spurs Growth: Saving and Investment by the Poor. In A. Solimano (ed.), *Social Inequalities: Values, Growth and the State*. Ann Arbor, MI: University of Michigan Press.

Bourguignon, F. 2001. The Pace of Economic Growth and Poverty Reduction. World Bank, Washington, DC. Mimeo.

Cornia, G.A., R. Jolly, and F. Stewart. 1987. *Adjustment with a Human Face*. Oxford, United Kingdom: Clarendon Press.

Dollar, D., and A. Kraay. 2000. Growth Is Good for the Poor. World Bank, Washington, DC. Mimeo.

Foster, J., and M. Székely. 2001. Is Growth Good for the Poor? Tracking Low Incomes Using General Means. Inter-American Development Bank Research Department. Mimeo.

Gallup, J.L., S. Radelet, and A. Warner. 1999. *Economic Growth and the Income of the Poor*. CAER II Discussion Paper No. 36. Harvard University, Harvard Institute for International Development, Cambridge, MA.

Inter-American Development Bank (IDB). 2000. *Economic and Social Progress Report: Development beyond Economics*. Washington, DC: Inter-American Development Bank.

———. 1998. *Economic and Social Progress Report: Facing up to Inequality in Latin America*. Washington, DC: Inter-American Development Bank.

———. 1996. *Economic and Social Progress Report: Making Social Services Work*. Washington, DC: Inter-American Development Bank.

Inter-American Development Bank Research Department (IDB-RES). 2000. Hacia una estrategia de desarrollo social en México. Inter-American Development Bank, Washington, DC. Mimeo.

Kanbur, R. 1987a. Structural Adjustment, Macroeconomic Adjustment and Poverty: A Methodology of Analysis. *World Development* 15(12): 1515-526.

———. 1987b. Measurement and Alleviation of Poverty. *IMF Staff Papers* 34: 60-85.

_____. 1985. *Poverty: Measurement, Alleviation and the Impact of Macroeconomic Adjustment.* University of Essex Discussion Paper No. 125. Essex, United Kingdom: University of Essex.

Londoño, J.L., and M. Székely. 2000. Persistent Poverty and Excess Inequality: Latin America 1970-1995. *Journal of Applied Economics* 3(1): 93-134.

Roemer, M., and M. Gugerty. 1997. *Does Economic Growth Reduce Poverty?* CAER II Discussion Paper No. 4. Harvard University, Harvard Institute for International Development, Cambridge, MA.

Sen, A. 1992. *Inequality Reexamined.* Oxford, United Kingdom: Oxford University Press.

_____. 1987. *The Standard of Living.* Cambridge, United Kingdom: Cambridge University Press.

_____. 1985. *Commodities and Capabilities.* Amsterdam: North-Holland.

Székely, M. 1998. *The Economics of Poverty, Inequality and Wealth Accumulation in Mexico.* London: MacMillan.

Székely, M., and M. Hilgert. 2001. The 1990s in Latin America: Another Decade of Persistent Inequality, but with Less Poverty. Inter-American Development Bank Research Department, Washington, DC. Mimeo.